The Campus History Series

THE CITY COLLEGE OF NEW YORK

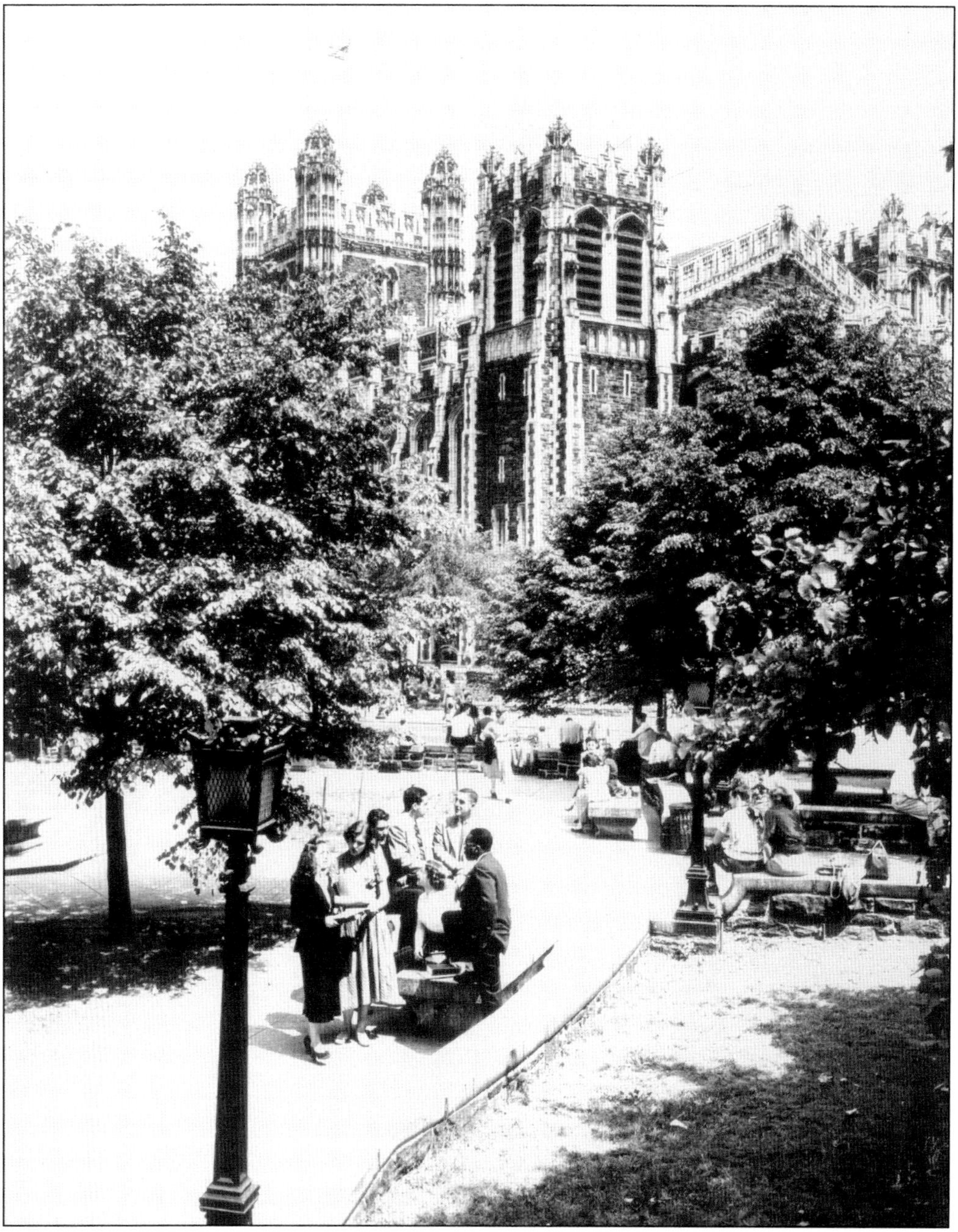

City College students gather at a bench in the quadrangle for relaxed discourse approximately in the year 1951. Surrounding them are the campus buildings designed by George B. Post. The towers of the Main Building, currently known as Shepard Hall, rise above the trees behind the group.

On the cover: Please see above. (Archives, The City College of New York, CUNY.)

The Campus History Series

THE CITY COLLEGE OF NEW YORK

SYDNEY C. VAN NORT

ARCADIA PUBLISHING

ISBN 978-0-7385-4930-9

Published by Arcadia Publishing
Charleston, South Carolina

Printed in the United States of America

Library of Congress Catalog Card Number: 2006931502

For all general information contact Arcadia Publishing at:
Telephone 843-853-2070
Fax 843-853-0044
E-mail sales@arcadiapublishing.com
For customer service and orders:
Toll-Free 1-888-313-2665

Visit us on the Internet at www.arcadiapublishing.com

To the students of City College past, present, and future.

Contents

ACKNOWLEDGMENTS

First and foremost, I would like to express my appreciation to assistant dean and chief librarian Pamela Gillespie, whose unwavering support of this project from the beginning has made it possible. I would like to thank Elena Sturman, the executive director of the City College Fund, and Donald Jordan, the executive vice president of the Alumni Association, for their interest in bringing this pictorial story of City College to the alumni and other friends of this great institution. I am grateful to Mary Lou Edmondson, the vice president and director of communication, and to Ellis Simon, the director of public relations, and his staff for their prompt response to my request for current images. These photographs bring the story of City College beyond the first 150 years of its history.

I would like to acknowledge the organizational skills of my predecessor, Prof. Emerita Barbara J. Dunlap, because without her extensive efforts to arrange the records of the institution and index the photograph collection, I could not have compiled all of the images presented in this work. I would like to convey appreciation to Erin L. Vosgien and the staff of Arcadia Publishing, who have provided the opportunity to share these images with a wider audience. I would like to thank the many photographers who have captured the college, its people, buildings, and events over the years. For their support and historical perspective on this project, I would like to convey my deep personal thanks to Richard M. Van Nort and Elizabeth I. Burns.

Unless otherwise stated, all images are courtesy of the archives of the City College of New York.

INTRODUCTION

The City College of New York, founded as the Free Academy, began as an educational and political experiment. The success of the experiment of the first public college in New York has been demonstrated by an expanding system of public colleges in New York City that were united as the City University of New York in 1961. The vision of a Democratic New York porcelain merchant and later the first American diplomat to the Empire of Japan, Townsend Harris, who adroitly and successfully lobbied public opinion and the New York State legislature as the chairman of the New York City Board of Education in a series of newspaper editorials created the first entirely tax-payer supported institution for higher learning in the country. In one such editorial published in the *Morning Courier* on March 15, 1847, he stated:

> No, Sirs, the system now pursued by that excellent society and by our ward schools is the true one, and may be advantageously applied to higher seminaries of learning. Make them the property of the people—open the doors to all—let the children of the rich and the poor take their seats together and know of no distinction save that of industry, good conduct, and intellect. A large number of the children of the rich now attend our public schools, and the ratio is rapidly increasing.

With the passage of the legislative bills in 1847, and the subsequent referendum approval by the voters of New York City, the working youth of the growing metropolis gained a means of entry into new professions. The city gained citizens committed to its welfare, as verified by the Ephebic Oath administered during the commencement ceremony. This unique, tuition-free institution was advantageous for young men residing in New York—immigrant and native alike—and soon became known as "The Poor Man's Harvard."

For the first 60 years, the students studied a curriculum resembling that of the Military Academy at West Point, where the first two college presidents, Horace Webster and Alexander Webb, had been trained. The classical curriculum, including such topics as history and philosophy, provided the basis for the College of Liberal Arts and Science. Their counterparts pursuing the scientific course, mechanical classes, were some of the first students to be trained in practical applied fields. These classes were the foundation for two of the flagship schools: the Grove School of Engineering (1919) and the School of Architecture, Urban Design, and Landscape Architecture (1962). Other divisions of the City College and their respective dates of establishment are as follows: the School of Education (1921), the School of Nursing (1969–1997), the Sophie Davis School of Biomedical Education (1973), and the Bernard M. Baruch School of Business and Public Administration (1919). Many of those trained by the institution kept their association by becoming tutors and subsequent professors, teaching future generations of young scholars.

The third president of the college, John H. Finley, brought the institution into the 20th century. He reformed the curriculum, moved many of the programs into the newly constructed neo-Gothic St. Nicholas Heights campus (dedicated in 1908) because the student body had outgrown the original building near Gramercy Park at Lexington Avenue and 23rd Street, and added a handsome athletic stadium reminiscent of a classical amphitheater in 1912. Some alumni gained recognition in various fields; there have been two Rhodes Scholars and nine Nobel laureates. Other alumni have been noted for their work in scientific research, legal theory, writing, and acting. The college continues to grow and offer new educational opportunities to a student body that has converged from all over the world to the campus in St. Nicholas Heights.

Creating a cohesive student life at a commuter campus has been challenging. One solution was the 1937 formation of the House Plan Association. This group operated three student houses providing facilities for clubs as well as student, faculty, and alumni interaction at weekly forums and other social events, but ceased during the 1970s. A rallying point for school pride has since become the athletic teams. The St. Nicholas Heights campus provided the facilities that allowed some of the coaches and players representing this college to achieve national prominence.

City College students were not reticent concerning local issues such as the college curriculum and global matters. Animated dialogues between students, students and faculty, and students and visitors from outside the college community have been hallmarks of City College activity for almost 160 years.

One

Origins

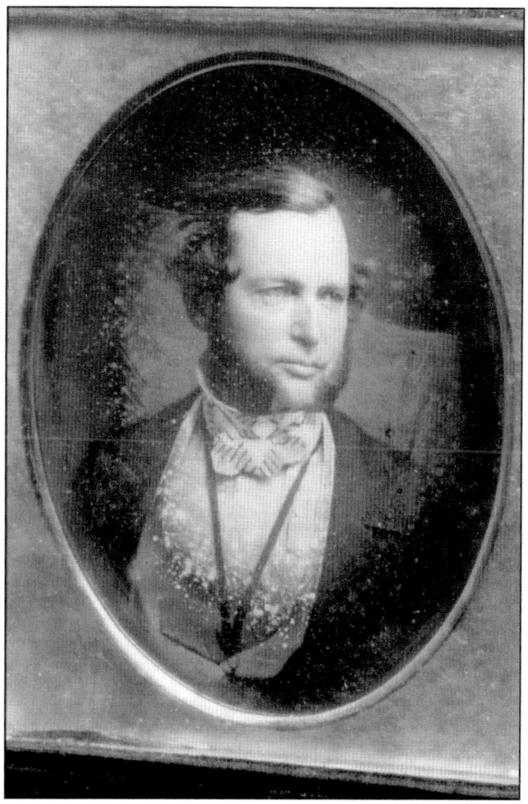

Townsend Harris, the founder of the Free Academy, is seen in this *c.* 1847 daguerreotype, taken when he was 43 years old. Harris wrote a series of columns that eventually prompted the New York State legislature to authorize the expenditure of the Literature Fund administered by the New York State Board of Regents to support a public institution of higher learning in New York. This legislation was passed in 1847 and approved by a referendum. Harris attended the opening ceremony for the new institution in 1849. About nine years after establishing the academy, Harris embarked on a new career as a diplomat. In 1856, following the directive of Secretary of State William Marcy, he called upon King Mongkut, Rama IV of Siam (reigned 1851–1868) and successfully negotiated a trade treaty. Harris sailed on to the empire of Japan and landed in the town of Shimoda to negotiate a treaty with the 13th Tokugawa Shôgun, Tokugawa Iesada (1824–1858). This Treaty of Amity and Commerce was signed and ratified by the U.S. Senate in 1858.

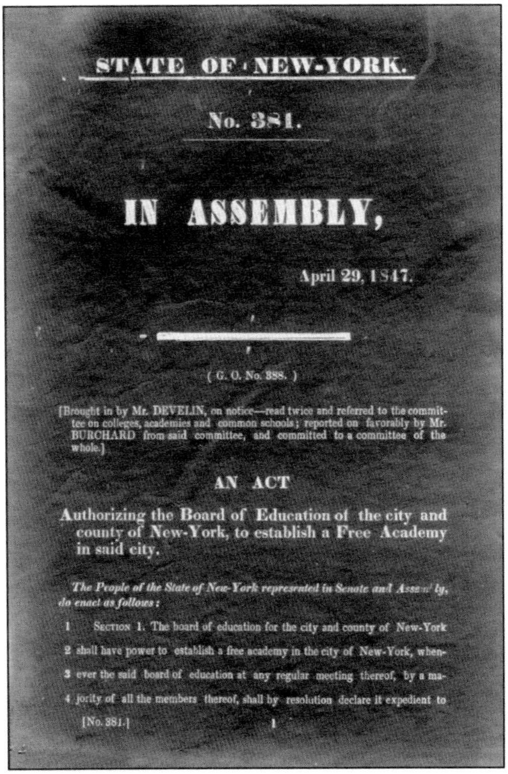
STATE OF NEW-YORK.

No. 381.

IN ASSEMBLY,

April 29, 1847.

(G. O. No. 388.)

[Brought in by Mr. DEVELIN, on notice—read twice and referred to the committee on colleges, academies and common schools; reported on favorably by Mr. BURCHARD from said committee, and committed to a committee of the whole.]

AN ACT

Authorizing the Board of Education of the city and county of New-York, to establish a Free Academy in said city.

The People of the State of New-York represented in Senate and Assembly, do enact as follows:

SECTION 1. The board of education for the city and county of New-York shall have power to establish a free academy in the city of New-York, whenever the said board of education at any regular meeting thereof, by a majority of all the members thereof, shall by resolution declare it expedient to

[No. 381.] 1

New York State Assembly bill No. 381 was approved on April 29, 1847, permitting the expenditures for a new higher education institution. On May 7, 1847, the two legislative bills were reconciled and passed, with approval "to establish a free academy in the city of New-York." The voters of New York considered the referendum in the judicial and school elections held on June 7, 1847, and passed it by a vote of 19,305 in favor and 3,409 against. The Commissioners of Common Schools, constituting a board of education for the city and county of New York, convened on June 16, 1847, to formalize the creation of the Free Academy. These New York State legislative acts are considered to be the charter documents of the City College of New York.

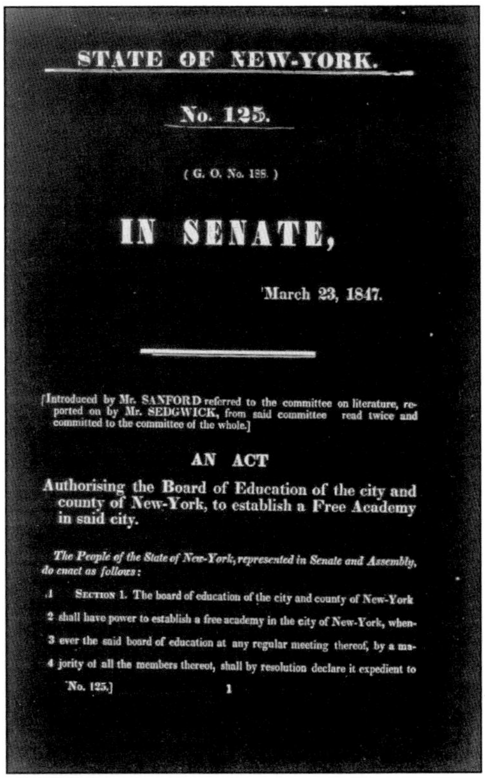
STATE OF NEW-YORK.

No. 125.

(G. O. No. 188.)

IN SENATE,

March 23, 1847.

[Introduced by Mr. SANFORD referred to the committee on literature, reported on by Mr. SEDGWICK, from said committee read twice and committed to the committee of the whole.]

AN ACT

Authorising the Board of Education of the city and county of New-York, to establish a Free Academy in said city.

The People of the State of New-York, represented in Senate and Assembly, do enact as follows:

SECTION 1. The board of education of the city and county of New-York shall have power to establish a free academy in the city of New-York, whenever the said board of education at any regular meeting thereof, by a majority of all the members thereof, shall by resolution declare it expedient to

No. 125.] 1

New York State Senate bill No. 125, authorizing financial support from the Literature Fund for a new institution of higher learning, passed on March 28, 1847.

The Free Academy Building, designed by James Renwick Jr., was home to the college from 1849 to 1907. Located at the corner of Lexington Avenue and 23rd Street, it is seen here in 1893, standing at an intersection as busy with pedestrians and traffic then as it is today. Measuring 80 by 125 feet, the Free Academy Building had such up-to-date conveniences as gaslights and running water piped in from the Croton Aqueduct. It was likely the first Gothic Revival college building on the east coast. Renwick, a young architect who would soon design St. Patrick's Cathedral, derived the form of this building after medieval town halls he had seen in Holland and Belgium and after King's College Chapel, Cambridge, England.

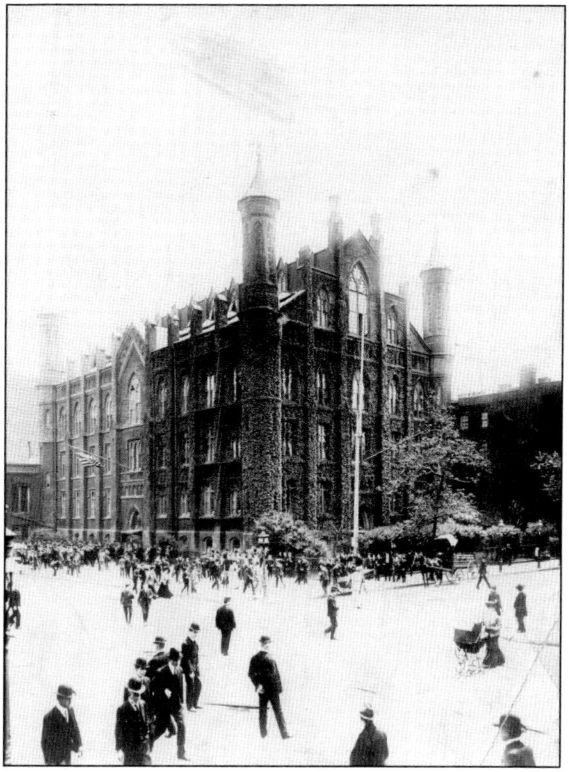

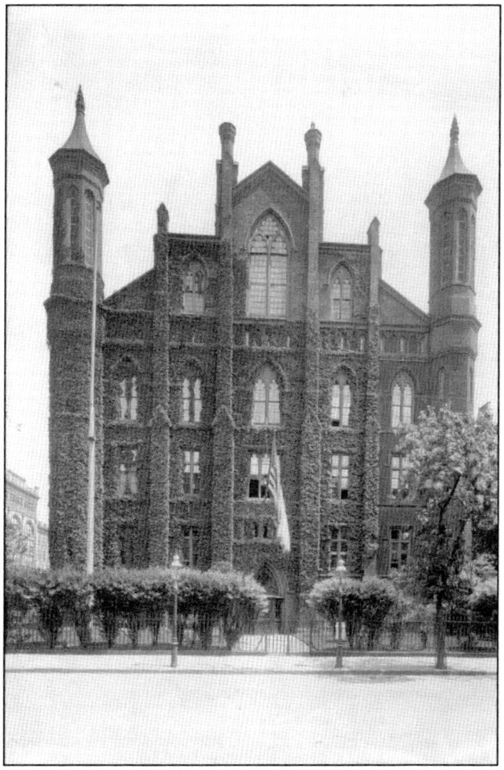

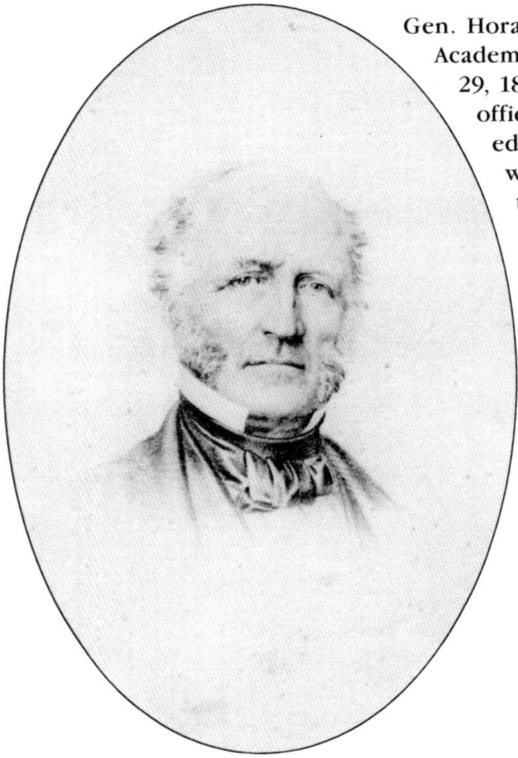

Gen. Horace Webster was the president of the Free Academy when the institution opened on January 29, 1849, until 1869. He was a teacher, presiding officer, and disciplinarian who believed in the educational "experiment [that] is to be tried, whether the highest education can be given to the masses, whether the children of the whole people can be educated." A former teacher of mathematics at the New York Military Academy at West Point, he encouraged the study of mathematics and science in an era when a "gentleman's education" concentrated on classical languages. The boys enrolled in the academy referred to him as "Pop," and he cautioned them to avoid alcohol and tobacco.

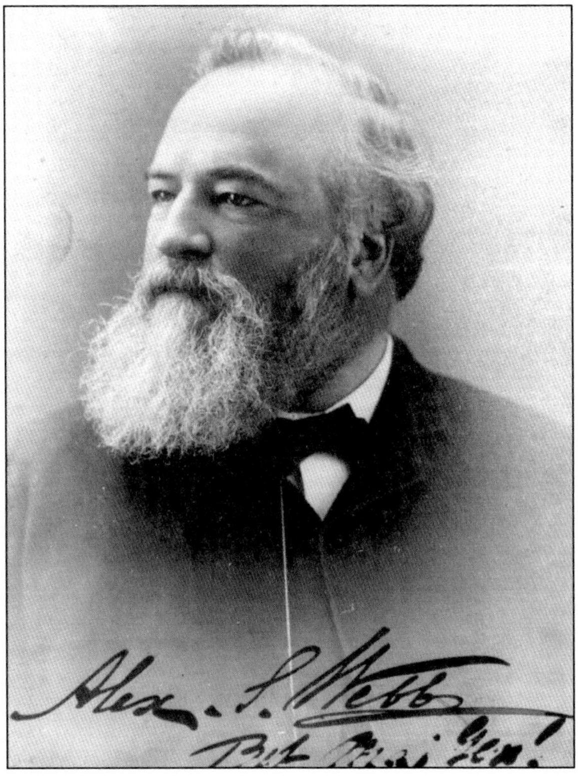

Gen. Alexander Stewart Webb received his education at West Point and taught mathematics there. He served the Union with distinction in the Civil War, particularly at the Battle of Gettysburg, garnering the Congressional Medal of Honor for "conspicuous personal bravery." He became the second president of the College of the City of New York. During his tenure from 1869 to 1902, a mechanical course was introduced into the curriculum, which laid the foundations for the Grove School of Engineering. Webster was opposed to the elective system, believing it suitable for graduate students but not for undergraduates. He worked hard to acquire the property in St. Nicholas Heights for a new campus. During these years, he became a founding member and the first president of the Westminster Kennel Club.

This ledger book records the names of the students who took the examination for admission to the first class in 1849. Note No. 195, John Hardie (or Hardy) as one accepted to be in the first group of 143 young men who entered the institution on January 27, 1849. Townsend Harris attended the opening ceremony. John Hardy was the salutatorian of the first graduating class on July 26, 1853. The commencement was held at Nilbo's Saloon that year. A founding member of the Associate Alumni Association and its first president in 1853, Hardy was elected to the New York State Assembly in 1860.

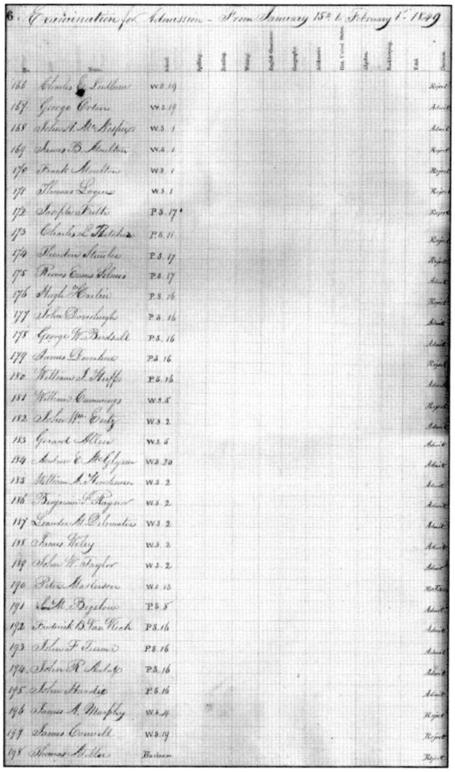

6. Examination for Admission – From January 15th to February 1st 1849

No.	Name	School	Spelling	Reading	Writing	English Grammar	Geography	Arithmetic	Hist. United States	Algebra	Bookkeeping	Total	Decision
166	Charles E. [illegible]	W.S. 19											Reject
167	George Orton	W.S. 19											Admit
168	John A. Mc[illegible]	W.S. 1											Admit
169	James B. Moulton	W.S. 1											Reject
170	Frank Moulton	W.S. 1											Reject
171	Thomas Logan	W.S. 1											Reject
172	Joseph Frith	P.S. 17											Reject
173	Charles L. Fletcher	P.S. 11											Reject
174	Theodore Stanley	P.S. 17											Reject
175	Reeves Evans Selmes	P.S. 17											Admit
176	Hugh Hartin	P.S. 16											Reject
177	John Dorsebugh	P.S. 16											Admit
178	George W. Birdsall	P.S. 16											Admit
179	James Dunbar	P.S. 16											Reject
180	William J. Stuff	P.S. 16											Admit
181	William Cummings	W.S. 5											Reject
182	John Wm. Ertz	W.S. 2											Admit
183	Gerard Allen	W.S. 5											Admit
184	Andrew E. McGlynn	W.S. 20											Admit
185	William A. Henderson	W.S. 2											Admit
186	Benjamin F. Raynor	W.S. 2											Admit
187	Leander M. Delamater	W.S. 2											Admit
188	James Wiley	W.S. 2											Admit
189	John W. Taylor	W.S. 2											Admit
190	Peter Masterson	W.S. 13											Not Ex[illegible]
191	A. M. Bigelow	P.S. 8											Admit
192	Frederick B. Van Vleck	P.S. 16											Admit
193	John F. Tieman	P.S. 16											Admit
194	John R. Rudolph	P.S. 16											Admit
195	John Hardie	P.S. 16											Admit
196	James A. Murphy	W.S. 4											Reject
197	James Connell	W.S. 19											Reject
198	Thomas Miller	Harlaem											Reject

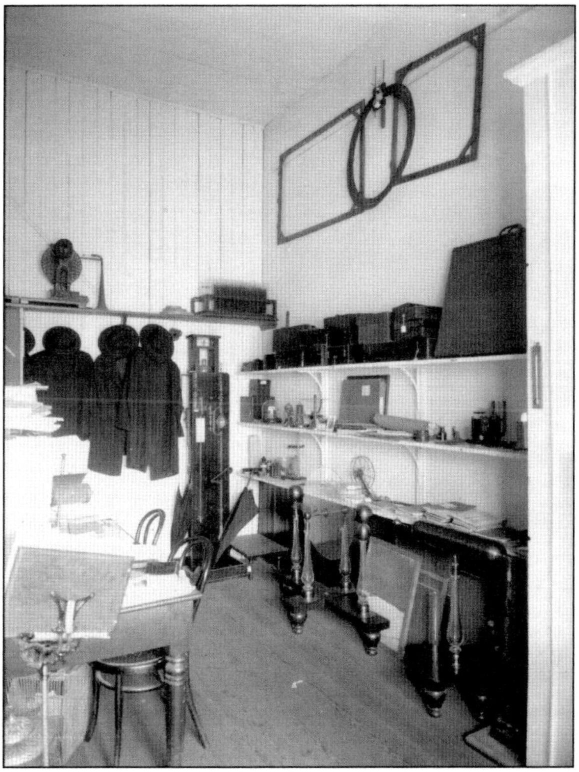

The small size of the coats hanging on pegs in a Free Academy classroom are mute testimony to the fact that the young men who enrolled in the Free Academy were often only 13 or 14 years of age. They took the admission exam after finishing their education in the New York Free School System, which covered grades one through eight.

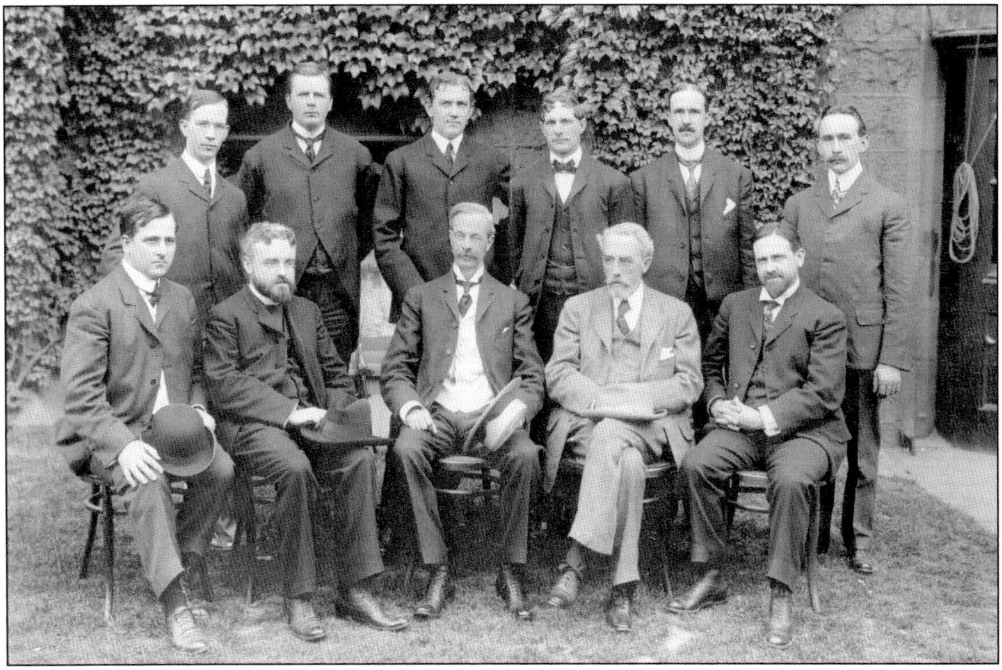

The history faculty of the College of the City of New York in 1905 included the following, from left to right: (first row) Thomas R. Moore, Livingston R. Schuyler, Henry P. Johnston, William G. McGuckan, and John R. Todd; (second row) Guy S. Snider, William B. Guthrie, Holland Thompson, Livingston B. Morse, Samuel C. Haight, and Nelson P. Mead.

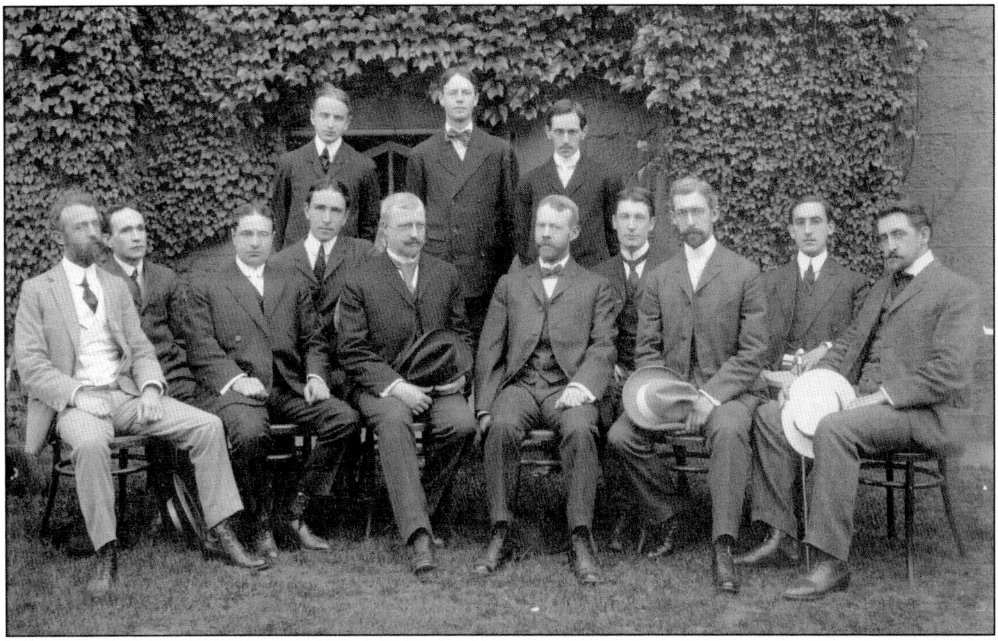

Members of the English department in 1905 were as follows, from left to right: (first row) Charles F. Horne, Earle F. Palmer, Edwin S. Brickner, Jarvis Keiley, Lewis F. Mott, Earnest N. Perrin, ? Sheridan, Harry C. Krowl, Henry Neumann, and Thomas G. Toaffe; (second row) Charles Galway, William B. Otis, and Felix Greulon.

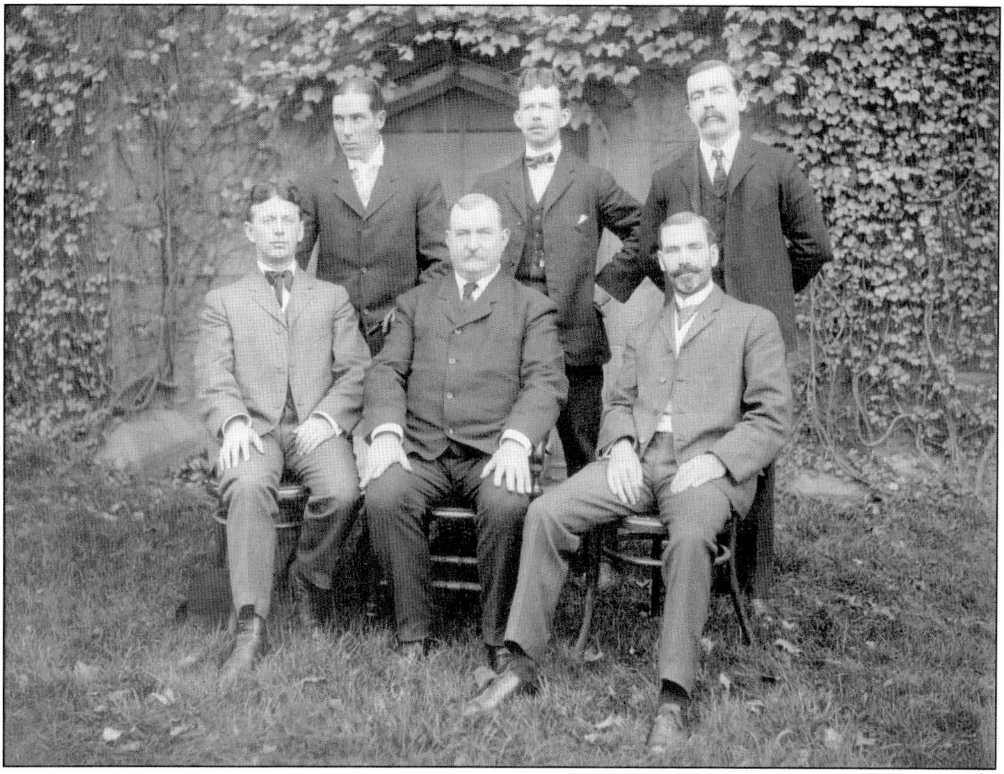

The faculty members who taught philosophy during the early 20th century included, from left to right, (first row) Walter E. Clark, John J. McNulty, and Stephen P. Duggan; (second row) ? Spaulding, George G. Scott, and Bernhard D. Saxe.

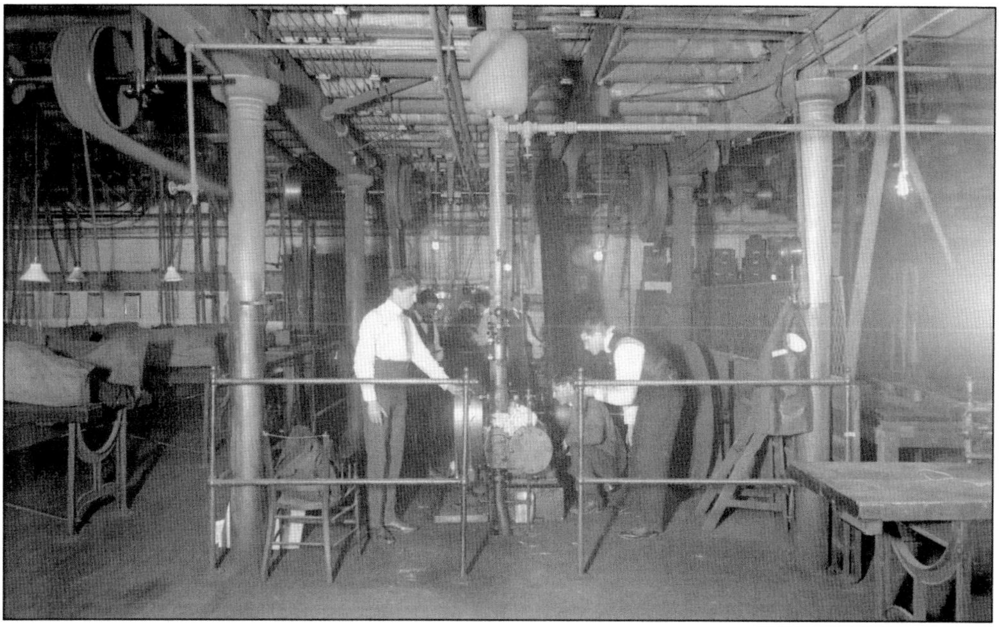

Students in Professor Alfred G. Compton's course examine an engine. The mechanical arts courses laid the foundations for the Grove School of Engineering.

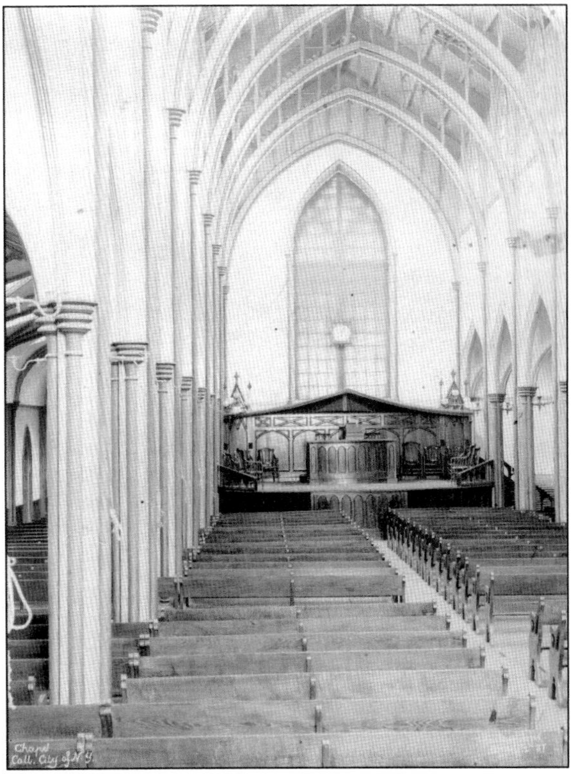

The chapel occupied the top floor of the Free Academy Building. Each class day, the college community gathered for a mandatory assembly and listened to Pres. Horace Webster or Pres. Alexander Webb read a Biblical passage. Spanned by wooden Gothic arched colonnades, this hall could accommodate 1,300 people.

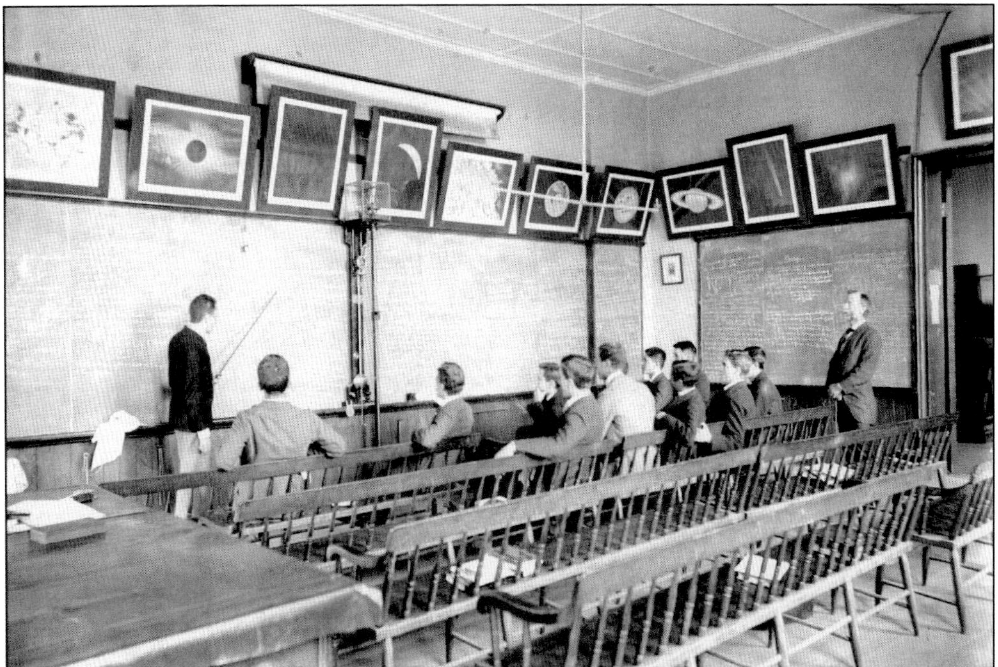

Astronomy was part of the natural history curriculum of the Free Academy. All academy classes included recitations, which were opportunities for the student to demonstrate to the professor how much lesson material had been memorized.

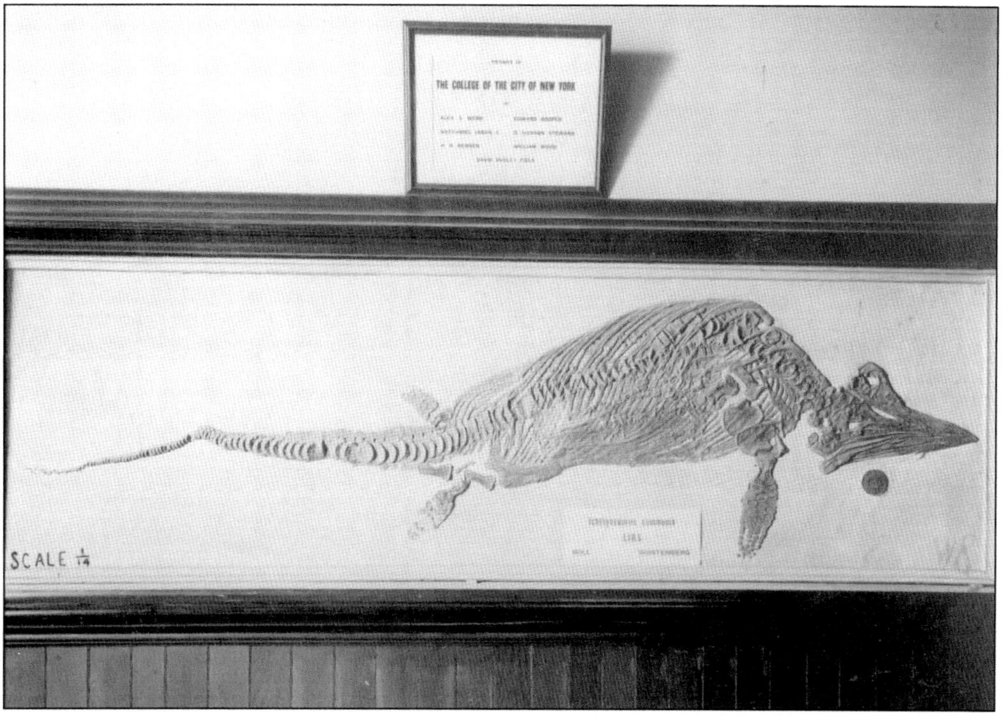

This *Ichthyosaurus communis* fossil specimen was adopted as a college mascot by many successive classes of the Free Academy.

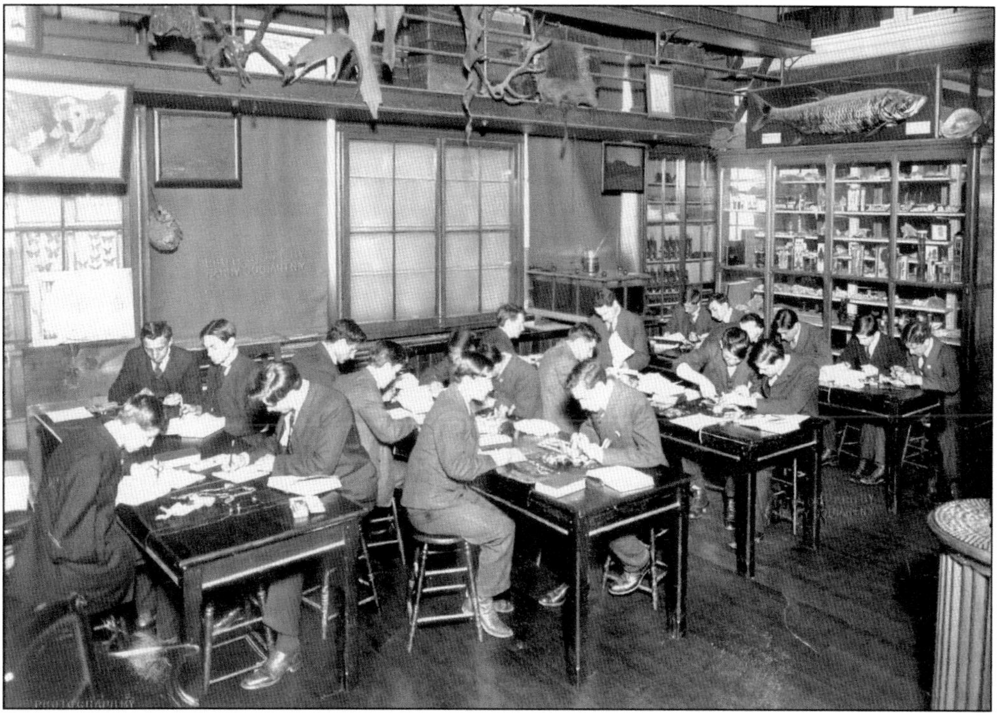

A class in the Natural History Hall, the east room of the Free Academy Building, is engaged in the work of dissecting and diagraming the results.

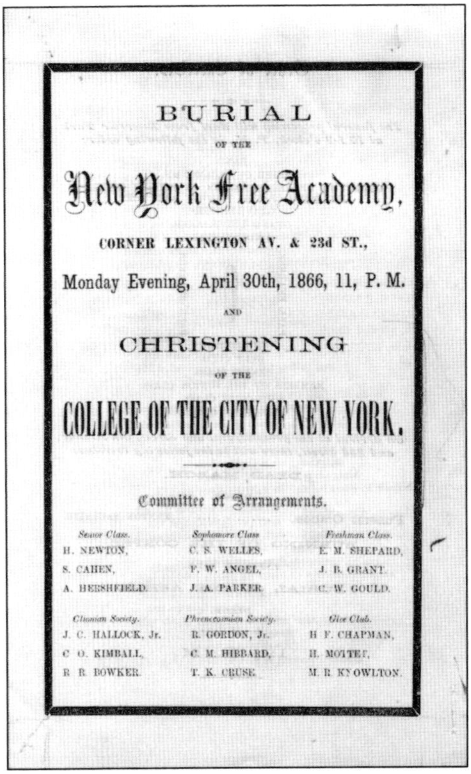

BURIAL

OF THE

New York Free Academy,

CORNER LEXINGTON AV. & 23d ST.,

Monday Evening, April 30th, 1866, 11, P. M.

AND

CHRISTENING

OF THE

COLLEGE OF THE CITY OF NEW YORK.

Committee of Arrangements.

Senior Class.	*Sophomore Class*	*Freshman Class.*
H. NEWTON,	C. S. WELLES,	E. M. SHEPARD,
S. CAHEN,	F. W. ANGEL,	J. B. GRANT.
A. HERSHFIELD.	J. A. PARKER.	C. W. GOULD.
Clionian Society.	*Phrenocosmian Society.*	*Glee Club.*
J. C. HALLOCK, Jr.	R. GORDON, Jr.	H F. CHAPMAN,
C O. KIMBALL,	C. M. HIBBARD,	H. MOTTEF,
R R. BOWKER.	T. K. CRUSE.	M. R KNOWLTON.

This brochure states that the Free Academy has been buried, only to be transformed into the College of the City of New York. A noisy procession of students down Fifth Avenue from 42nd Street to 23rd Street on April 30, 1866, announced to residents that the college they had voted to support with taxes had gained a new name.

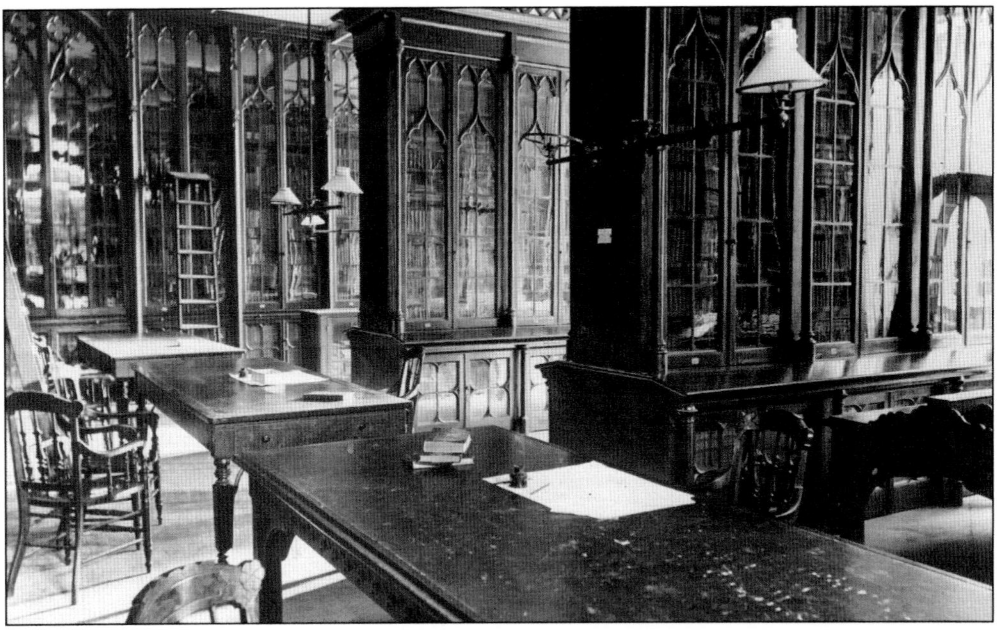

The original institutional library provided limited access to members of the college community. Students could check out one book between 8:30 and 9:00 a.m. on alternate Fridays upon presenting a detailed form with three faculty signatures. Books were to be returned between 3:00 and 3:30 p.m. on alternate Fridays. Professors could borrow up to six books at one time, while tutors were allowed only three.

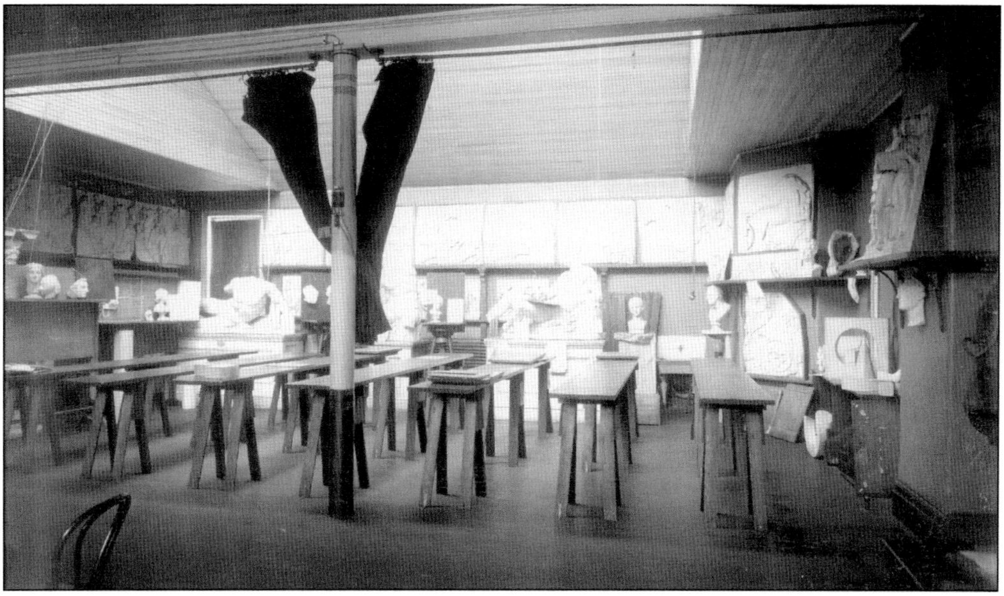

In the Old Drawing Room, casts of Parthenon sculptures from the pediment and the frieze are on display. These sculptures were used as models for the drawing classes that were part of the curriculum for both the arts and the science students. Prof. P. P. Duggan made the most of whatever talent his students possessed. This set of plaster casts, taken in the 1830s from the marble originals in the British Museum, was presented by Charles M. Leupp, Esq., to the college in 1852 as one of the first of its kind to come to the United States.

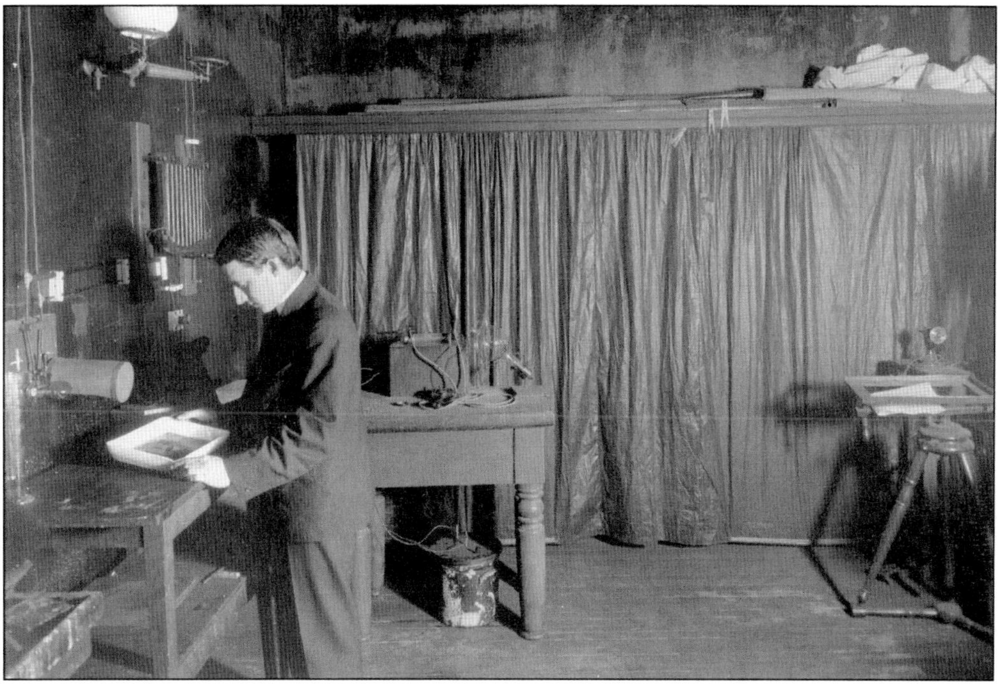

Students in a dark room are engaged in photographic work. Photography has been an interest of City College students since the days of the Free Academy. Classes in photographic technique are currently offered by the Department of Art.

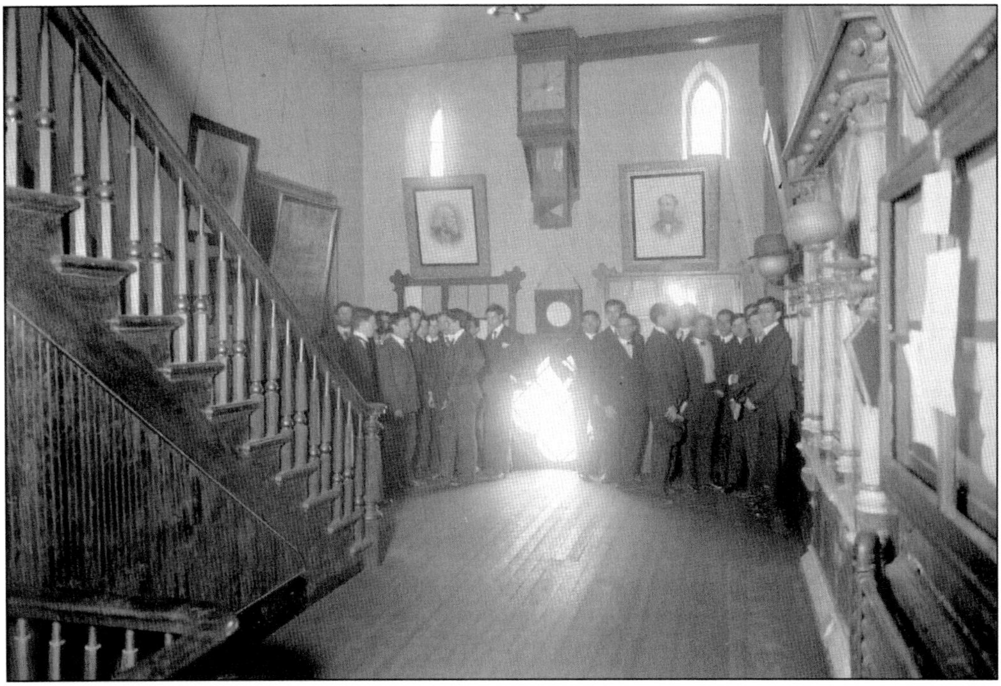

Free Academy students stand in the corridor. The memorial tablet recording the names of those students who died fighting for the Union in the Civil War is on the wall to the right.

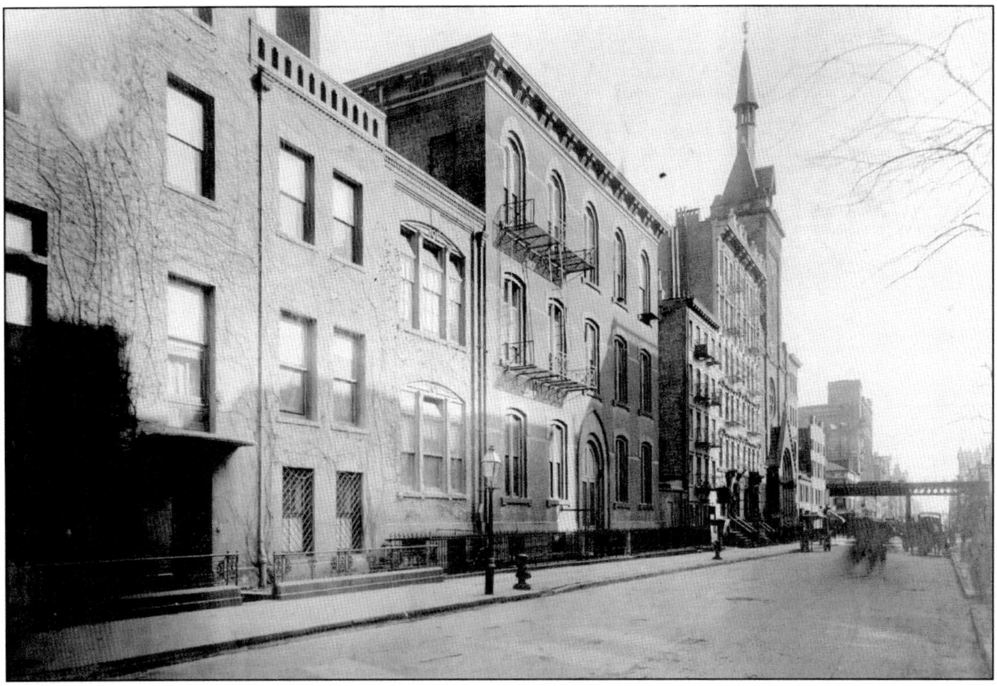

The Free Academy rapidly outgrew the 125-by-80-foot space provided by the original building, therefore expanding to the east and south. The student body had grown from 768 to 1,969 by the time Gen. Alexander Webb left office in 1902. Looking east along 23rd Street, this view shows some of the space acquired by the growing institution in the Gramercy Park neighborhood.

Two

From a Guild Hall to Grotesques

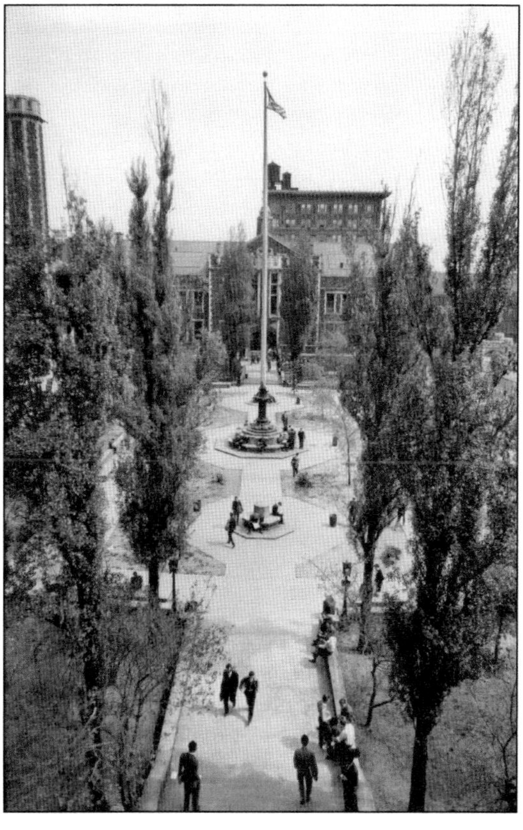

In 1898, George B. Post garnered the commission to construct a new campus. The trustees and alumni on the competition jury "found themselves led to the belief that the kinship of Post's Collegiate Gothic design was associated with the medieval images of Oxford and Cambridge." Post chose a striking combination of building materials for the new campus: gneiss excavated from the construction area itself and terra-cotta ornamentation. Grotesque sculptural elements designed by G. Grandellis include figures engaged in activities reflecting the academic disciplines studied within. These buildings, constructed between 1903 and 1907, form the quadrangle flanked by the Main Building (now Shepard Hall) and constitute the St. Nicholas Heights campus. A flagpole is seen in the center of the quadrangle in this northward view from Wingate Hall. In 1981, the New York Landmarks Preservation Commission designated these buildings as landmarks. In 1985, the quadrangle buildings were placed on the State and National Register of Historic Places.

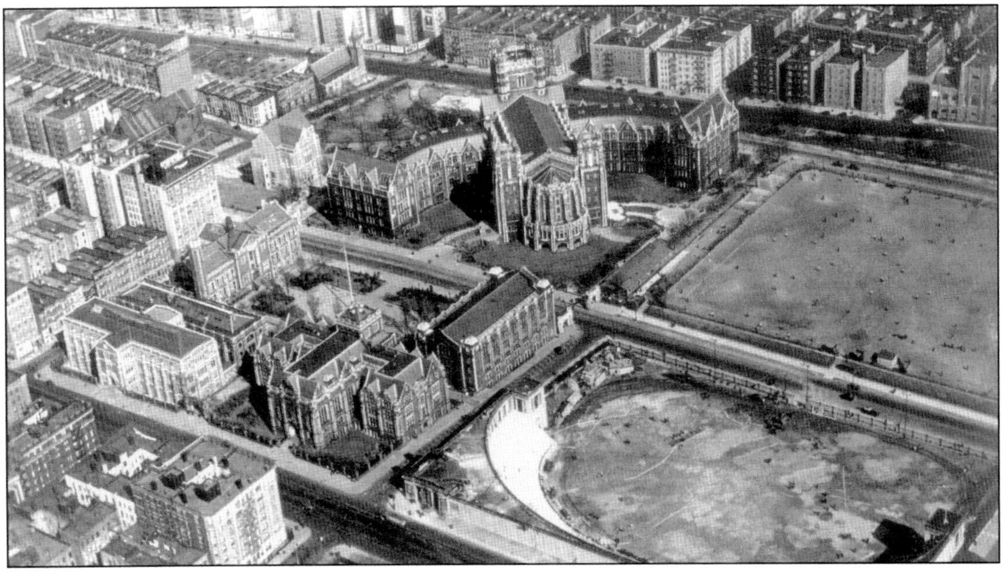

The City College campus is seen from the air around 1937 (above) and about 1986 (below). The Post-designed buildings lie to the north, and flanking them to the south in the 1937 view is the curve of Lewisohn Stadium. In the 1986 view, the stadium has been replaced by North Academic Center. The Post buildings include Harris Hall, named for the founder of the institution, Townsend Harris. It was meant to accommodate the young men engaged in preparatory work as students of the Townsend Harris Hall High School who, upon completion of their three-year course of study, were guaranteed a place in the freshman class of City College. Next to Harris Hall is the former School of Technology (later engineering) building, designated in 1955 Alfred G. Compton Hall, with a smokestack for a power-generating station now inactive. To the right of these structures is the original chemistry building, named Baskerville Hall in honor of early chemistry professor Charles Baskerville. To the east of the quadrangle building is Shepard Hall, originally the Main Building, named in honor of an alumnus and trustee Edward M. Shepard (class of 1869). Finally, denoting the southern boundary of this area is Wingate Hall, named for George Wingate (class of 1858). (Above, City College Archives; below, Philip Carvalho.)

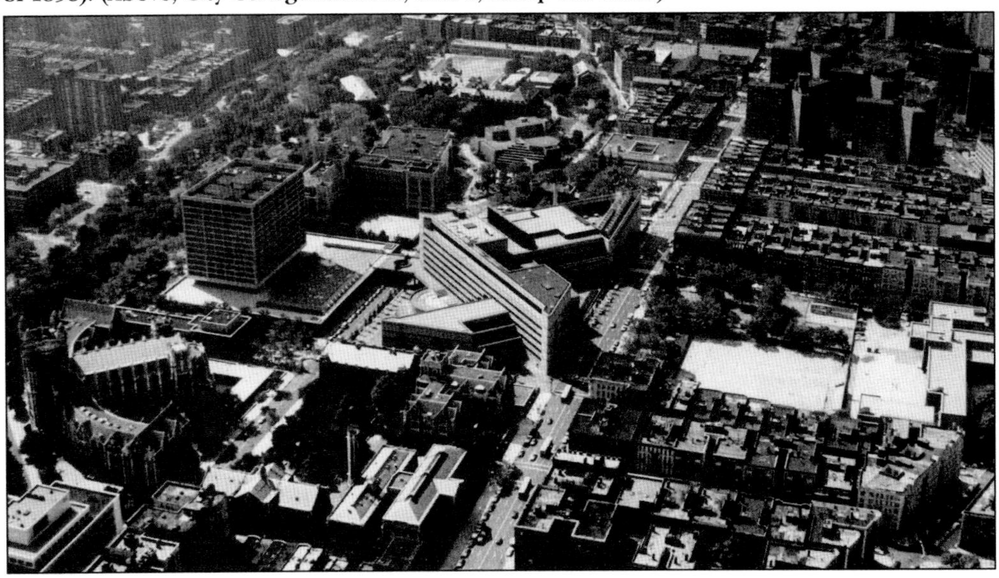

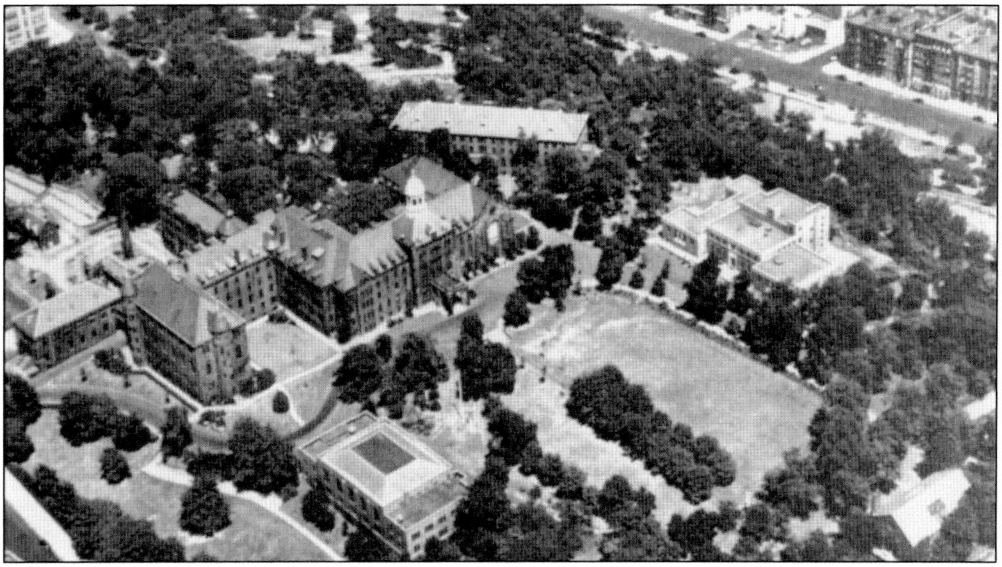

When Manhattanville College decided to relocate to Westchester, City College was given the opportunity to acquire the grounds and buildings of the Manhattanville College of the Sacred Heart, shown here. The board of higher education passed a resolution urging New York City mayor William O'Dwyer and the board of estimate to purchase the property of Manhattanville College as an addition to the college in 1949. Alumni Association president Jacob Shapiro (class of 1911) mounted a campaign for public support. On June 29, 1950, the campaign reached its goal and the board of estimate voted for acquisition. After renovation, this part of the campus, with facilities for liberal arts education, opened in fall 1955.

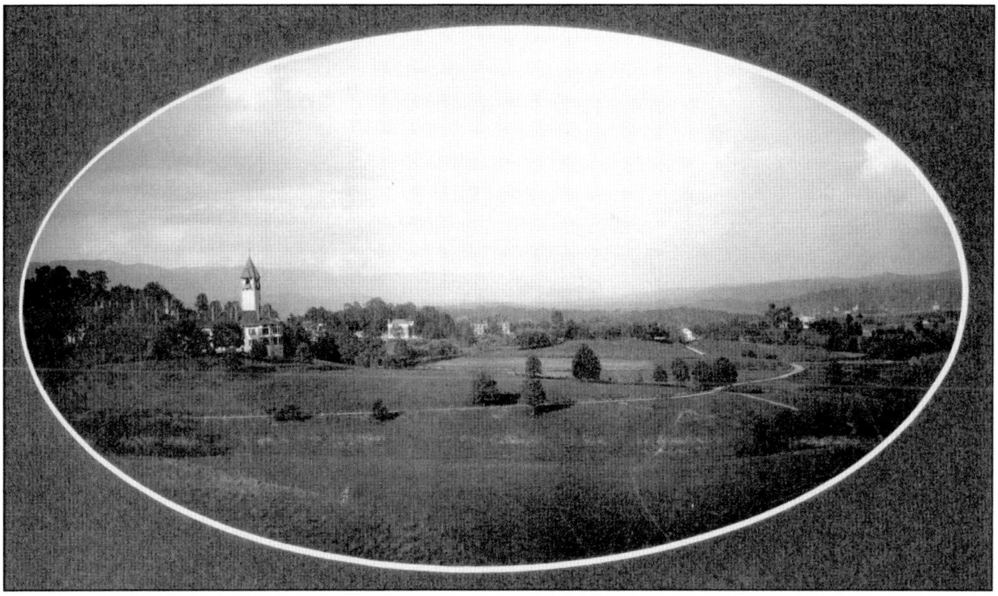

This *c.* 1860 view depicts the Female Academy of the Sacred Heart, which became known as Manhattanville College in 1917. Taught by nuns, young ladies came to this institution far from the growing city for fresh air and a quiet neighborhood. Construction began on the main building in 1847, the same year that the Free Academy was founded. Manhattanville College became the neighbor of City College when the uptown campus in St. Nicholas Heights was occupied in fall 1907.

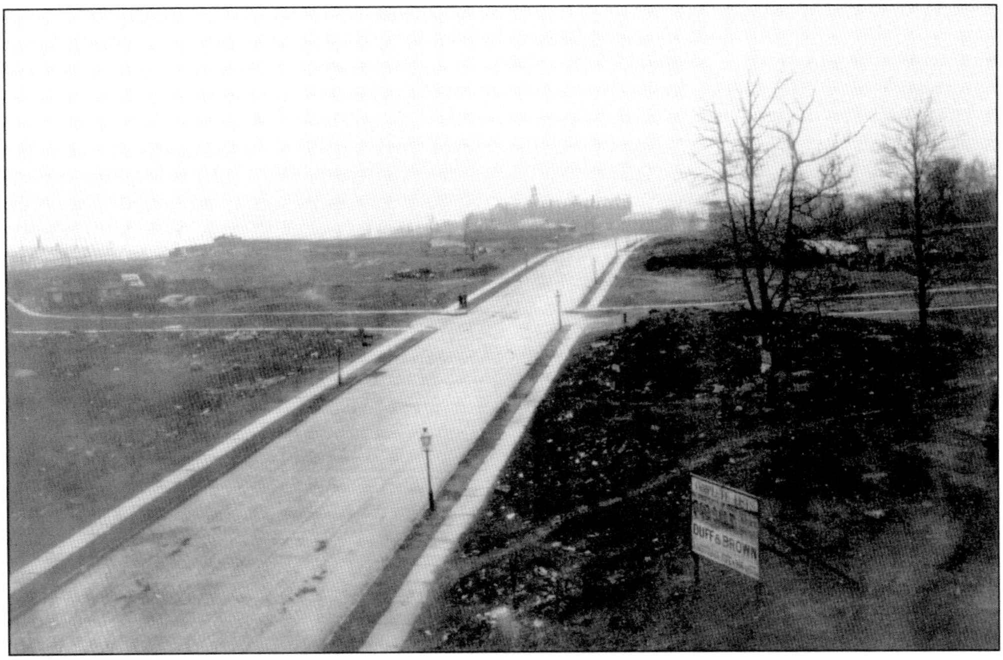

A *c.* 1900 view of Convent Avenue looks south toward the Female Academy of the Sacred Heart and the Gatehouse, or Croton Aqueduct System pumping station, on 135th Street. Six undeveloped parcels of land, which included this area, were purchased by New York City with appropriations from the state legislature for the development of the new campus.

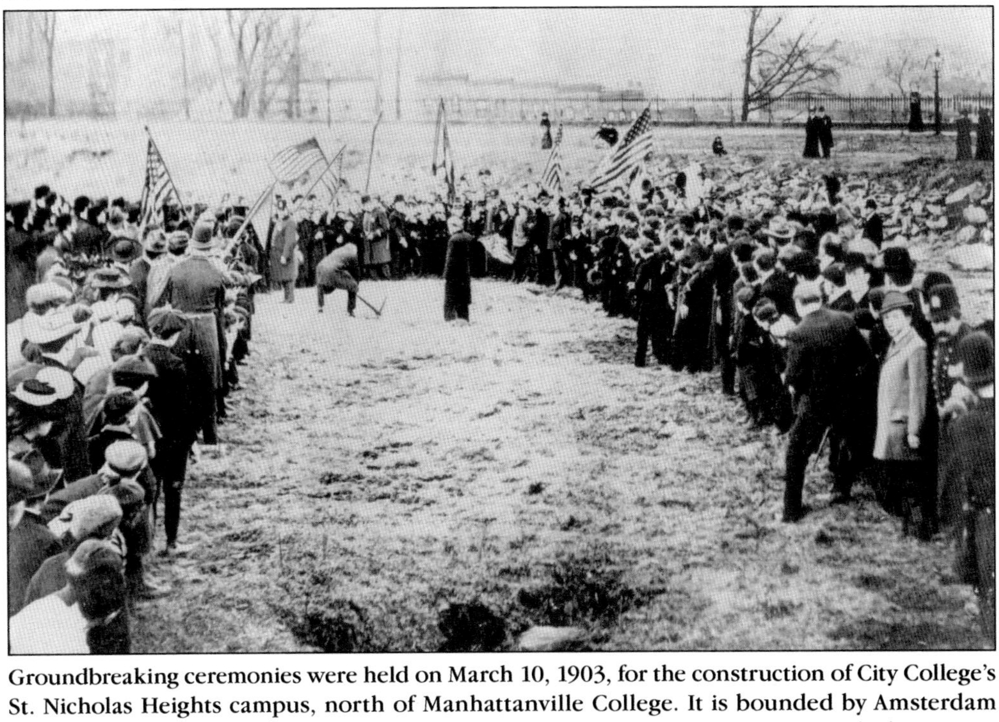

Groundbreaking ceremonies were held on March 10, 1903, for the construction of City College's St. Nicholas Heights campus, north of Manhattanville College. It is bounded by Amsterdam Avenue to the west, St. Nicholas Terrace to the east, 138th Street to the south, and 140th Street to the north.

The cornerstone for the Main Building was laid on September 29, 1903, by New York City mayor Seth Low. During the ceremony, Low employed a silver trowel made by Tiffany and Company.

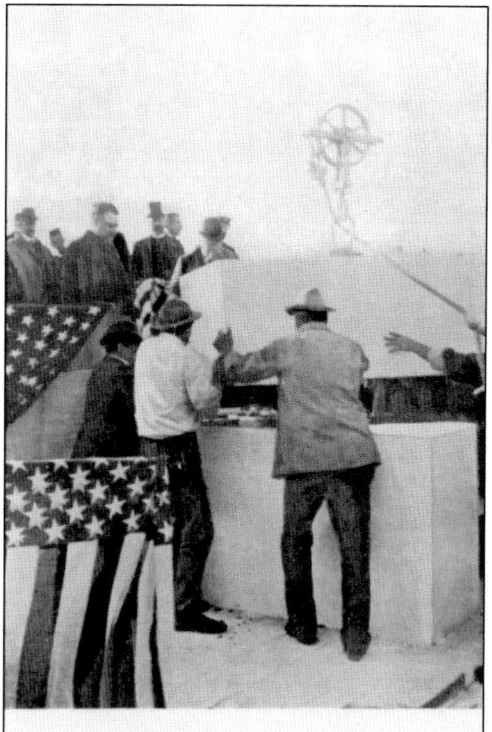

LAYING OF CORNER STONE TO NEW COLLEGE

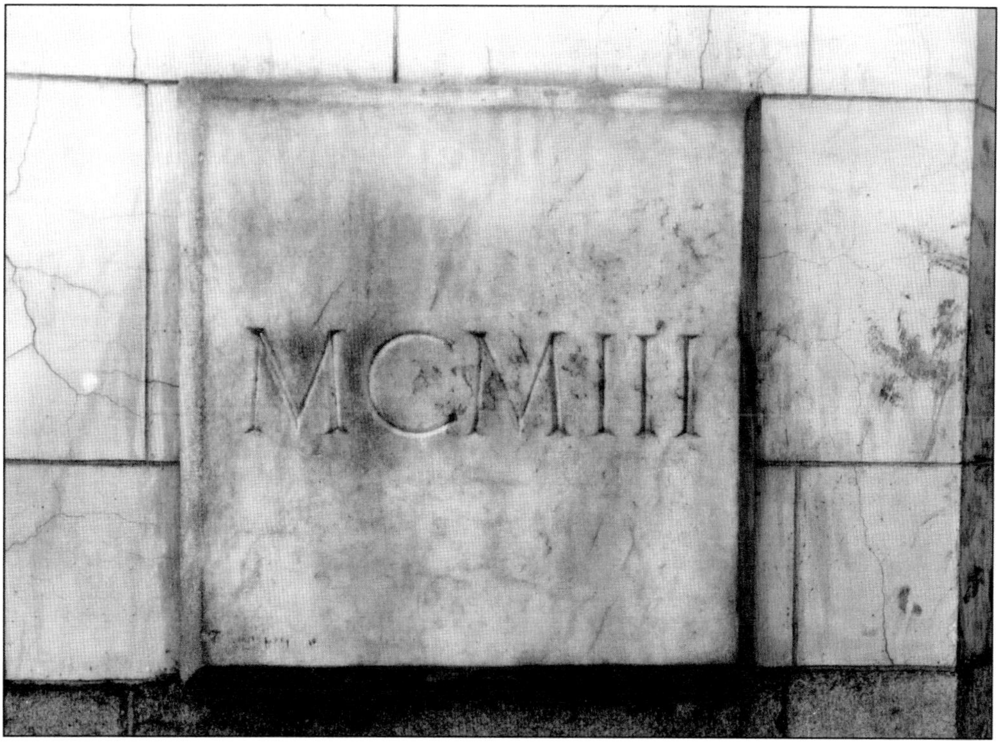

The cornerstone of the Main Building displays the 1903 date of installation.

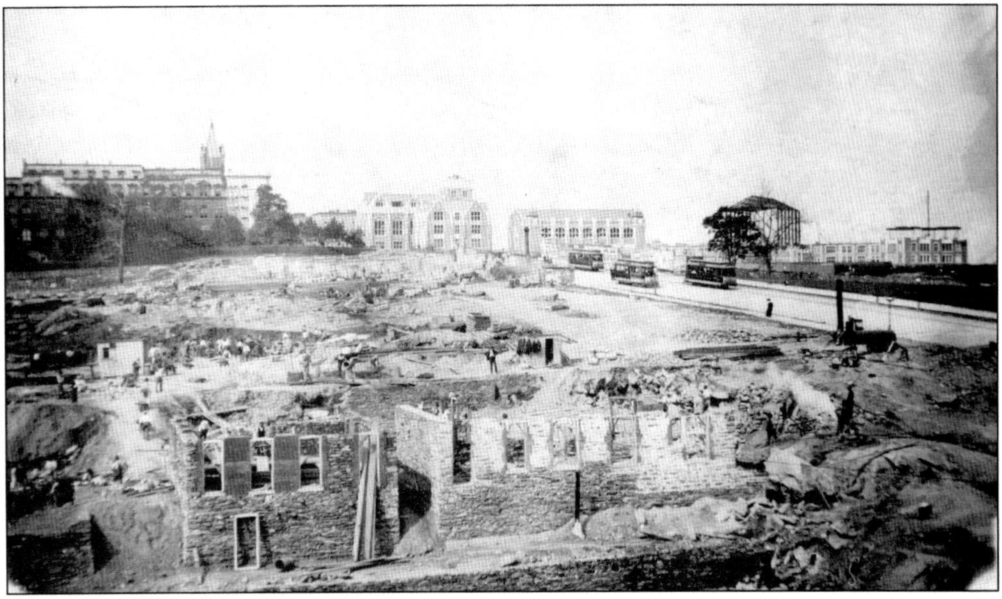

The campus buildings were constructed between 1903 and 1907. Although ground had been broken on March 10, 1903, construction contracts were not signed until later that year. Excavation and masonry work was behind schedule by April 1904, making an autumn completion date impossible. The work progressed slowly due to delays in the foundation work. The clashes among the contractors and between the contractors and client did not contribute to the swift progress of such a large building project.

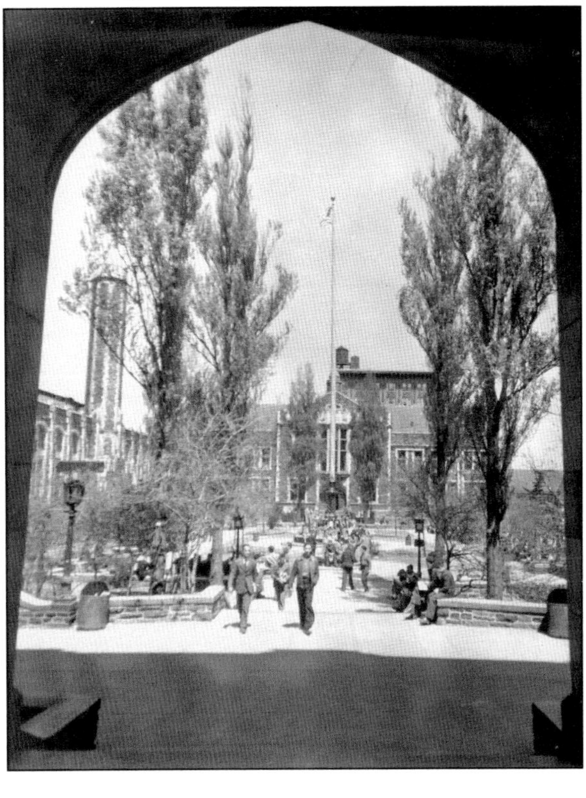

The quadrangle buildings of the campus were completed in time for classes to be held on the new campus in fall 1907. They were officially dedicated the following May. In this photograph, City College students of the 1930s walk between the buildings to their next classes.

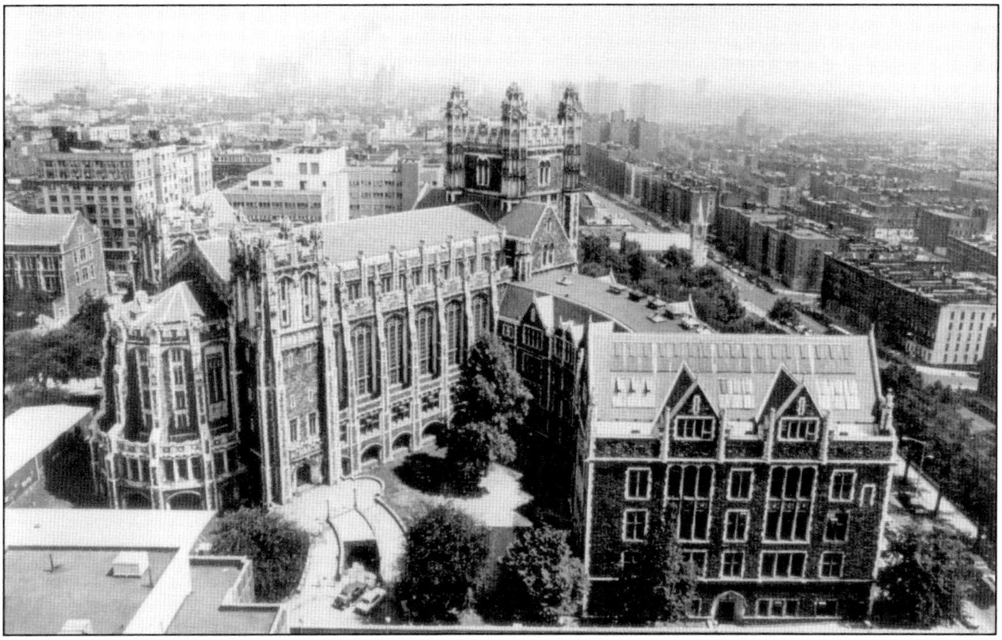

Shepard Hall, the original Main Building, seen from an elevated view point (above) and looking east from Convent Avenue (below), was meant to be the focus of the campus. The Gothic Great Hall, sitting along the central axis, included seating for 2,200 members of the community gathering for ceremonial occasions. The two curving wings for classrooms attached just behind the eastern face of the building. The structure housed the administrative offices, the library, and the classrooms for those disciplines not taught in the other four buildings.

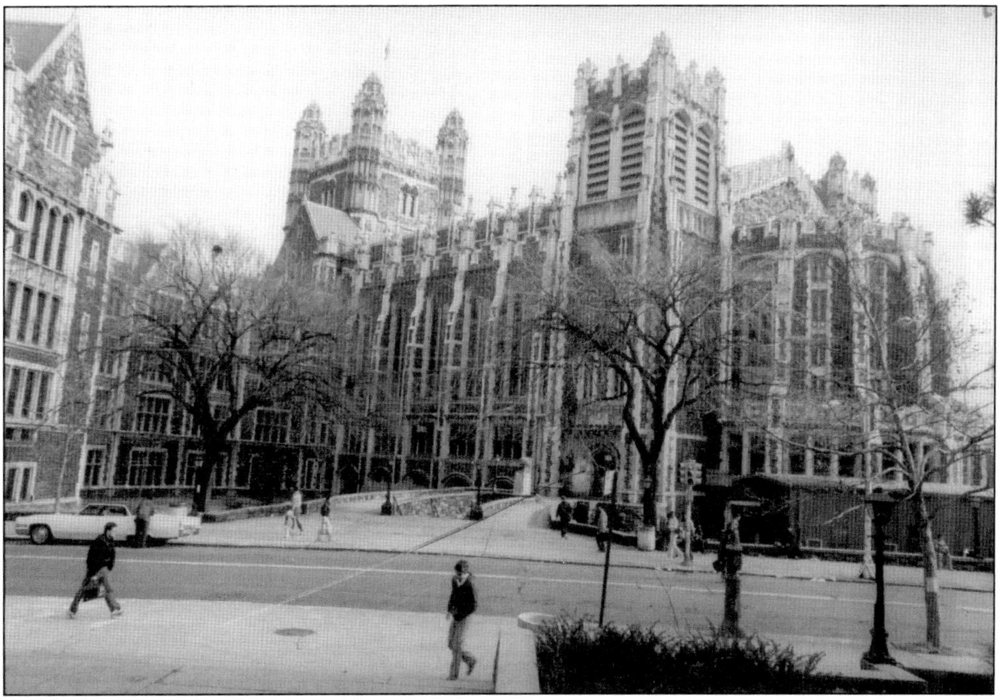

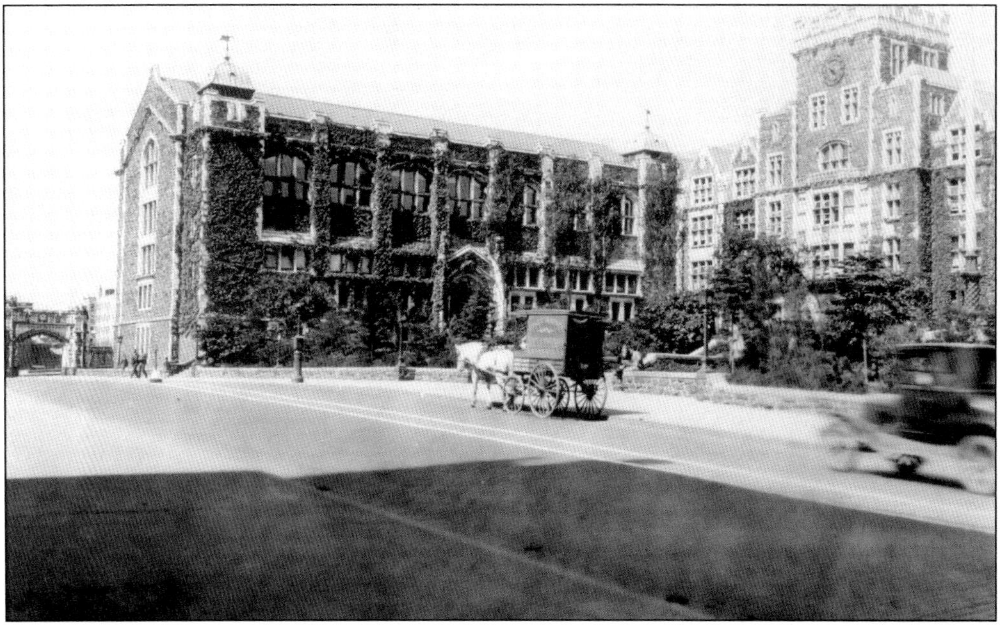

Wingate Hall, pictured soon after completion in 1907 for the Department of Physical and Health Education, featured a gymnasium and swimming pool on the lower level. The gymnasium provided indoor practice space for the basketball team for the first time since it was established in 1904. Additional facilities in the building allowed for other athletic pursuits.

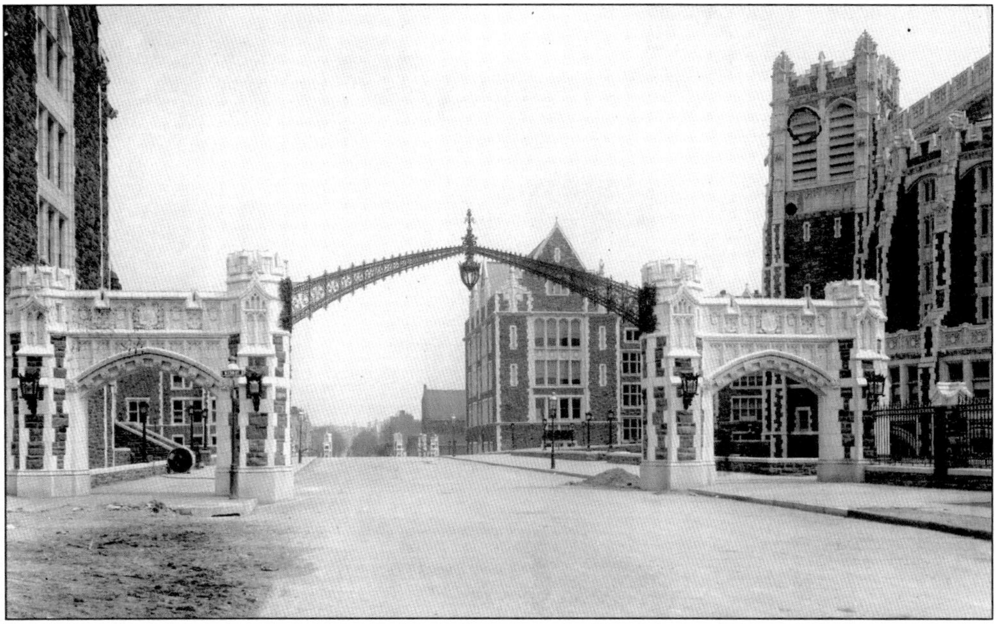

The George Washington Gate, spanning Convent Avenue at 138th Street, is one of three gates designed by George B. Post to unify the campus. The other two are the Hamilton Gate at 140th Street and Convent Avenue, which refers to Hamilton Grange, Alexander Hamilton's former home located to the north of the campus on Convent Avenue, and the Henry Hudson Gate on Amsterdam Avenue between Harris and Compton Halls.

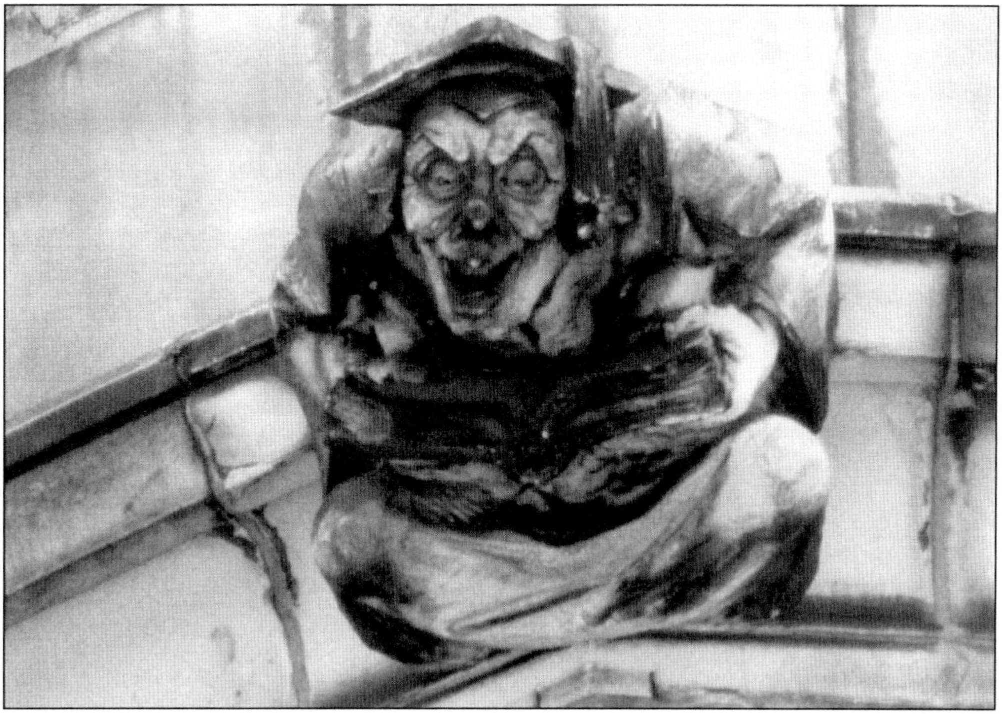

Many of the grotesque sculptures designed by G. Grandellis decorating the Collegiate Gothic buildings are engaged in activities that reflect the academic pursuits of the community. Above, a figure pauses while reading a book, while below, another pours a substance into a flask during an experiment. (Martin Sacks.)

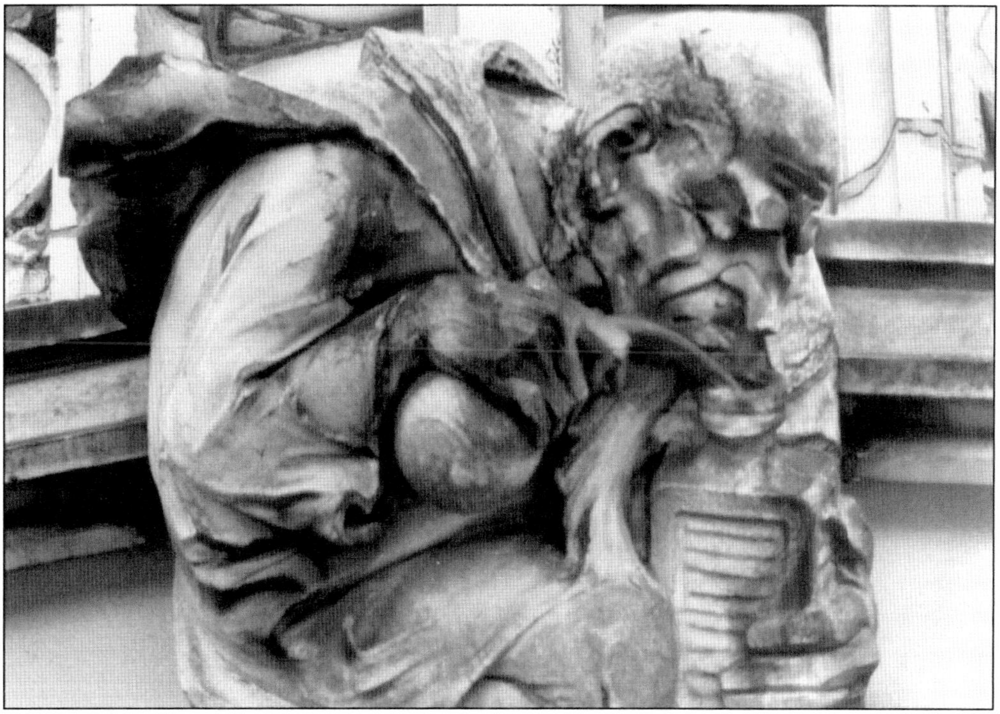

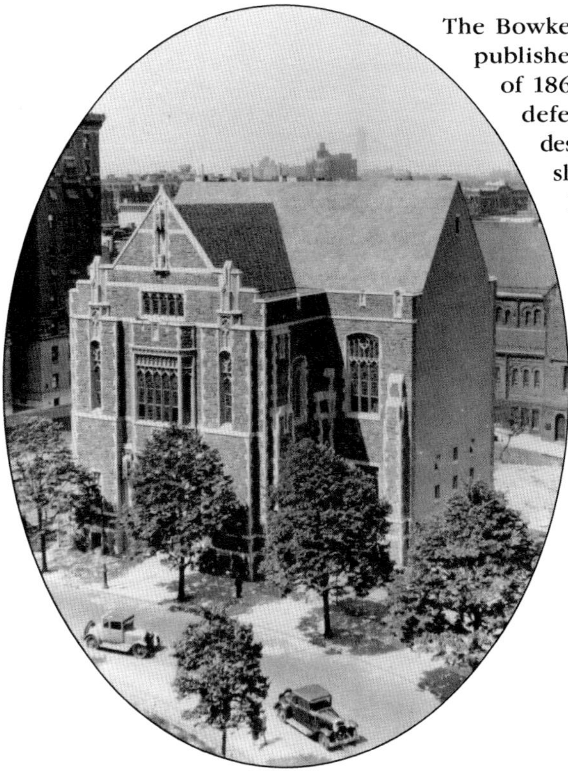

The Bowker Alumni Library, named in honor of publisher Richard Rogers Bowker of the class of 1868, was intended to remedy the major defect in George Post's original campus design—the lack of a library. The Depression slowed the rate of alumni giving, and the 1937 segment remained unfinished. When the Manhattanville campus was purchased, the location of the library at the extreme northern end of the site became inconvenient. Pres. Buell Gallagher determined that a totally new structure should be built in the middle of the campus. Thus, the original Morris Raphael Cohen Library was finished in 1957, and Bowker was demolished to make room for David B. Steinman Hall.

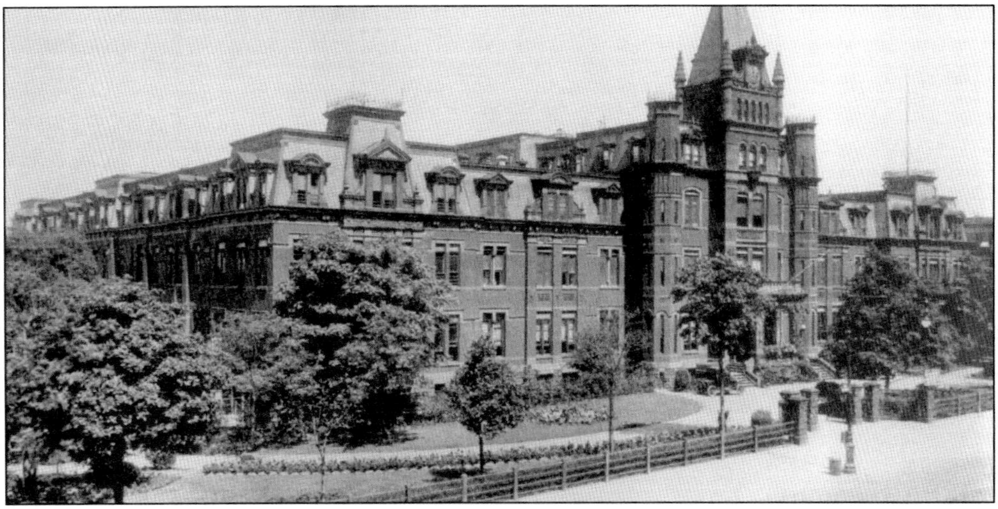

The Hebrew Orphan Asylum building, designed by William H. Hume, opened in 1883 across Amsterdam Avenue from what was to become the location of Lewisohn Stadium. This institution housed up to 1,250 children (mostly 9 to 11 years old) and staff members. By 1941, the population had dwindled to 607 children, who were dispersed to other city agencies and foster homes. In 1943, the building was purchased by New York City and then assigned to City College as a classification center and barracks for 3,000 soldiers under the new name of Army Hall. At the end of World War II, it was reconverted to provide accommodations for up to 500 male members of the student population, a number of sorely needed classrooms, and storage for a portion of the college's library collection.

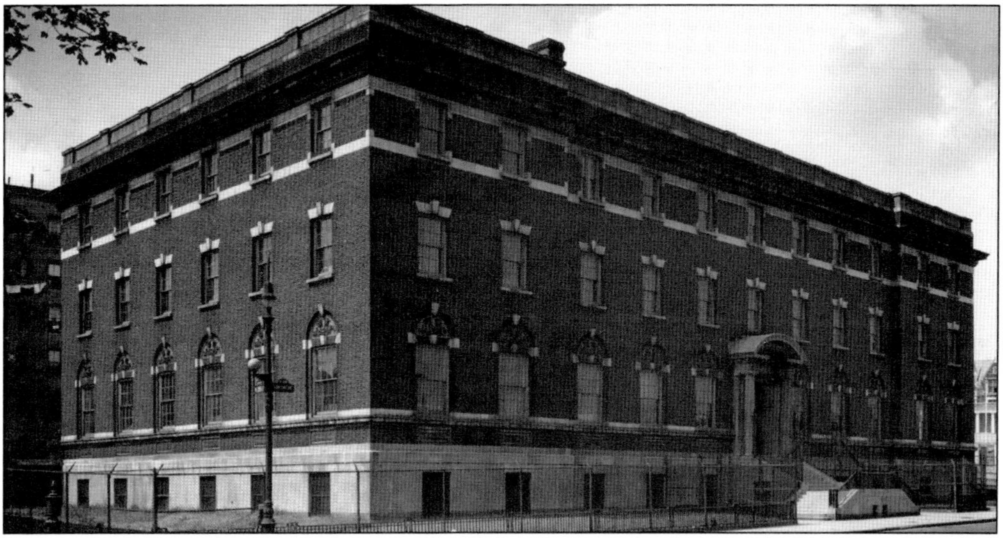

Paul Klapper Hall was designed by William Robins as the Protestant Episcopal Orphan Asylum. Constructed in 1905, the three-story brick building was turned over to City College in 1946 and remodeled for the Department of Hygiene. In 1949, it was again altered for the School of Education. At that time, the structure was renamed in honor of the distinguished professor and dean of the School of Education, Paul Klapper. He graduated from the College of the City of New York in 1904 and joined the faculty in 1907 as a tutor in education, making his career in the department as professor (1921) and dean (1928) until he departed to become the president of Queens College in 1937.

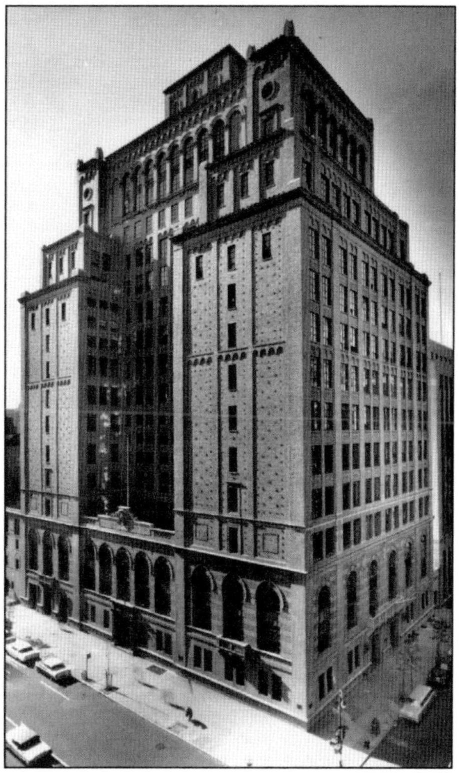

This structure replaced the original Free Academy Building at the corner of Lexington Avenue and 23rd Street. It was constructed between 1927 and 1929 for the commerce school.

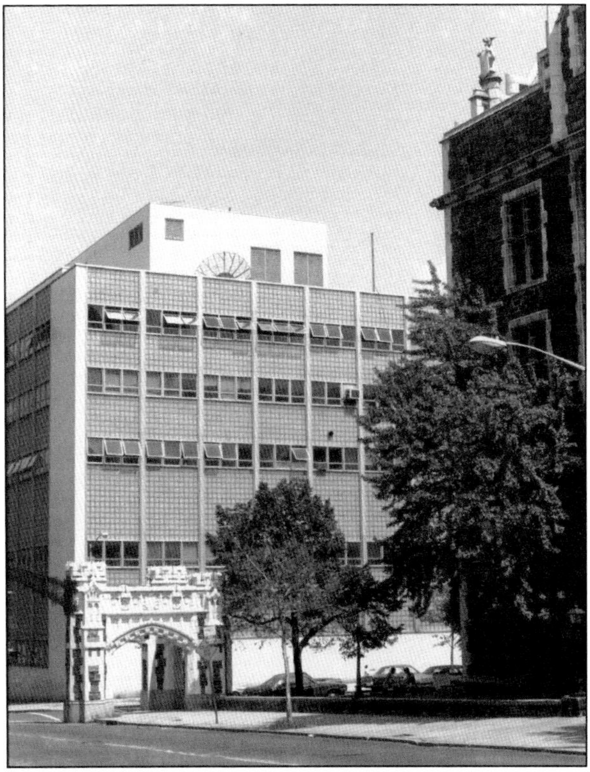

David B. Steinman Hall was named in honor of a member of the class of 1906. The new technology building was designed by architects and engineers Lorimar and Rose, who completed the structure in 1960. Steinman Hall consists of 280,000 square feet of classrooms, laboratories, administrative offices, and an auditorium. The Grove School of Engineering is considered to be the third largest in the nation. The school offers undergraduate and master's degrees in biomedical, chemical, civil, electrical, and mechanical engineering.

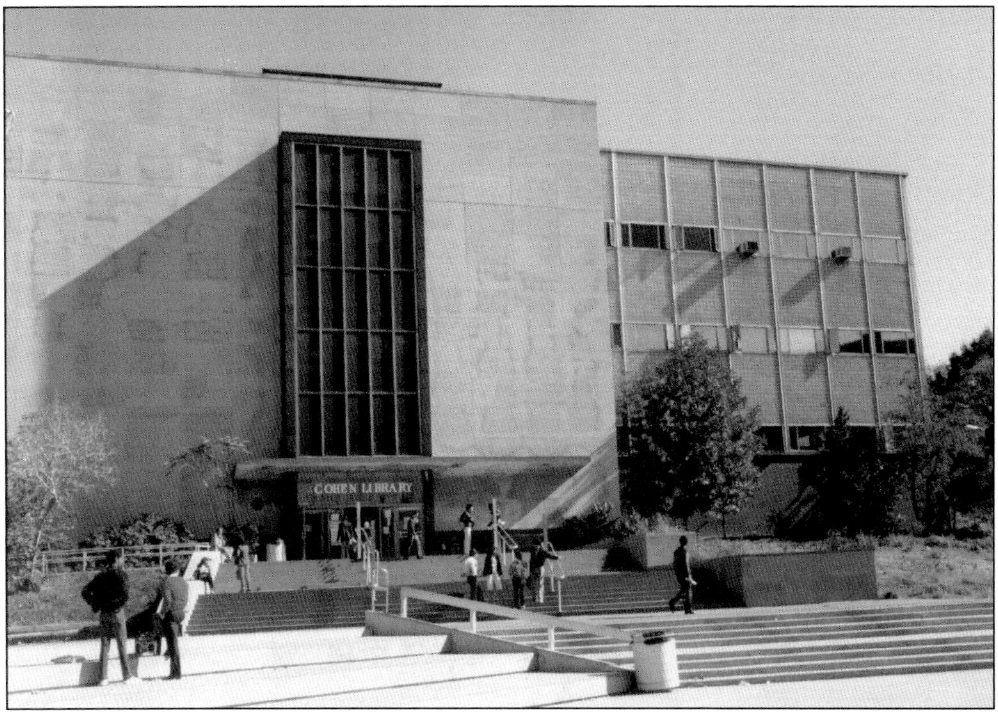

The original Morris Raphael Cohen Library building is seen here. It is set to become the home of the School of Architecture, Urban Design, and Landscape Architecture.

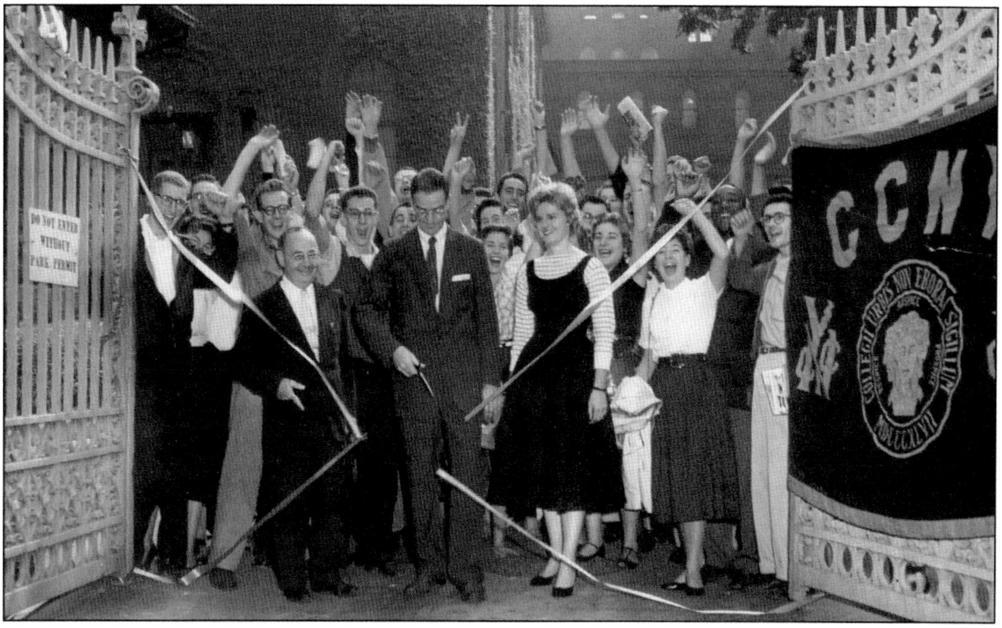

City College acquired the campus of the Manhattanville College of the Sacred Heart in 1950. The buildings were remodeled and, in the fall of 1955, formed the new south campus for programs in the humanities disciplines. Gloria Kingsley, the first woman to become president of the uptown day student government, participated in the ribbon-cutting ceremony to officially open the new campus with college president Buell Gallagher.

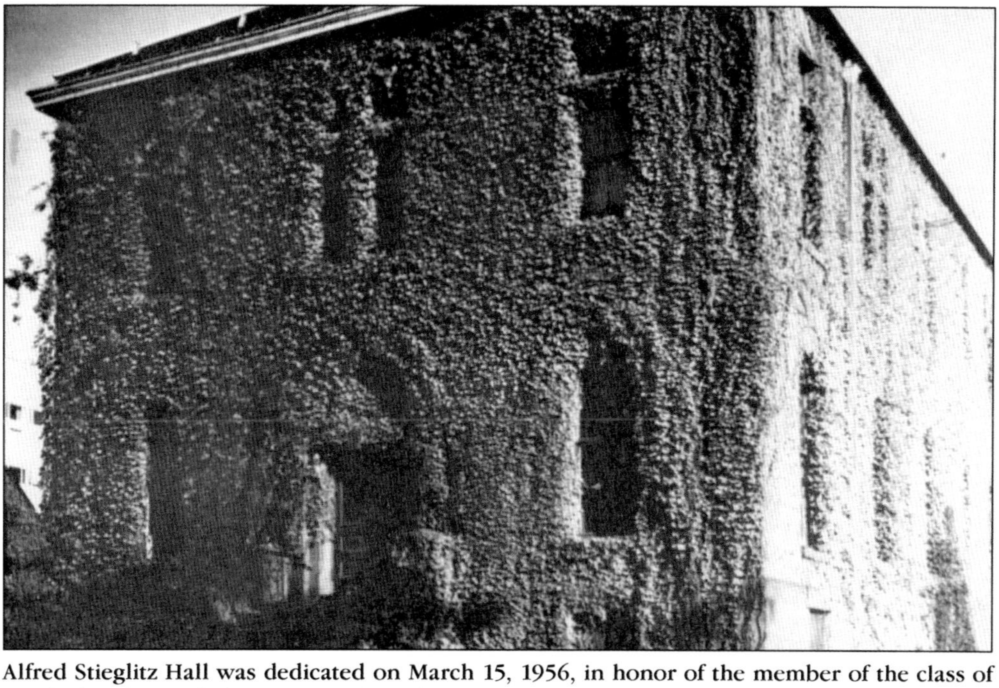

Alfred Stieglitz Hall was dedicated on March 15, 1956, in honor of the member of the class of 1884 who advanced photography along the lines of contemporary developments in painting. This south campus building served as the home of the Institute of Film Technique under the direction of Hans Richter for many years.

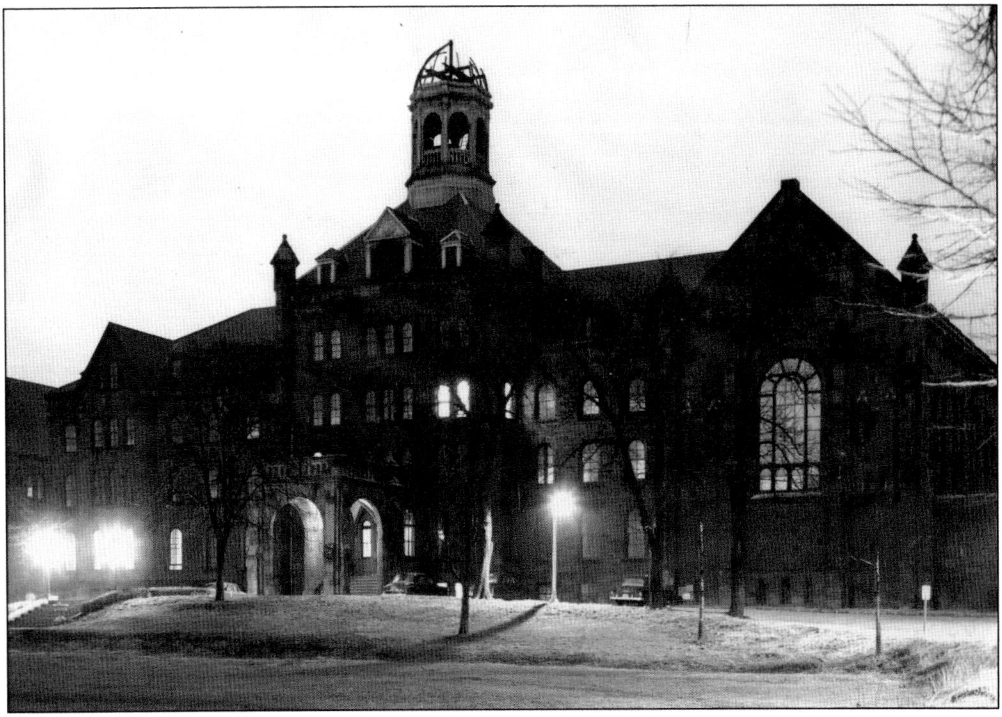

The John H. Finley Student Center, named for the college's third president, John Huston Finley, was built from 1888 through 1890 by Manhattanville College to serve as its main building. It replaced the original structure erected after 1847. City College acquired the building in 1950, then refurbished and reopened it for classes in 1955. It was demolished in 1983.

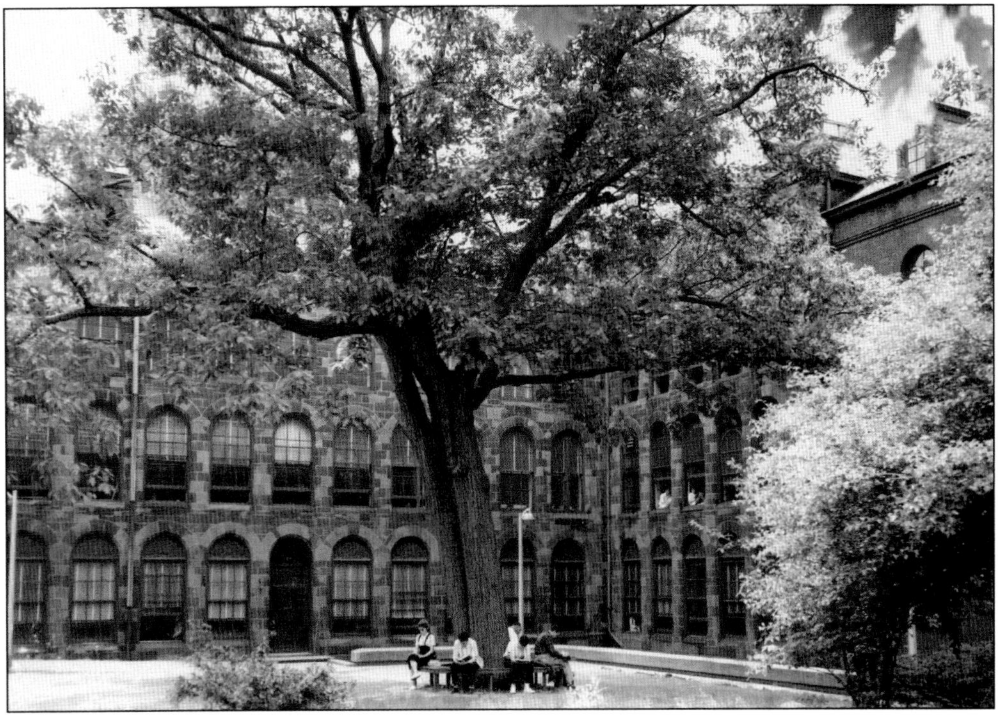

The first Arnow Theater, as it was designated by City College, was originally a chapel for Manhattanville College. Here, damage is inspected following the fire on May 8, 1969. The large window would subsequently be boarded. This fire, that started in a second floor closet, was of suspicious origin and it damaged the Rubin Goldmark wing of the John H. Finley Student Center. It was one of three fires set in south campus buildings after the college had reopened after being closed for two weeks due to an occupation of the south campus by a coalition of African American and Puerto Rican students.

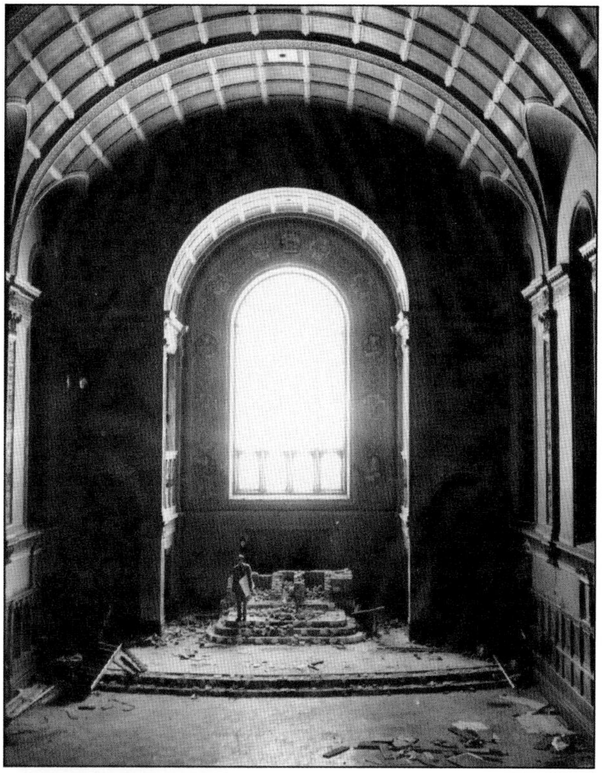

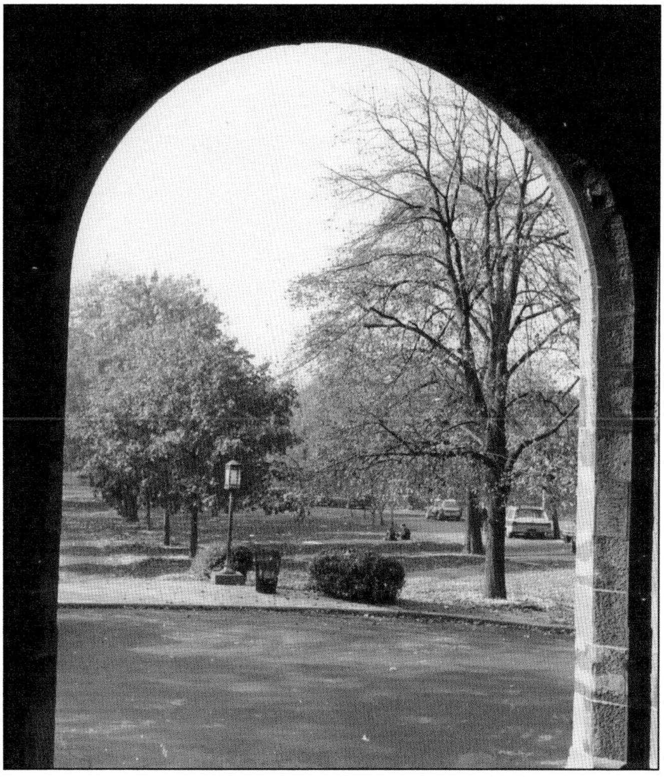

The grounds of the south campus are seen from the porch of Wagner Hall. The numerous trees give the impression of a grand country estate rather than a space in an urban environment.

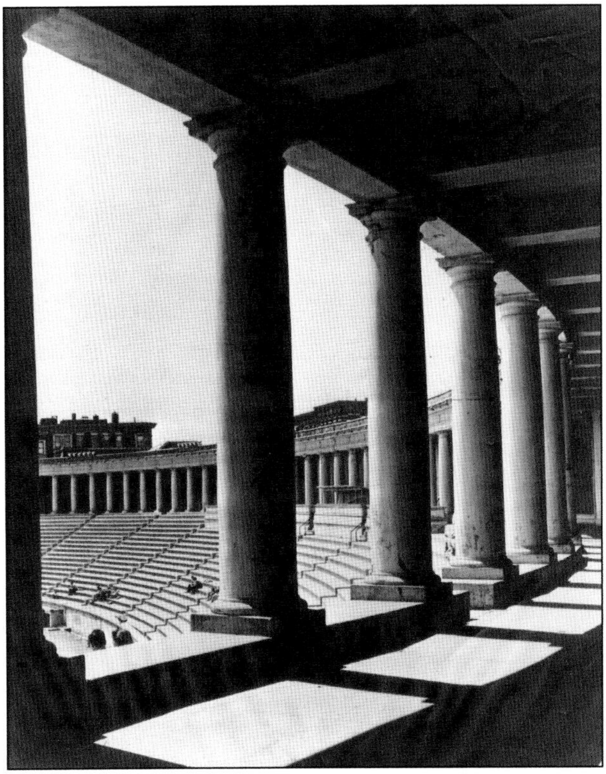

Designed by Arnold W. Brunner to resemble a classical amphitheater and constructed of concrete, this stadium was the fulfillment of Pres. John H. Finley's dream. The dream would not have been realized without the generosity of Adolph Lewisohn, a leading industrialist who came to New York as a teenager from his native Germany. A summer concert series was inaugurated in this great public space with a production of *Aida* in 1917 and continued until 1966 under the leadership of Minna "Minnie" Guggenheimer. The stadium was the site of City College athletic events and commencement ceremonies. From its inception, it was more than a City College institution; it became a municipal and even a national meeting place, just as donor and college authorities desired.

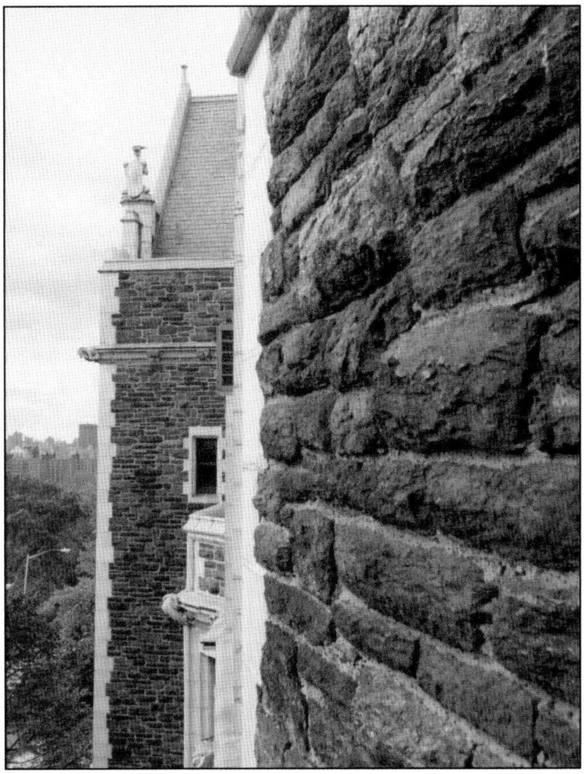

The view from the window of Room 408 in Shepard Hall highlights one of the grotesque sculptures on a pedestal decorating the corner of the roof line.

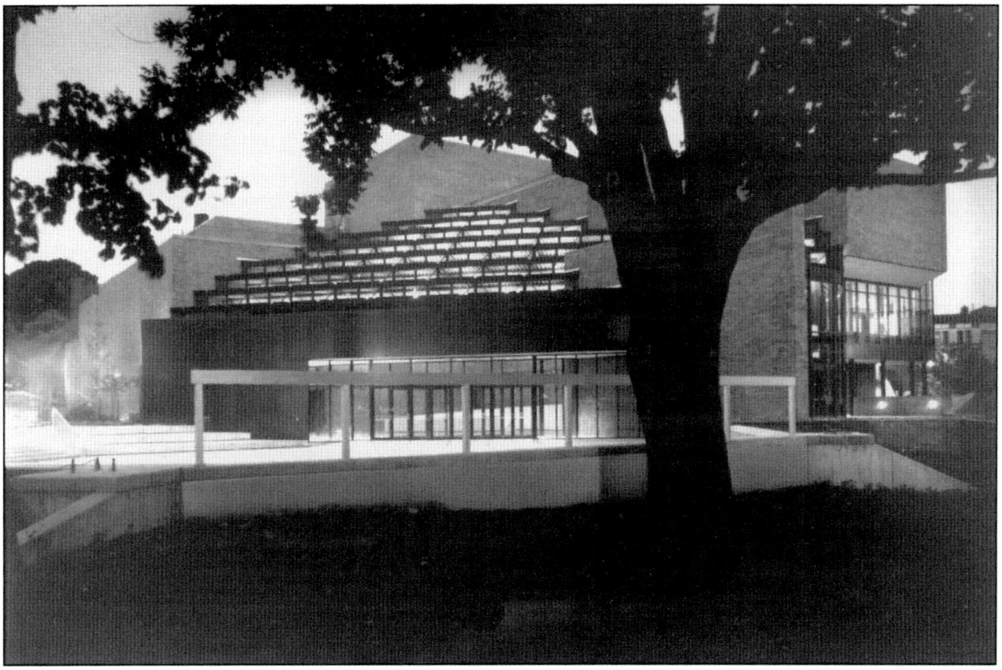

Aaron Davis Hall opened as a performing arts center in 1979. Designed by Abraham Geller, the building is situated in the northwest quadrant of the south campus.

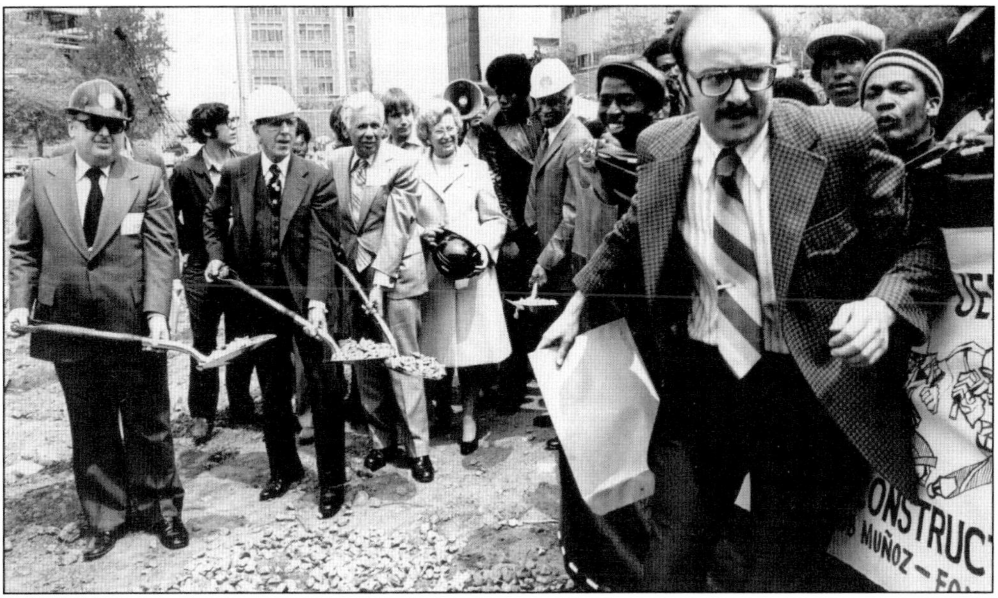

Members of the college administration break ground for the construction of Aaron Davis Hall in 1975.

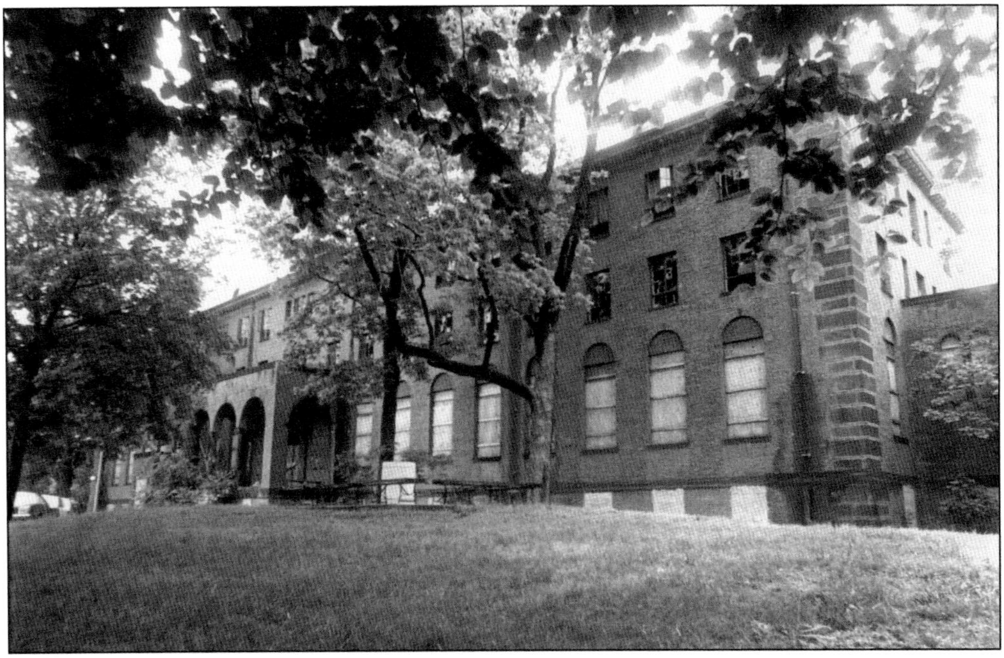

Robert F. Wagner Hall was built in 1937 as a dormitory for the young ladies attending Manhattanville College. After City College acquired the building in 1950, it was remodeled for classroom and office space in 1953 and named in honor of Robert F. Wagner Sr., a member of the class of 1898. It was demolished in 1991.

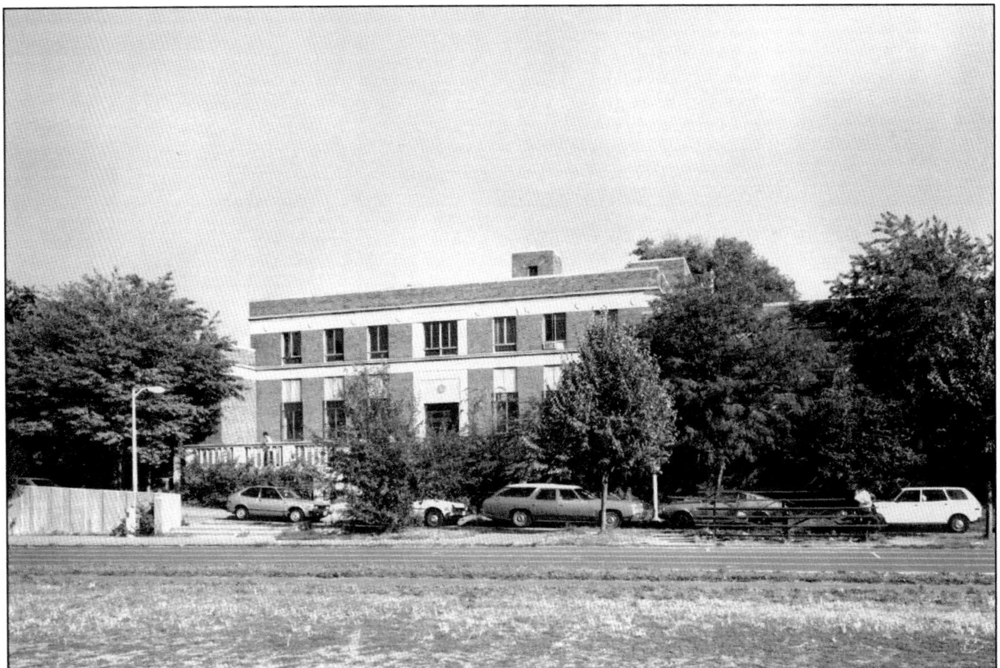

Mark Eisner Hall, named for the chairman of the board of higher education in the 1930s, was constructed in 1937 to house the library collection of Manhattanville College. It was altered to become the City College art department in 1953.

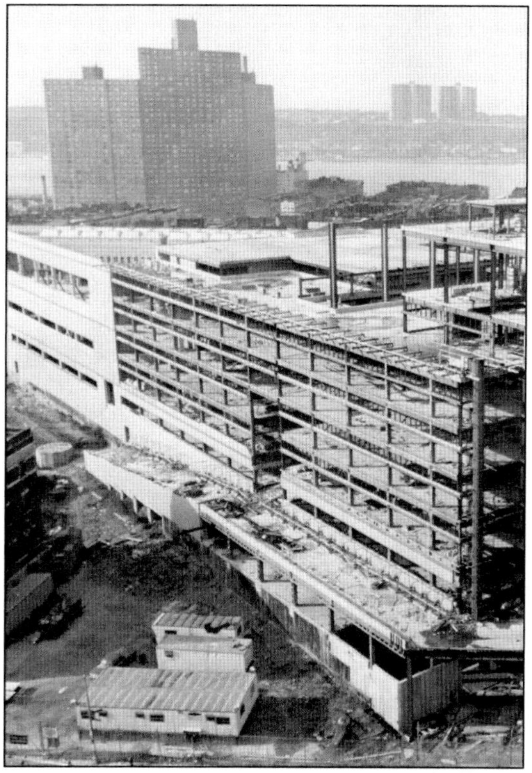

Designed by John Carl Warnecke and Associates, the North Academic Center provided expanded classrooms, program administrative space, and a new home for the Morris Raphael Cohen Library. On the former site of Lewisohn Stadium, the building's construction proceeded slowly (1975 view to the right) due to financing problems created by the New York City fiscal crisis of the mid-1970s. The facility opened in 1984 and has functioned as the location for most of the programs in the humanities and the School of Education and the Morris Raphael Cohen Library.

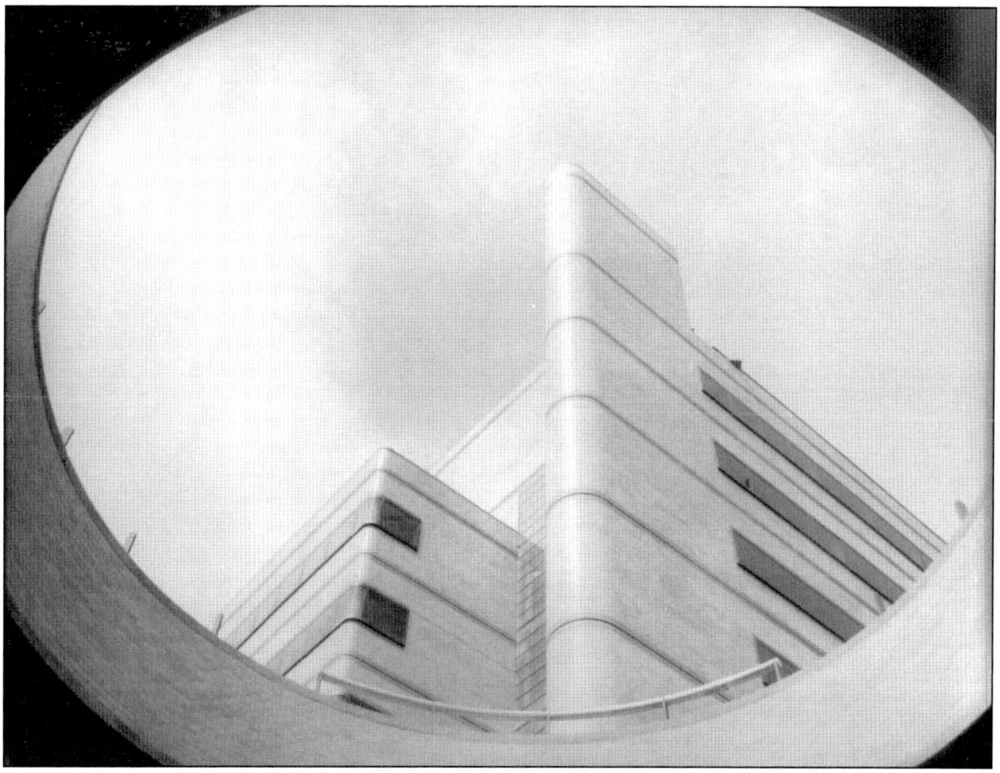

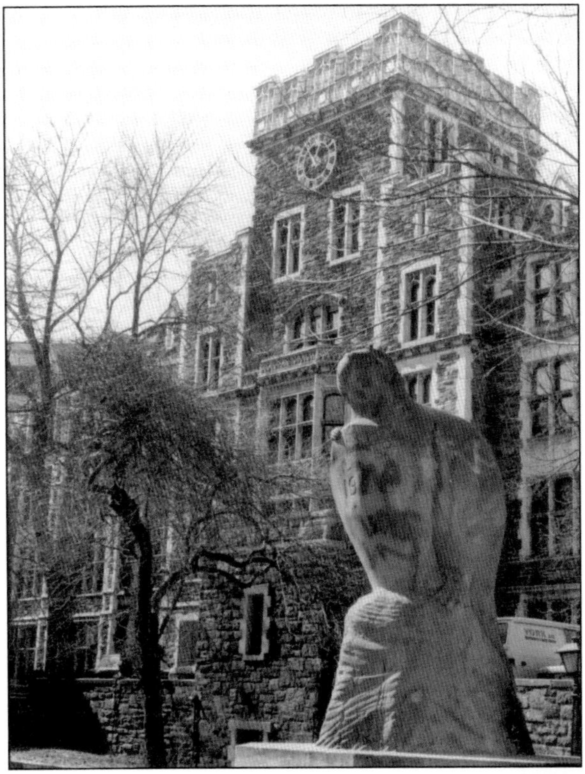

A statue of the college mascot, the beaver, created by Robert I. Russin was given to City College by the class of 1953 and placed on the south campus. In 1983, it was moved to the quadrangle and sited where the flagpole once stood. More recently, the beaver sculpture has been removed and replaced by another flagpole. (Lynne Chu.)

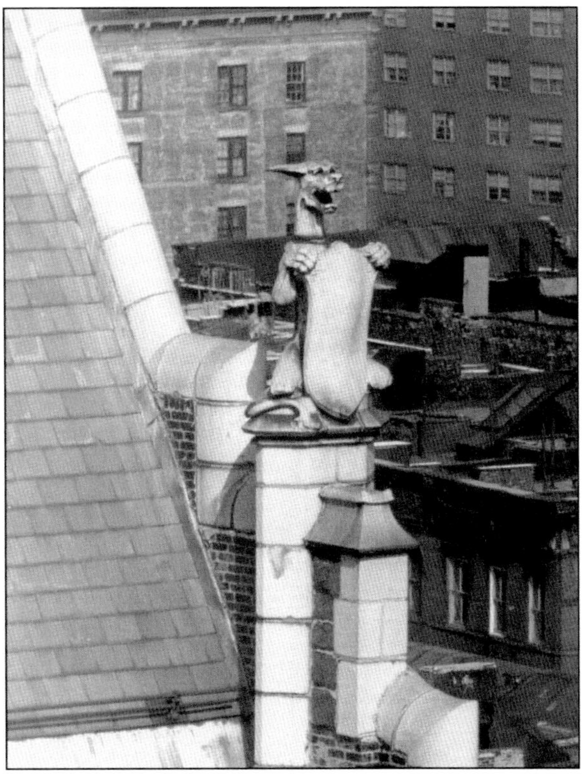

A grotesque sculpture of a dog holding a shield tops another corner of Shepard Hall. (Martin Sacks.)

Three

Building Student Life at a Commuter Campus

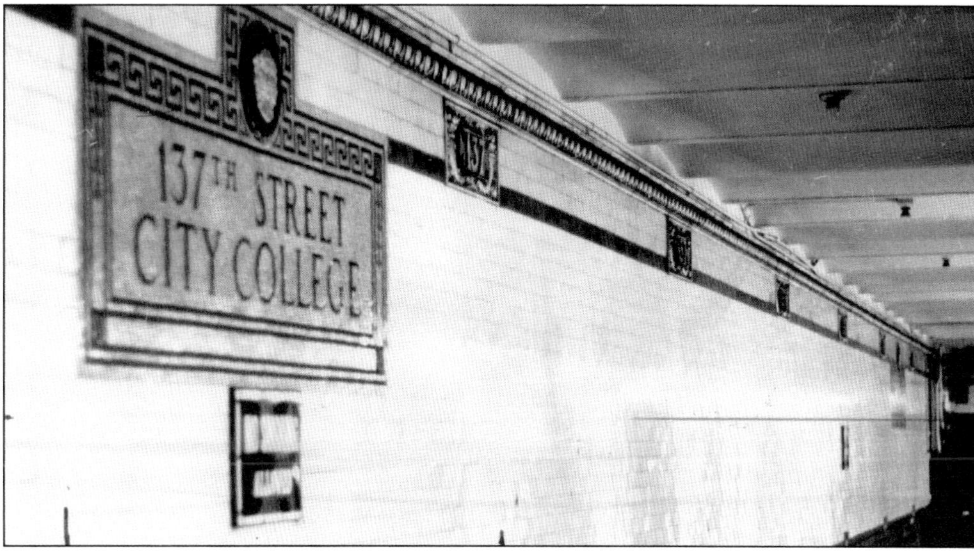

Generations of students traveling to City College have disembarked at the 137th Street and Broadway subway station for the No. 1 local IRT (Interborough Rapid Transit). They would have seen this mosaic, depicted in 1922, identifying the station as the one for "The College of the City of New York" and exhibiting the college seal. This facility first opened in 1903. In 1916, a petition was circulated calling for the designation of the station for City College. The petition was successful, as this mosaic continues to attest. The other important links to the Hamilton Heights campus are the IND (Independent) stations at 135th and 145th Streets and St. Nicholas Avenue. These public transportation lines have provided access for hundreds of City College students seeking higher education at the City University campuses.

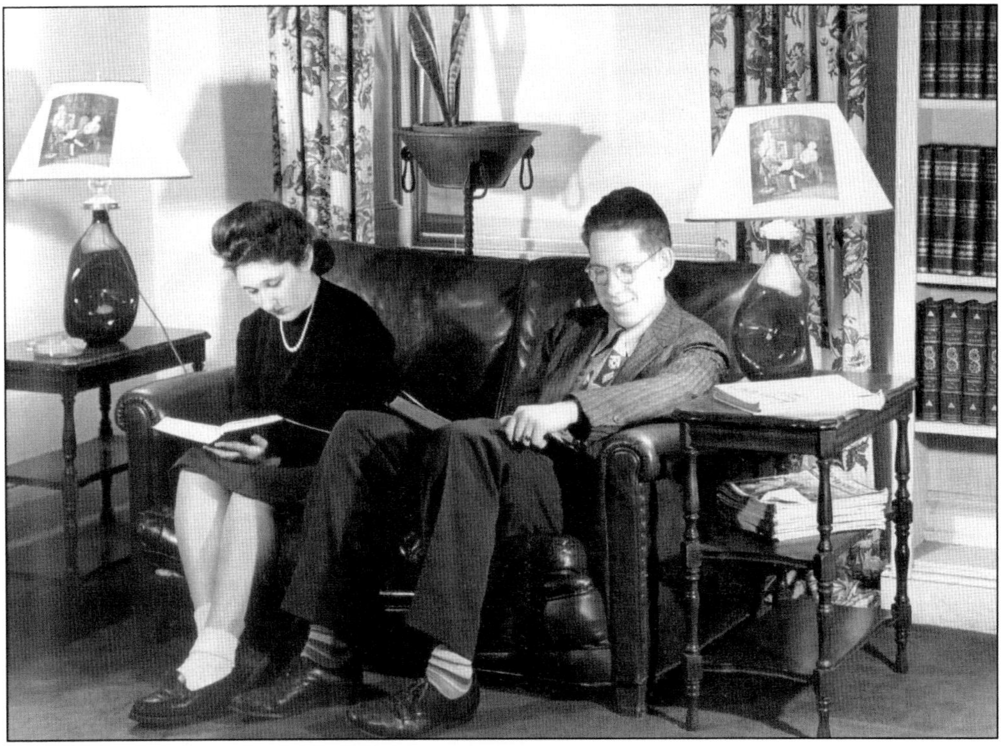

Faculty members of the House Plan Association are seen here in the 1940s.

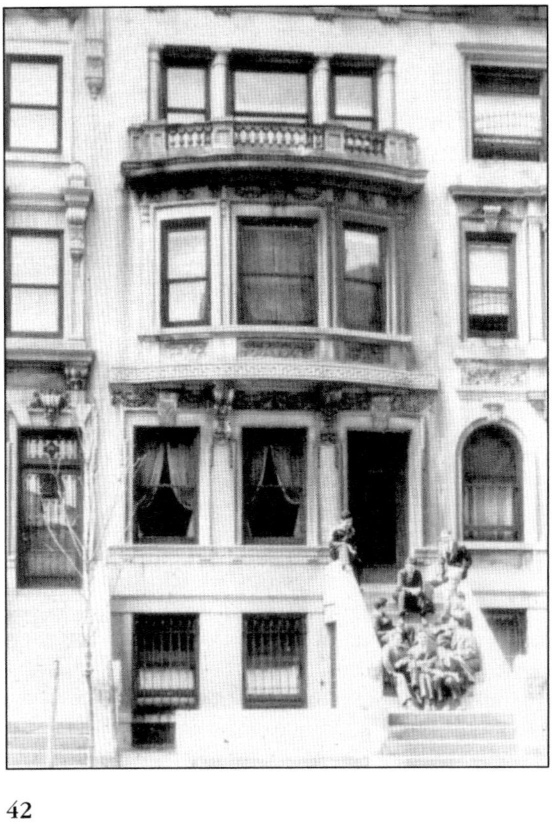

The House Plan Association was established in order to promote social relationships and activities among the students and between the students and faculty. Students were assigned to a small group known as a house at freshmen registration. The student-run association sponsored a variety of social, educational, and athletic programs. It operated out of the houses it owned near the college: 292 and 295 Convent Avenue. A House Plan Association house operated near the downtown Business School campus as well.

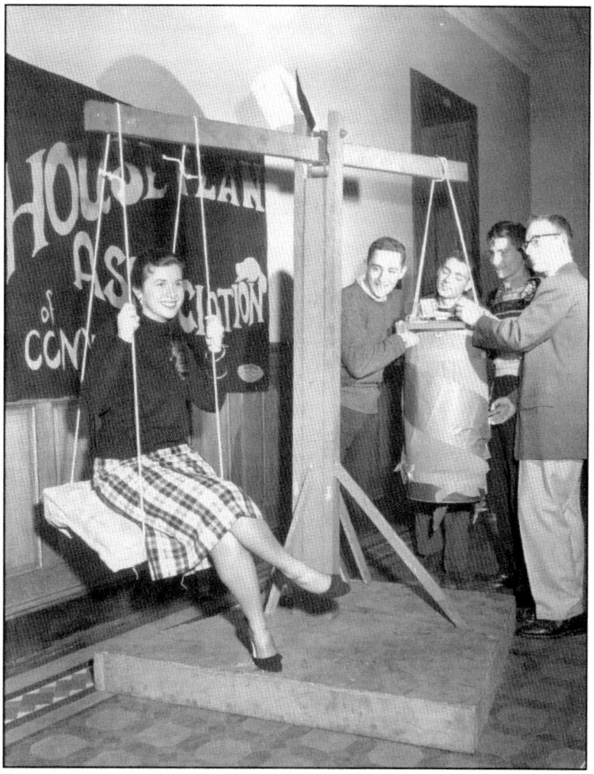

One of the biggest activities organized by the House Plan Association was the annual Carnival on an evening in December. The balance game was popular with City College students at the Carnival, seen here around 1951. (Conrad Waldinger.)

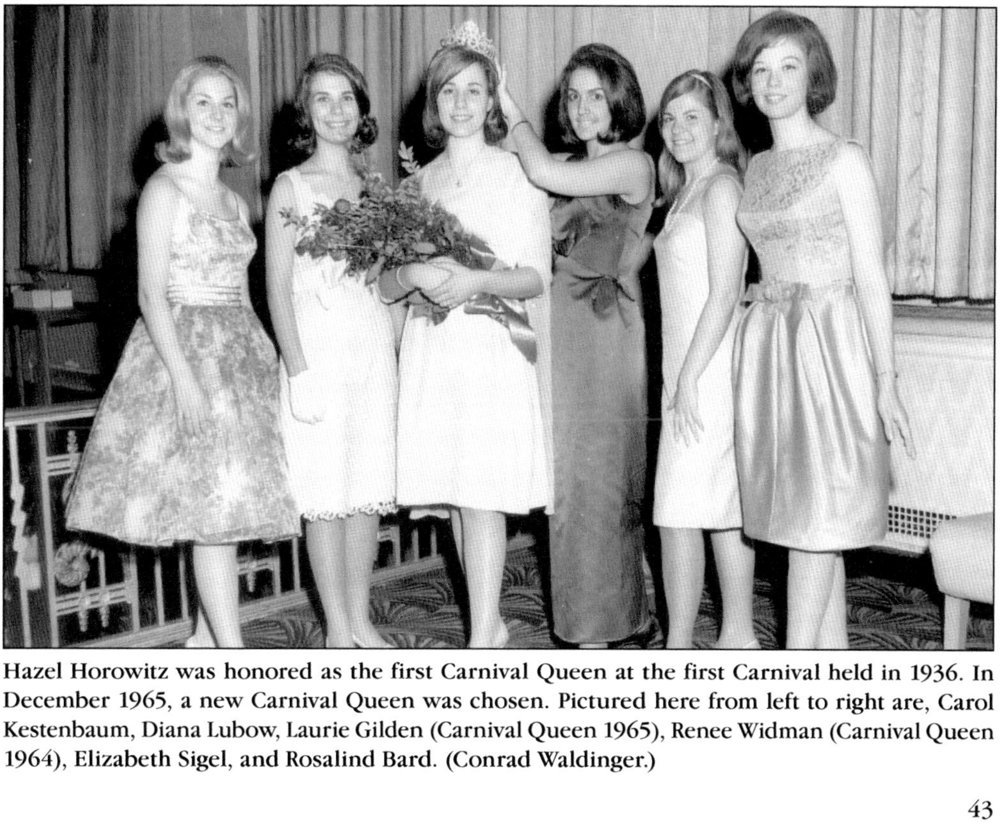

Hazel Horowitz was honored as the first Carnival Queen at the first Carnival held in 1936. In December 1965, a new Carnival Queen was chosen. Pictured here from left to right are, Carol Kestenbaum, Diana Lubow, Laurie Gilden (Carnival Queen 1965), Renee Widman (Carnival Queen 1964), Elizabeth Sigel, and Rosalind Bard. (Conrad Waldinger.)

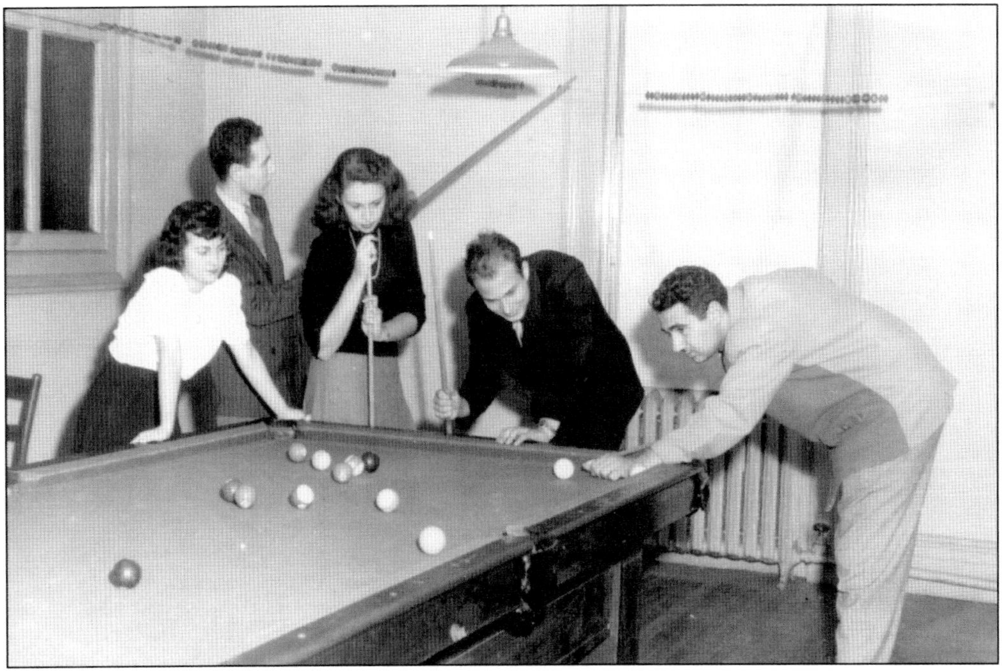

The House Plan Association created an atmosphere for relaxed interchange among members of the student body. The group was concerned with the development of students' physical, social, and intellectual lives. Students are playing a game of pool (above), and gathered around a piano (below).

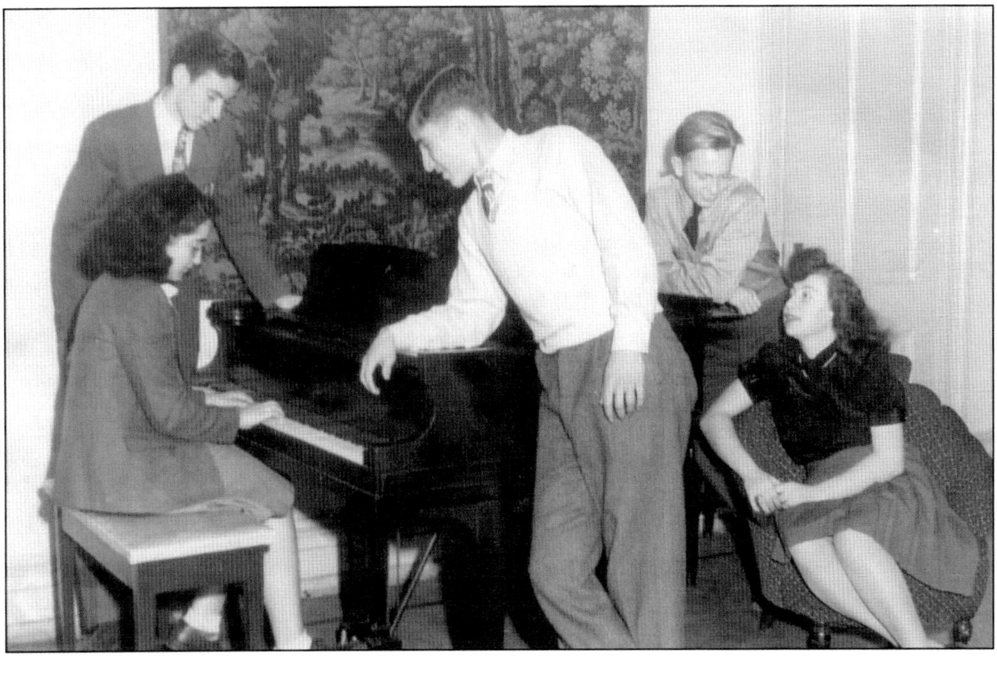

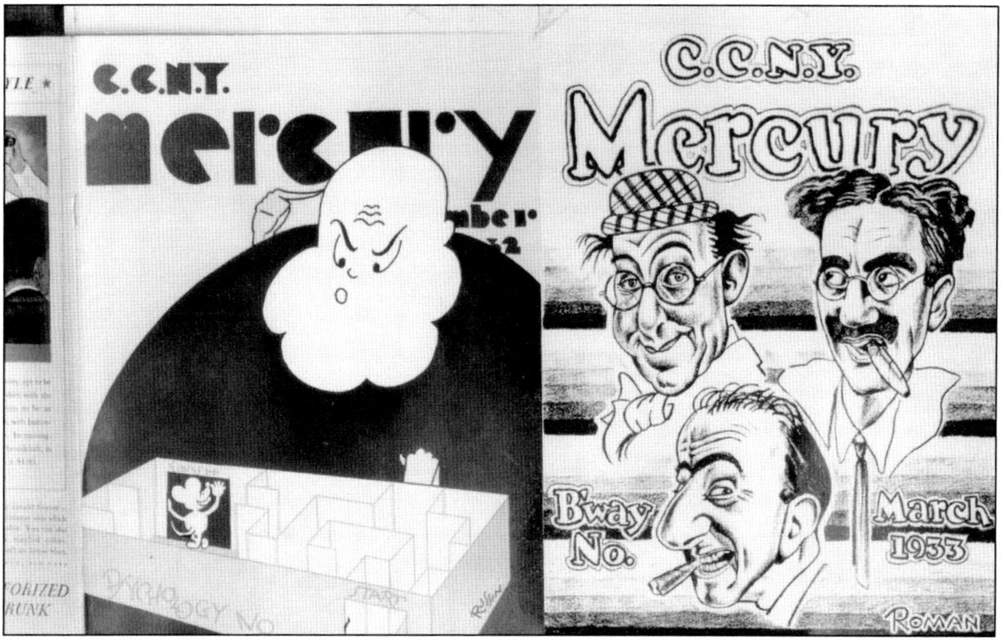

Beginning in 1880, the *Mercury* presented events of college life to its readers. After the advent of the *Campus* in 1907, the *Mercury* became a literary and humor magazine and left the reporting of current campus events to the new publication. The covers of the December 1932 and March 1933 editions reflect the linear graphic design of the art deco era.

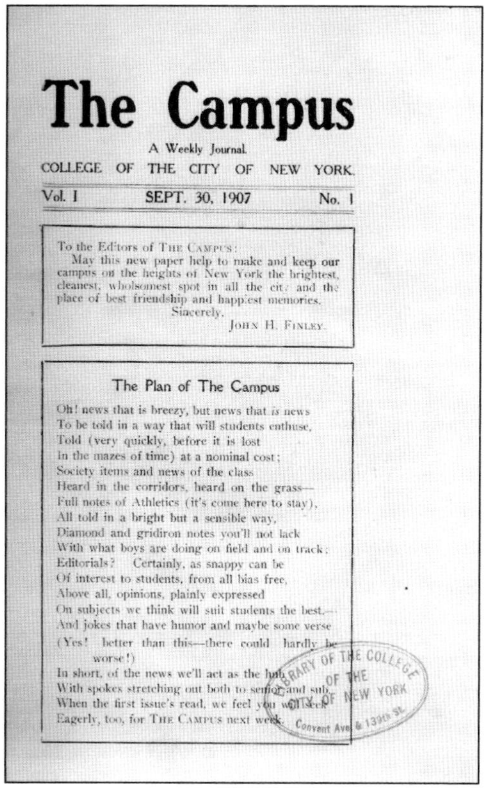

The Campus

A Weekly Journal.

COLLEGE OF THE CITY OF NEW YORK.

Vol. I SEPT. 30, 1907 No. 1

To the Editors of THE CAMPUS:

May this new paper help to make and keep our campus on the heights of New York the brightest, cleanest, wholsomest spot in all the city and the place of best friendship and happiest memories.

Sincerely,

JOHN H. FINLEY.

The Plan of The Campus

Oh! news that is breezy, but news that *is* news
To be told in a way that will students enthuse,
Told (very quickly, before it is lost
In the mazes of time) at a nominal cost;
Society items and news of the class
Heard in the corridors, heard on the grass—
Full notes of Athletics (it's come here to stay),
All told in a bright but a sensible way,
Diamond and gridiron notes you'll not lack
With what boys are doing on field and on track;
Editorials? Certainly, as snappy can be
Of interest to students, from all bias free,
Above all, opinions, plainly expressed
On subjects we think will suit students the best.—
And jokes that have humor and maybe some verse
(Yes! better than this—there could hardly be worse!)
In short, of the news we'll act as the hub
With spokes stretching out both to senior and sub.
When the first issue's read, we feel you will seek
Eagerly, too, for THE CAMPUS next week.

The *Campus* was founded when classes started on the new St. Nicholas Heights campus. The first page of the first issue, September 30, 1907, prints an expression of support from Pres. John H. Finley and an outline in verse explaining the aims of the publication. The *Campus* is one of the oldest student newspapers still being published at an American college today.

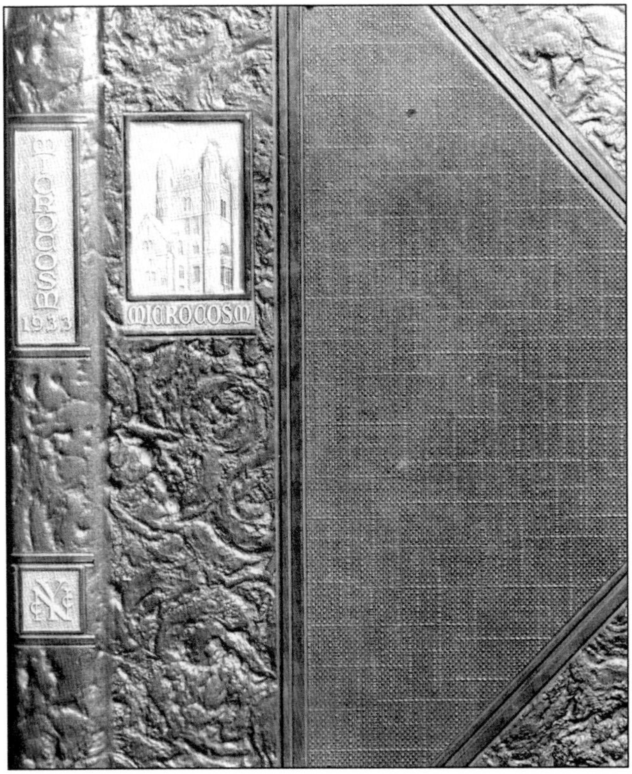

Microcosm debuted in 1858 as a record of student activities. This publication, which eventually became the yearbook, did not gain official recognition until it was issued under the auspices of the Student Council in 1911. In 1923 it became the senior class publication. Dynamic graphic design, as displayed on this 1933 issue, has been a hallmark of the covers for many years.

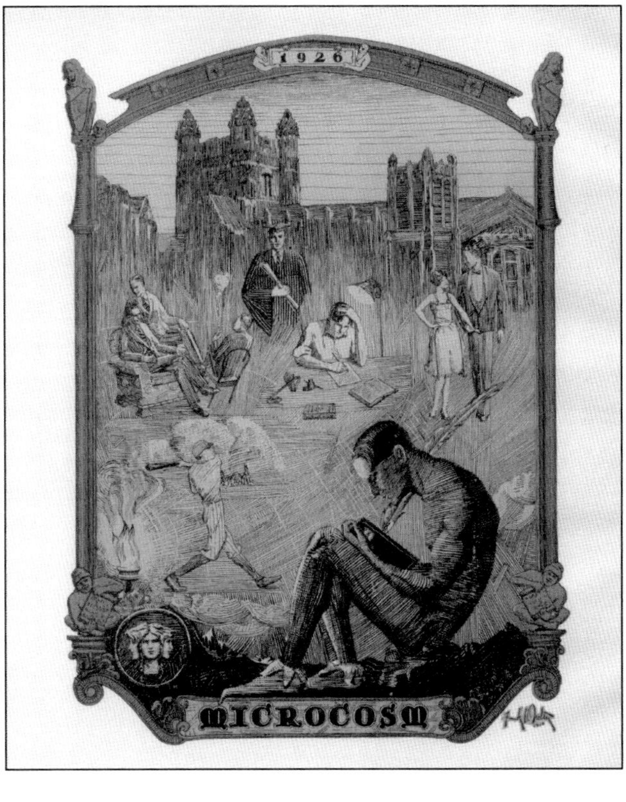

The frontispiece for the 1926 *Microcosm* was created by Frank Netter, a member of the art staff and editor of the yearbook in 1927, his senior year. His lively cartoons were a boon to *Mercury* as well. Netter earned a medical degree from New York University in 1931 and eventually became the world's leading medical illustrator.

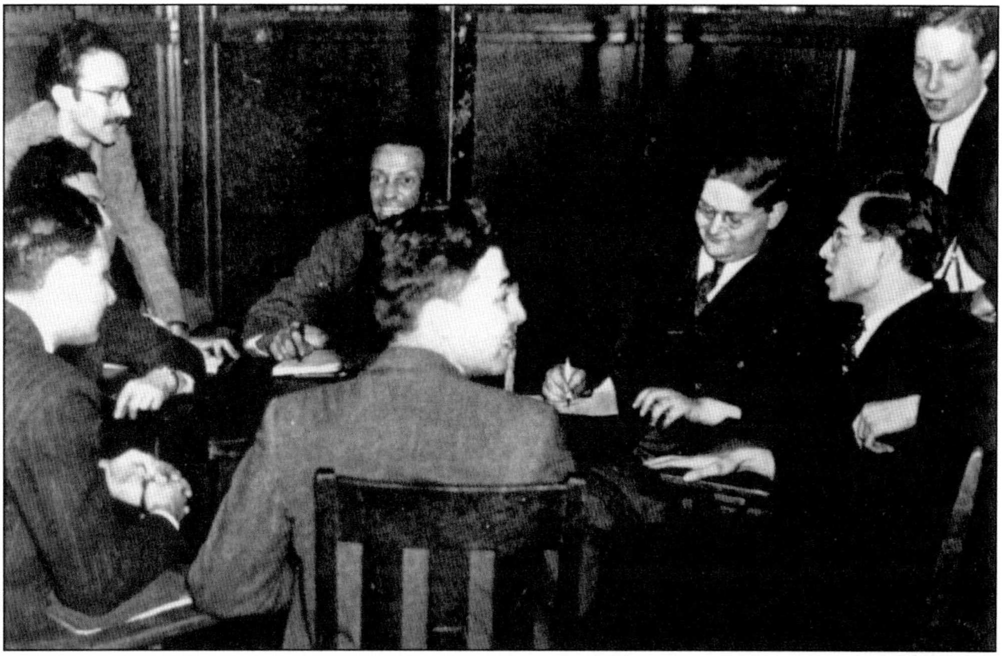

Irving Kristol (class of 1940) stands on the far right during a meeting of the Student Council under the leadership of William L. Rafsky. It was in the atmosphere of heated political discussion that he encountered contemporaries Nathan Glazer (class of 1944), Daniel Bell (class of 1939), and Irving Howe (class of 1940).

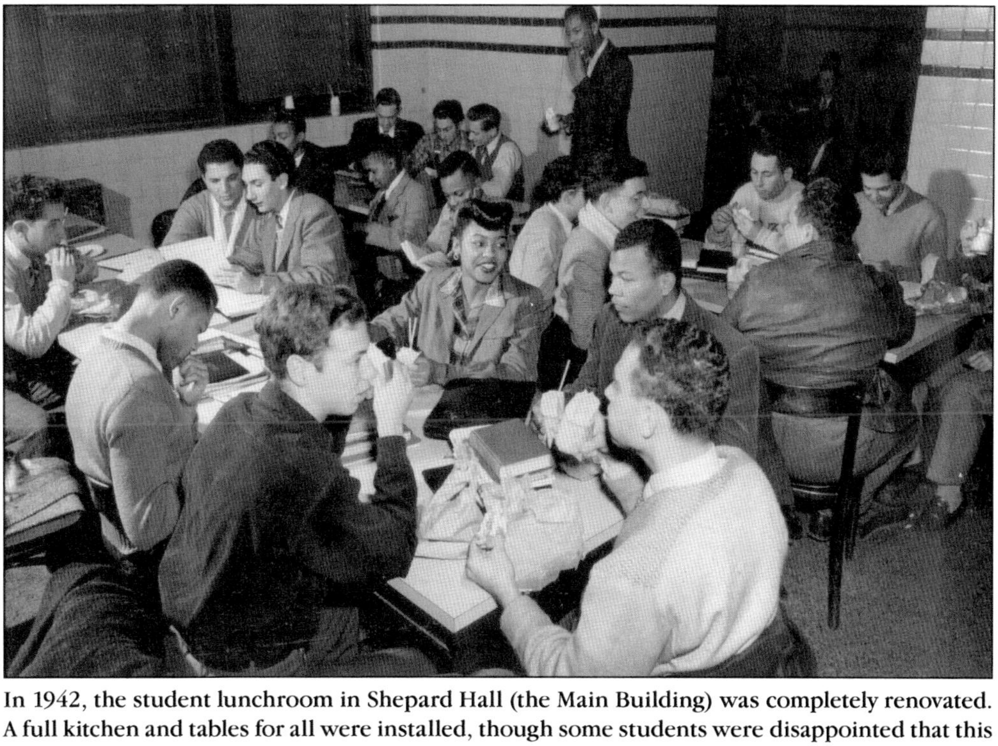

In 1942, the student lunchroom in Shepard Hall (the Main Building) was completely renovated. A full kitchen and tables for all were installed, though some students were disappointed that this facility closed at 8:00 p.m.

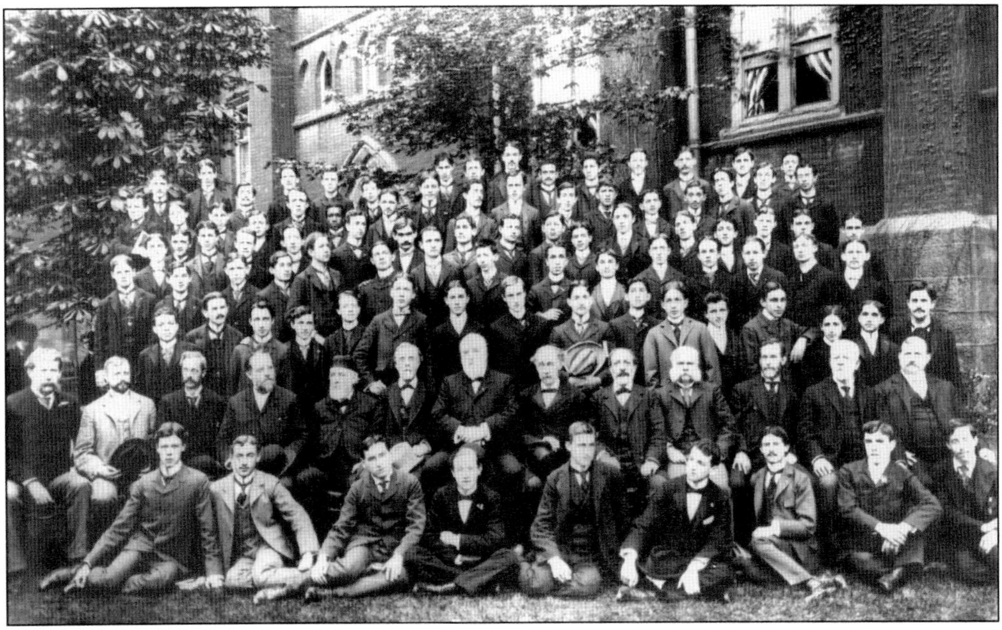

The class of 1898 included Robert F. Wagner Sr. Serving as a U.S. senator from New York for 23 years, Wagner led the drive for social and labor legislation during the New Deal—which certainly reflected well on his alma mater. He became the first chairman of the National Labor Board, which Pres. Franklin Roosevelt had authorized to help spur recovery during the Depression. Wagner also served as president of the City College Alumni Association.

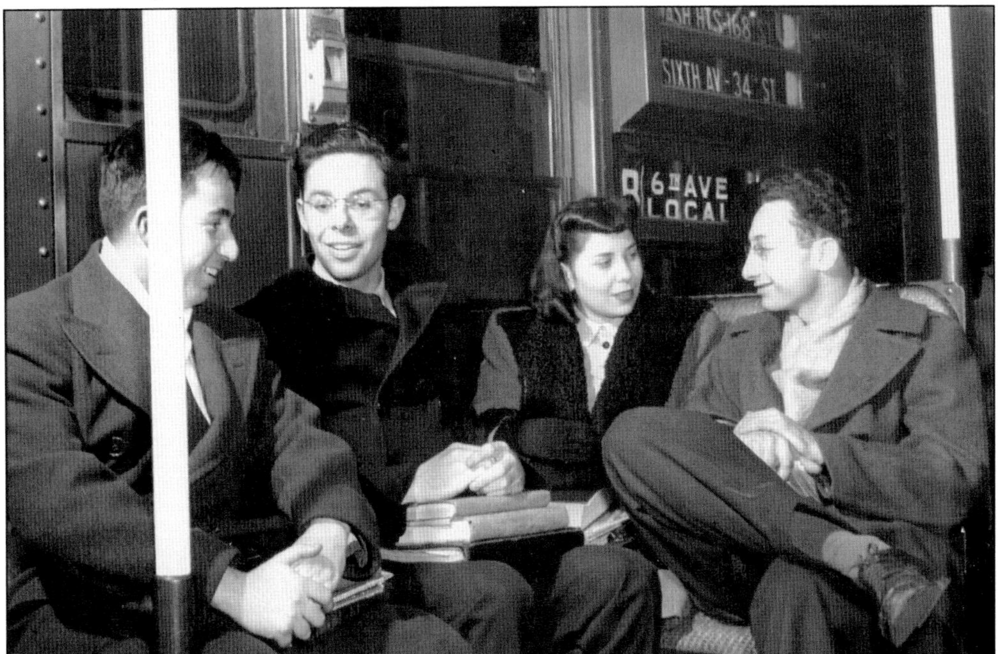

Students ride the IND B subway line, the local service line for the Avenue of the Americas and Sixth Avenue. The stations closest to City College are at 135th Street and St. Nicolas and 145th Street and St. Nicholas Avenue.

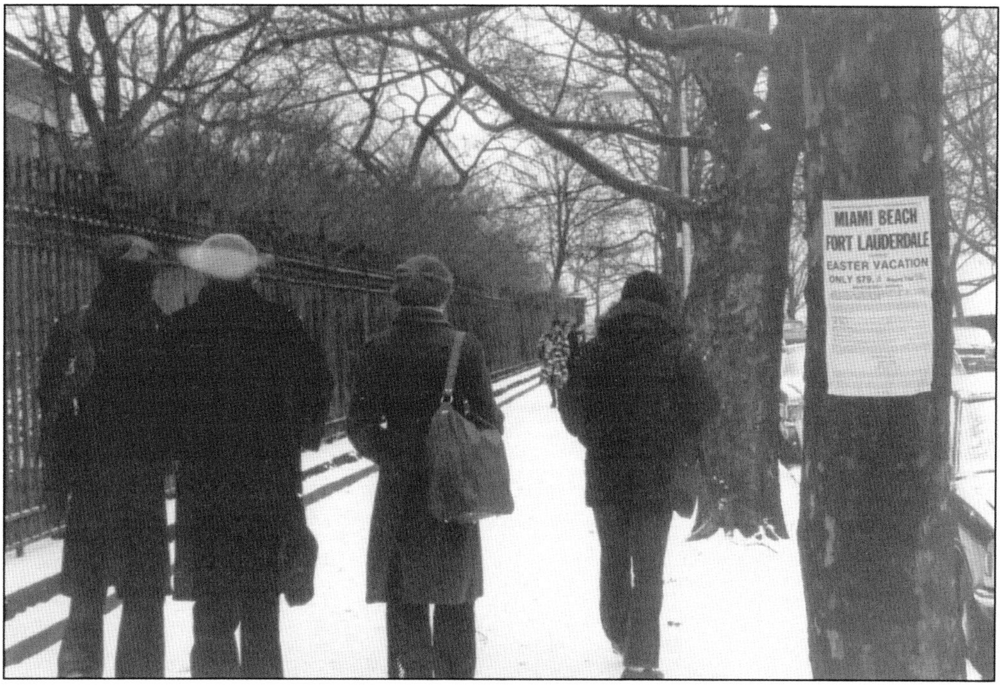

On a winter day in the 1970s, these students are likely longing for the Fort Lauderdale–Miami Beach vacation that is advertised on a nearby tree.

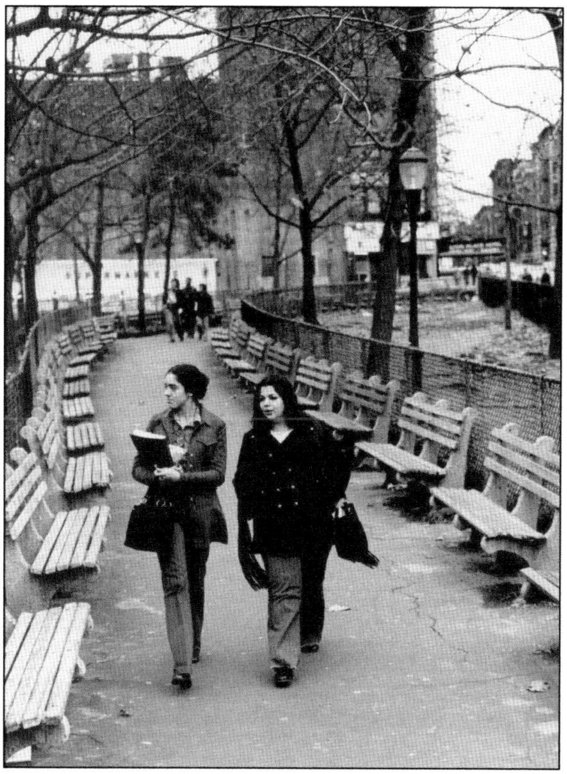

Two young women carry their books on their way to the campus in 1972. (James Shields.)

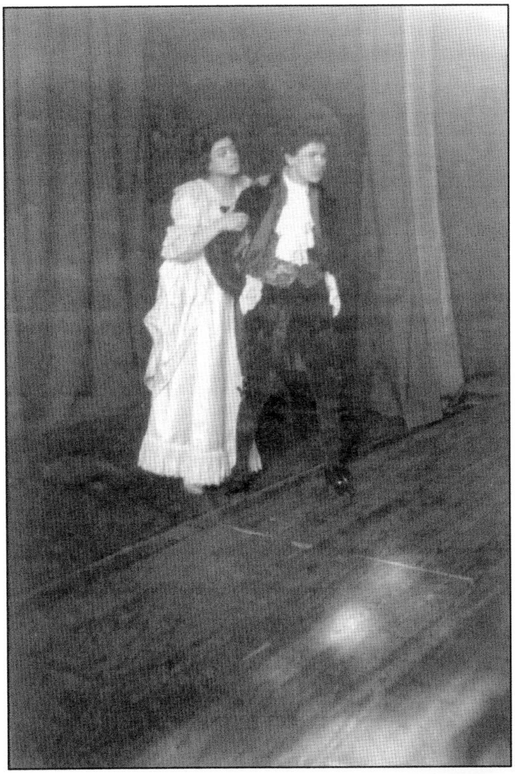

Dramatic productions have been performed at the college since the early 20th century. Thomas G. Taaffe, who joined the English department in 1901, staged *She Stoops to Conquer* with Martin D. S. Peterson as Tony Lumpkins and Harold Lewken as Constance.

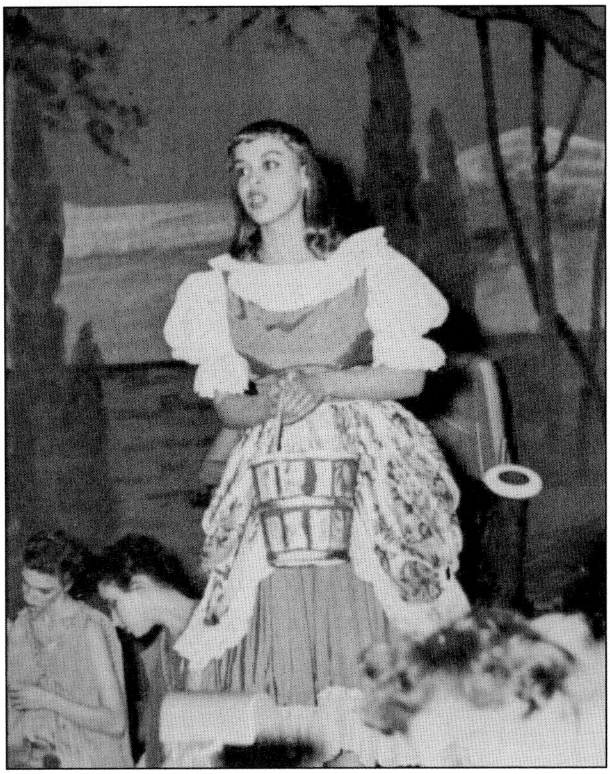

City College's Gilbert and Sullivan Society mounted a production of *Patience* in 1960.

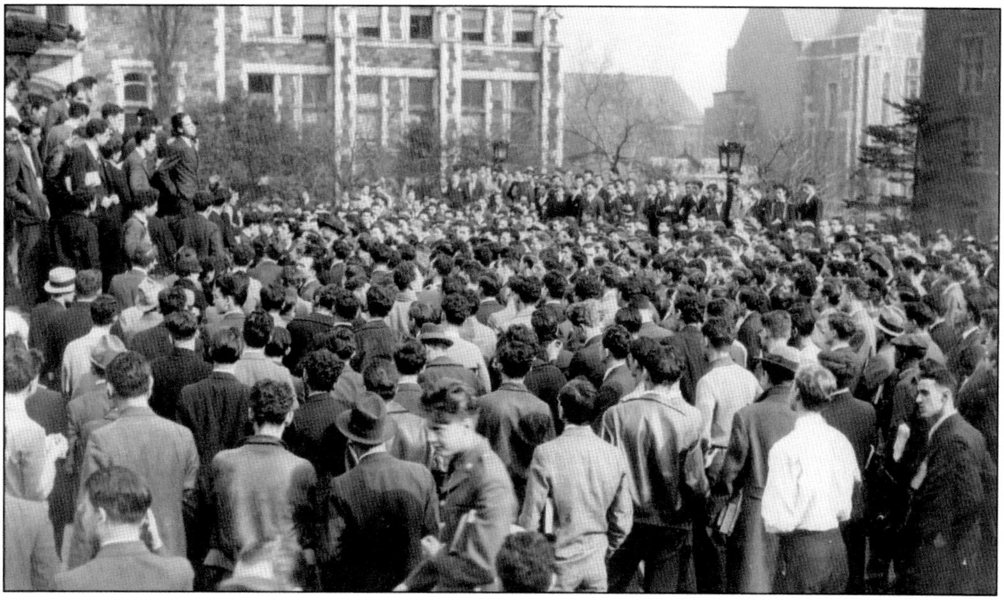

On October 9, 1934, a special assembly was held in the Great Hall to host a delegation of students from Italy. These students represented the fascist regime of Benito Mussolini. Members of the City College student body felt that it was inappropriate for the administration to recognize the Italian government. A protest was held in October to oppose the visit. In response, 21 students were either suspended or expelled. On November 20, 1934, a rally was held in the quadrangle to request that these students be reinstated.

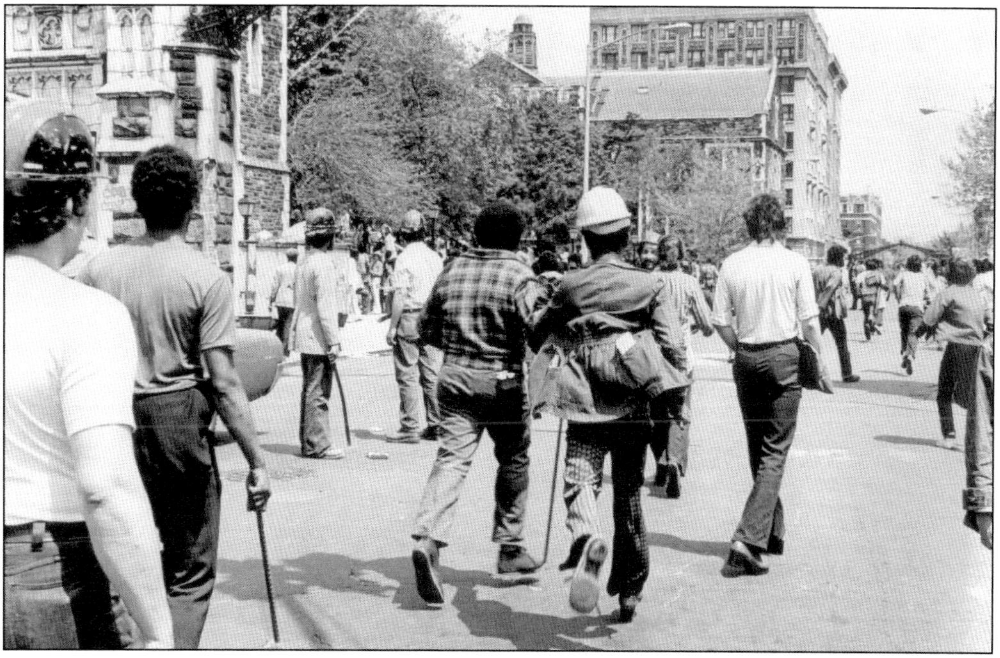

Students formed a coalition with unionized construction workers during the building of the North Academic Center in 1975. The workers and students felt that those who were constructing this great building for the municipal college should more accurately reflect the ethnic mix of New York City.

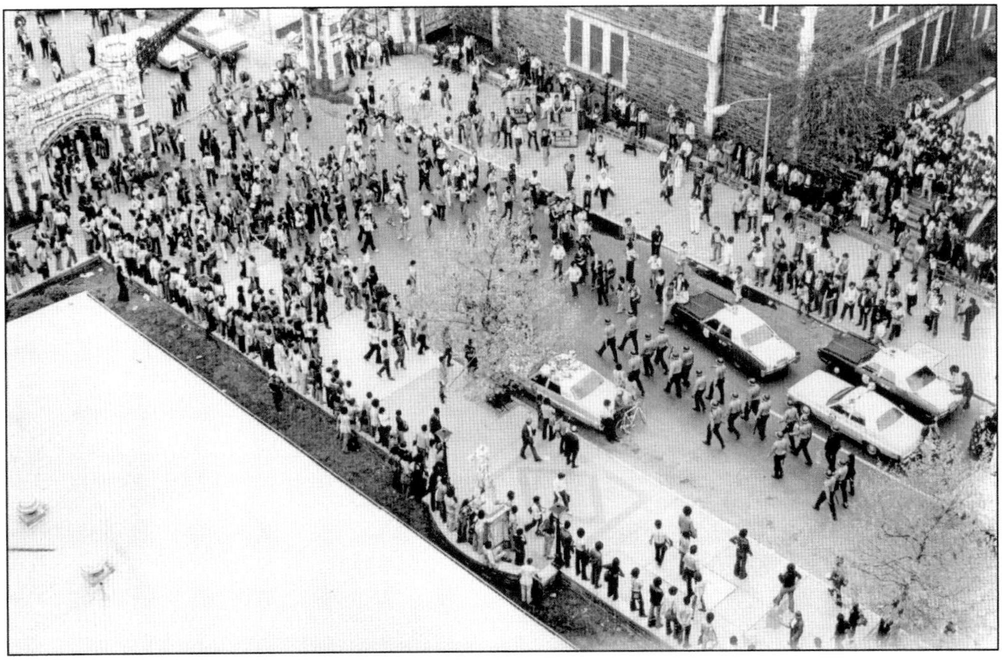

Along with the entire City University System, the college instituted an open admission policy in 1970 in response to the student sit-in of the previous year. Now, a place would be available to any graduate of a New York City high school in the City University System. At this time, students expressed desire for more relevant courses in the curriculum, such as those concerning various ethnic groups. Additional debate and unrest were caused by the imposition of tuition for the first time in the university's history in 1976 due to New York City's fiscal crisis.

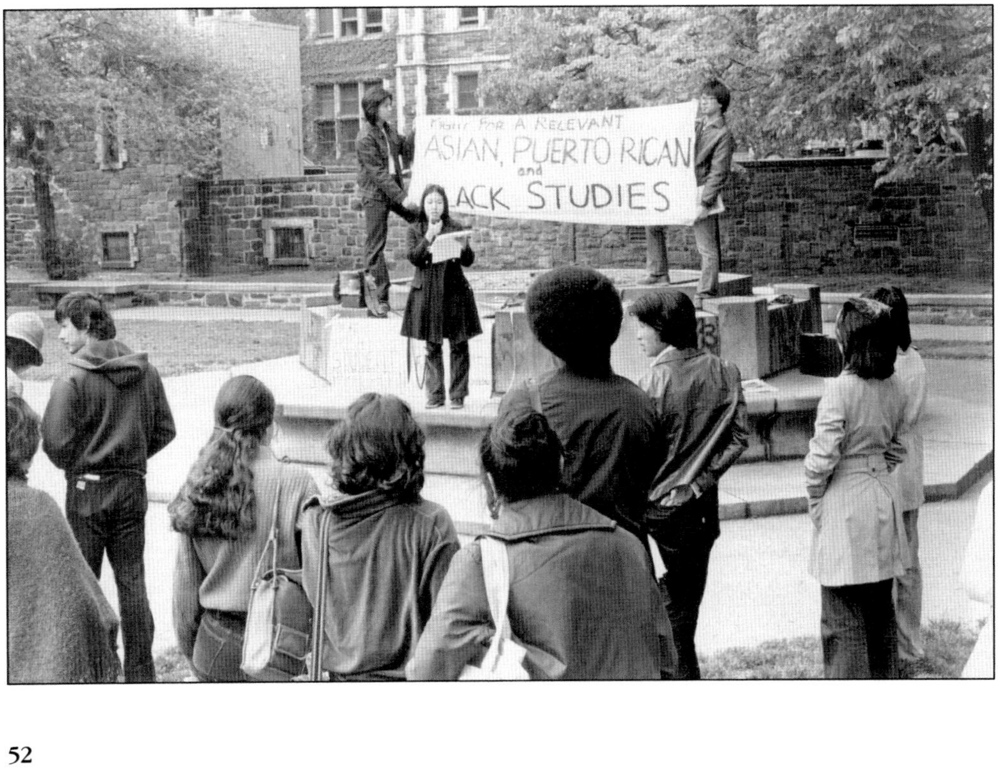

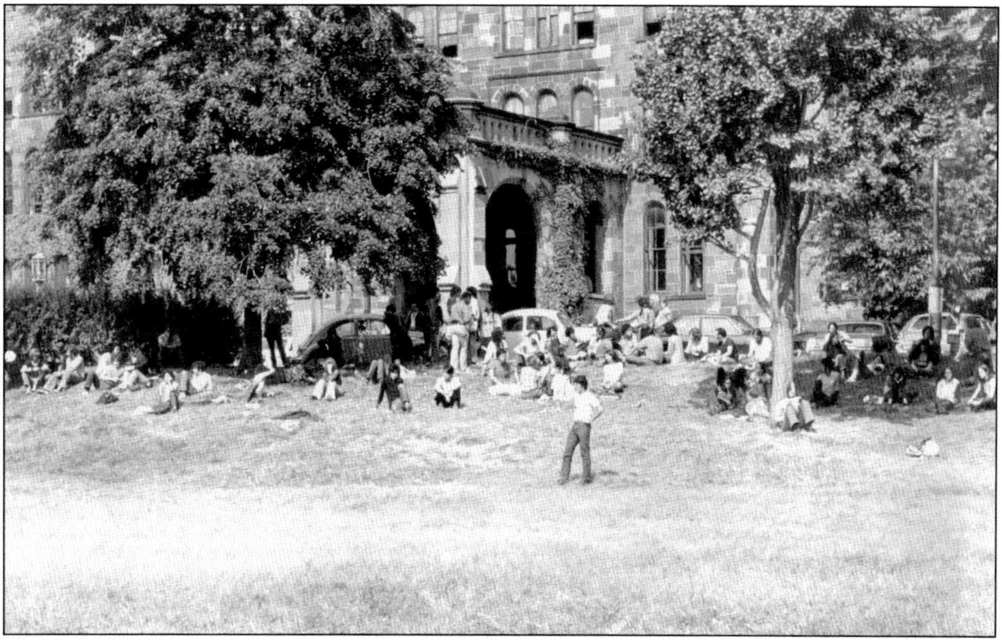

The south campus provided many areas for relaxed interaction among the students. Some gathered under the trees by the entrance to the John H. Finley Student Center (above), while others lounged on the lawn (below).

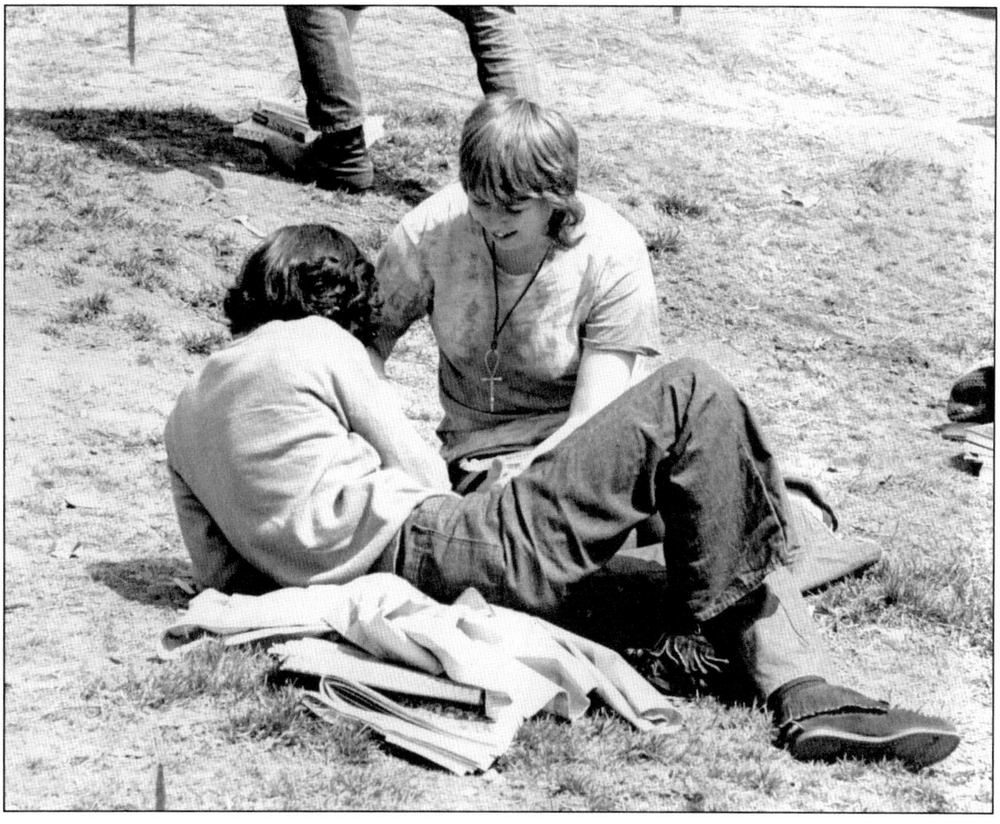

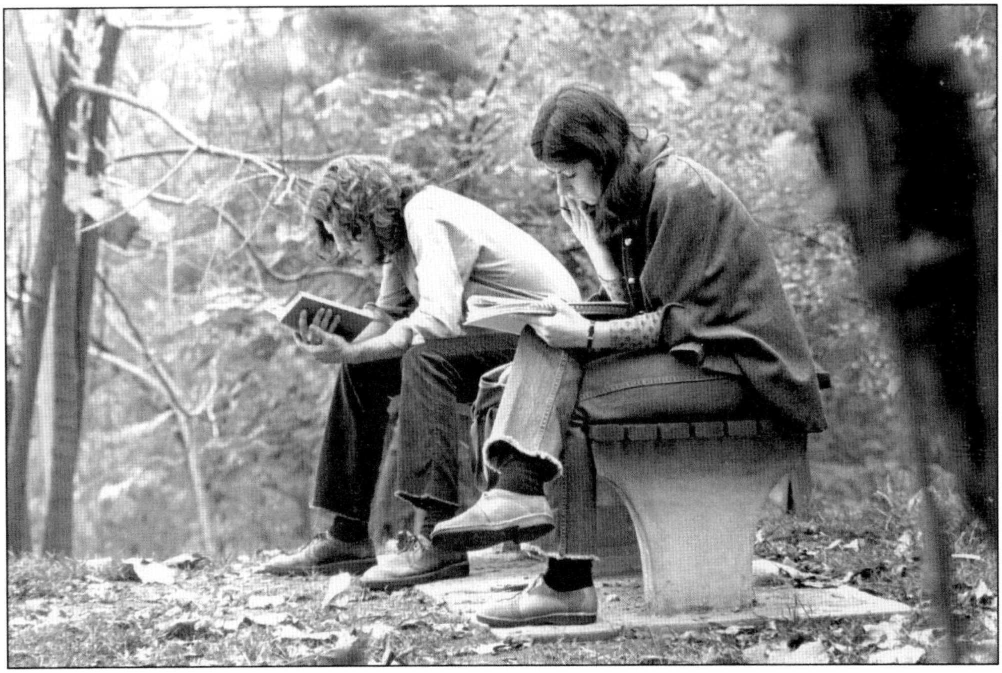

Students enjoy the south campus in 1968. This quiet atmosphere was not in evidence the following spring when a sit-in occurred on south campus for two weeks.

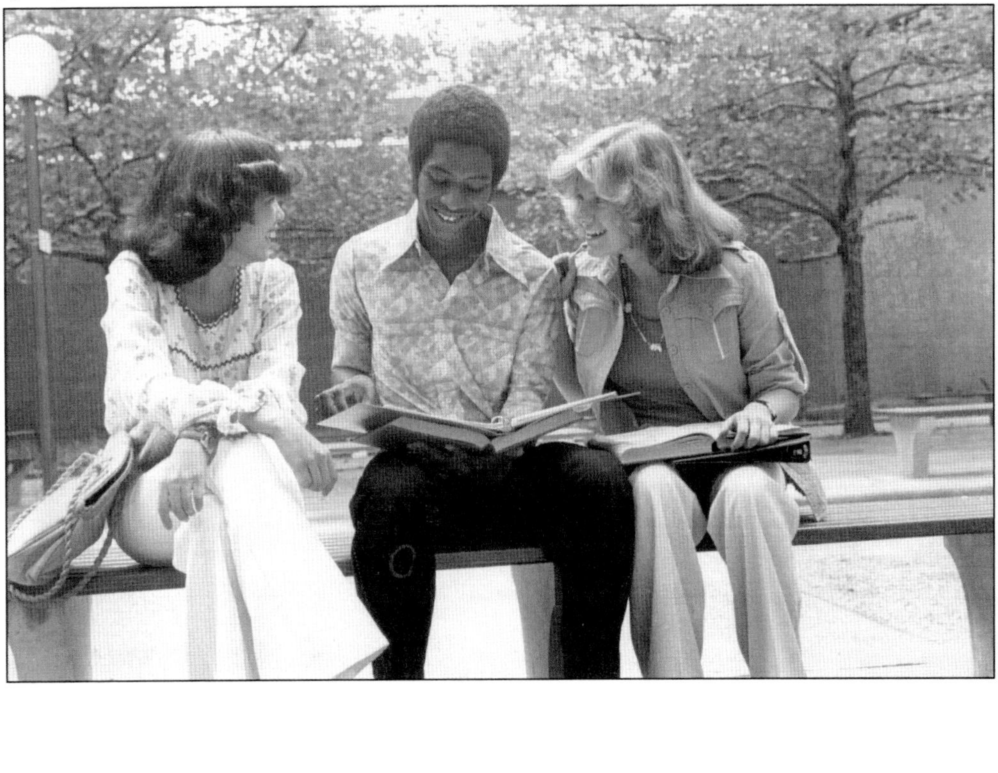

These students sitting on the steps leading to Finley Hall seem to have forgotten that the campus is located in a major urban center. (Conrad Waldinger.)

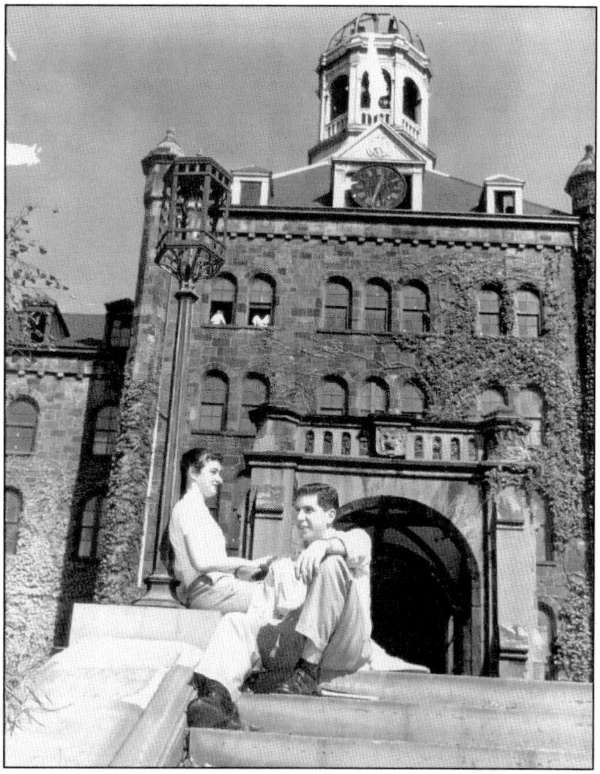

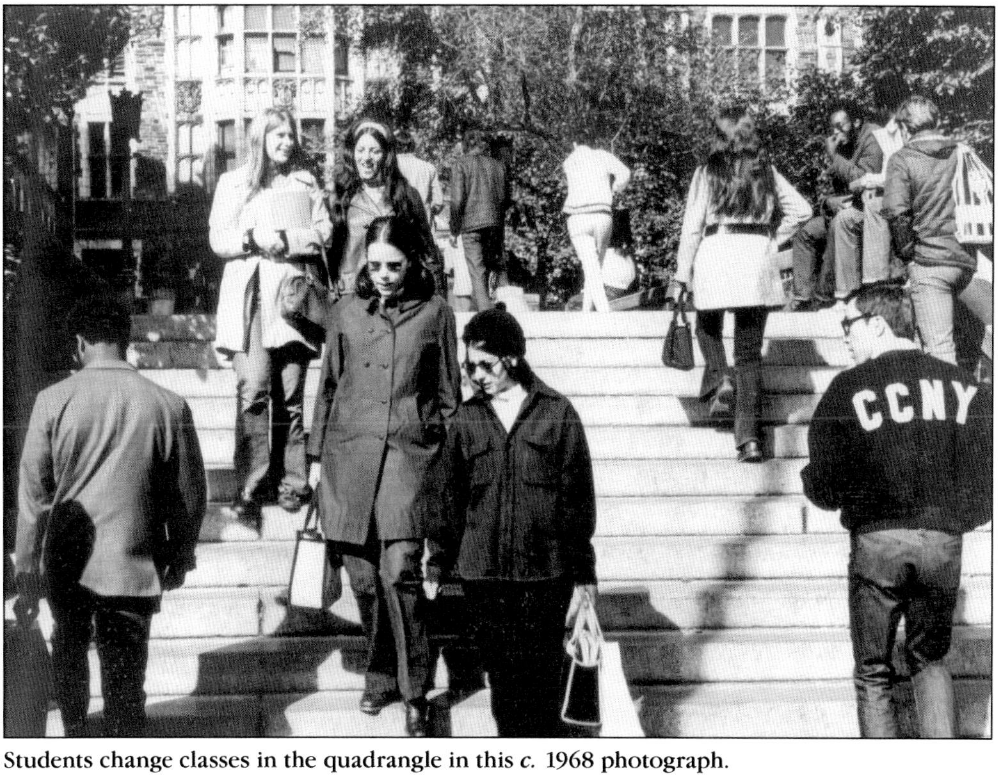

Students change classes in the quadrangle in this *c.* 1968 photograph.

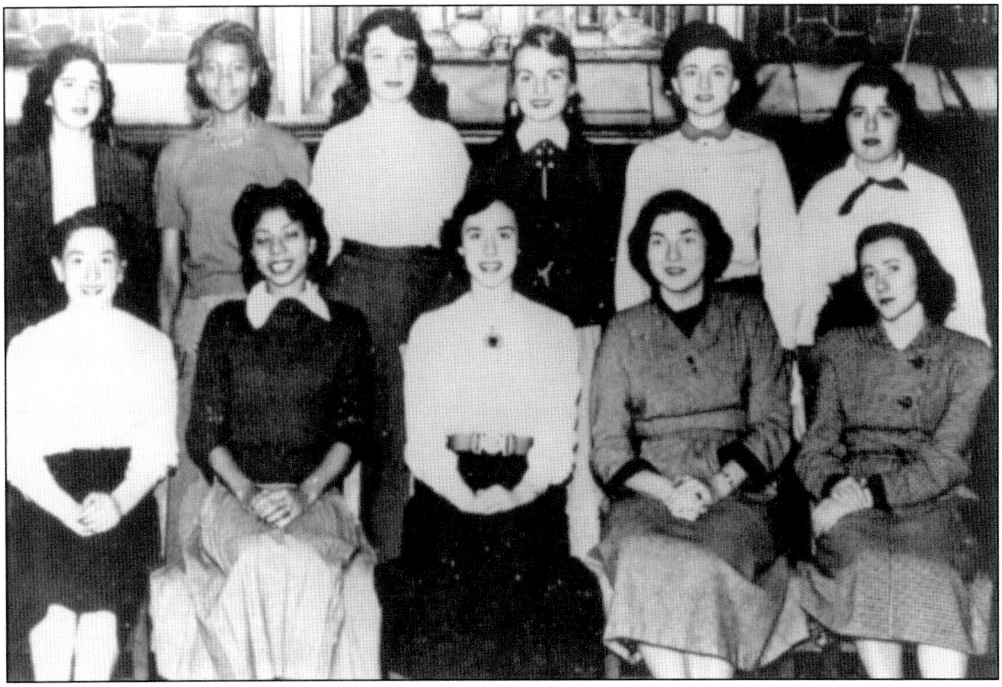

Women were first admitted to the School of Technology in 1938, and nine had enrolled by January 1940. By 1950, the women in the school were able to establish a chapter of the Society of Women Engineers, as seen here.

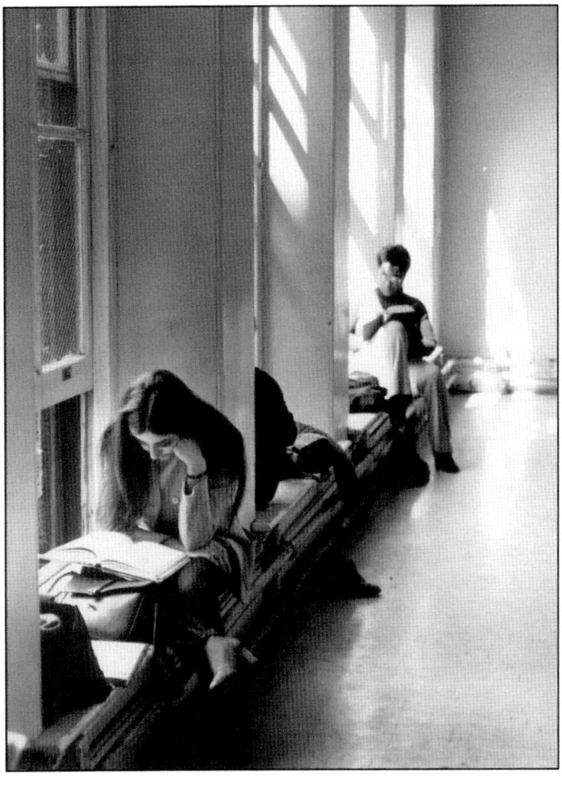

City College students have always had to find what time they can to study between the demands of their classes and the jobs they work to help pay for educational expenses. Here, three students take advantage of a corridor's window seats to catch up on their reading in 1972. (Photograph by James Shields.)

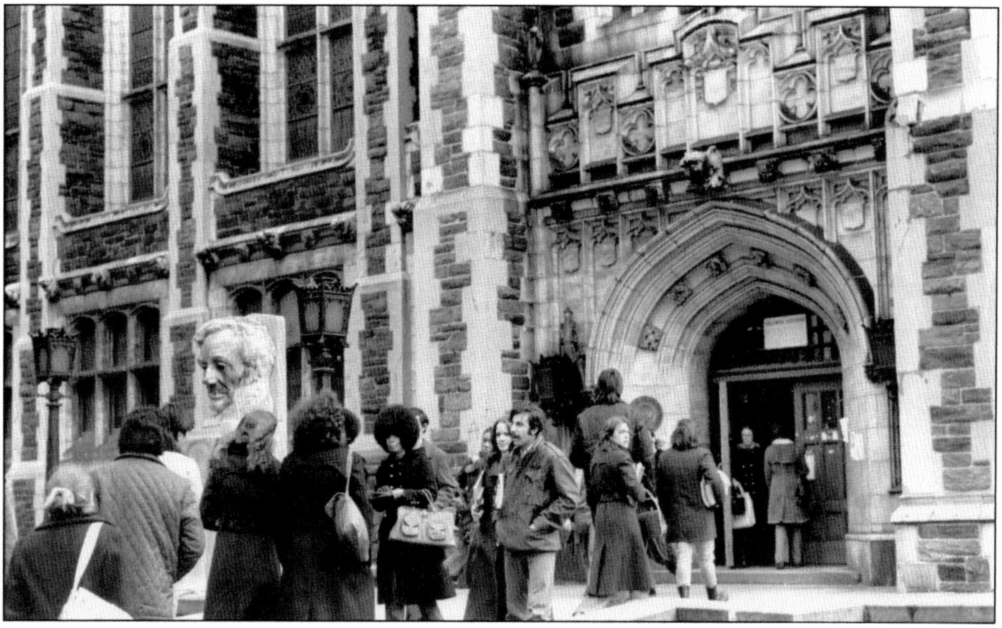

Students enter and exit Shepard Hall in 1972. They are walking past the bronze head of Abraham Lincoln, presented to the college by artist John Gutzon-Mothe Borglum on December 23, 1908, during an assembly in the Great Hall. This bronze piece was one of just three cast in the early 20th century from the 1907 marble portrait; the other two are at Lincoln's grave and at the White House. (Photograph by James Shields.)

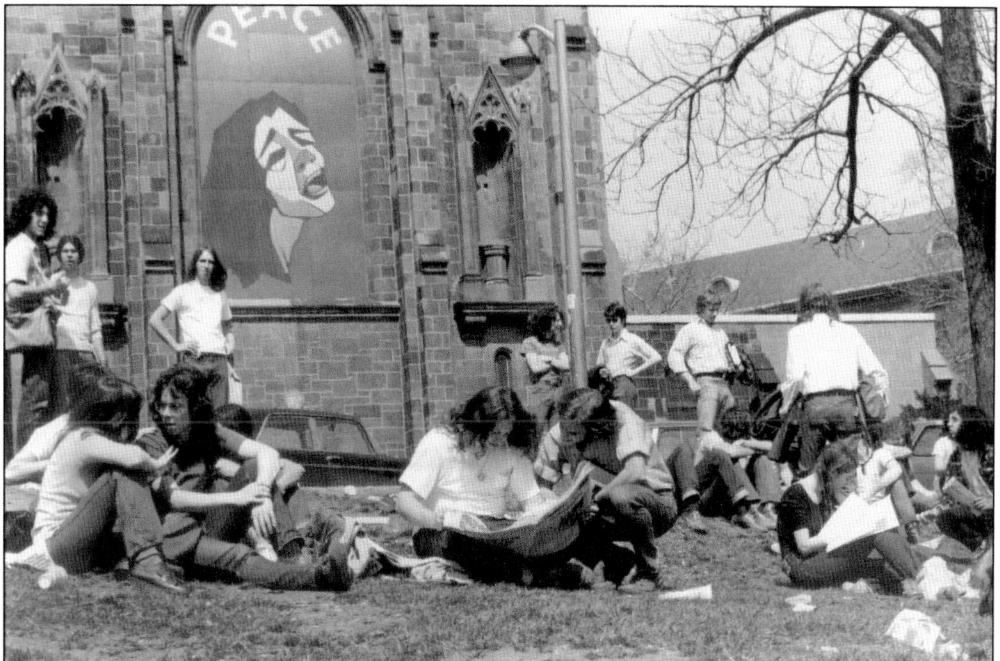

The Peace Window, shown here in 1972, was a mural painted on the wooden boards that replaced the stained-glass window of the Arnow Theater. The window had been damaged due to the fire that occurred during the 1969 student occupation of that wing of Finley Hall. (James Shields.)

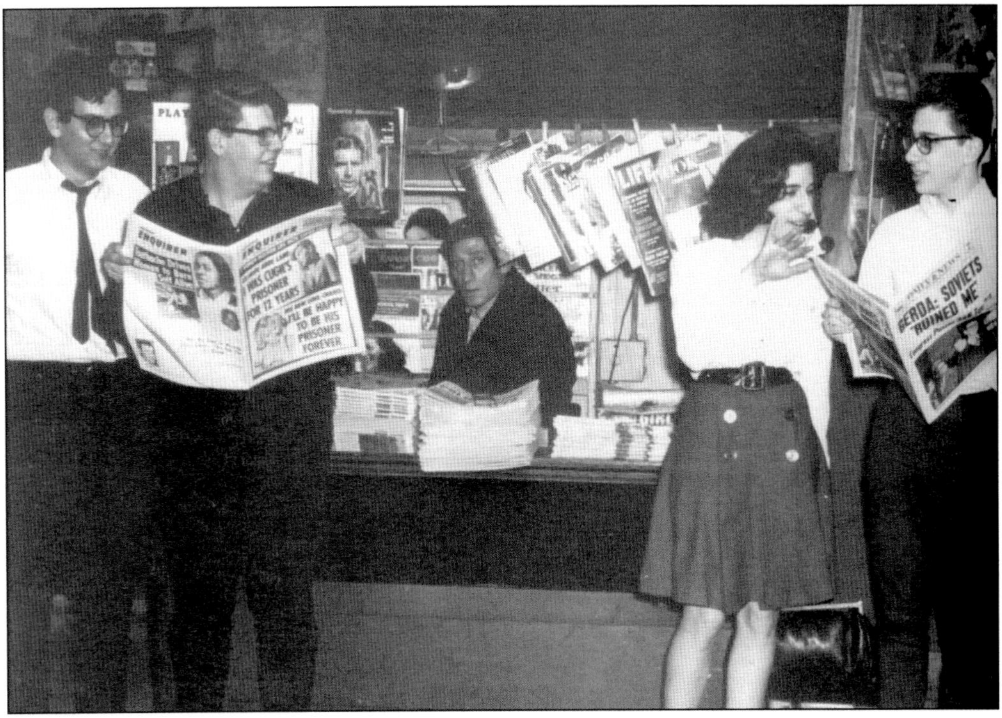

The students of the downtown campus's School of Business had their own newspaper, which began in 1932 and was known as the *Ticker*.

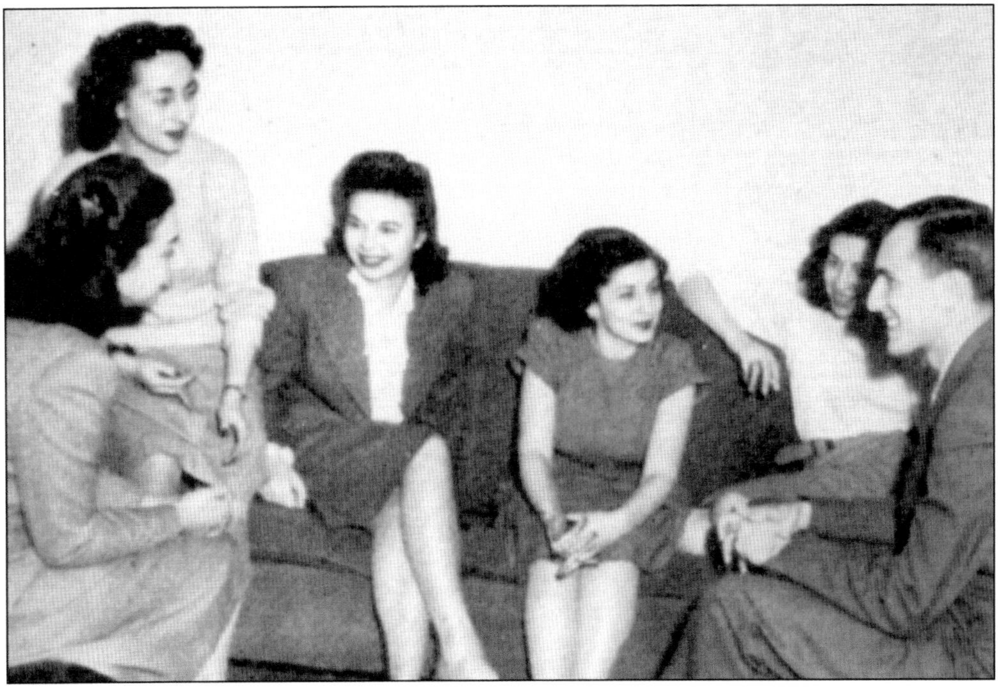

Business school students regularly took time out of their schedules studying accountancy and management in order to participate in self-government. Here, members of the 1947 Class Council discuss issues during a meeting.

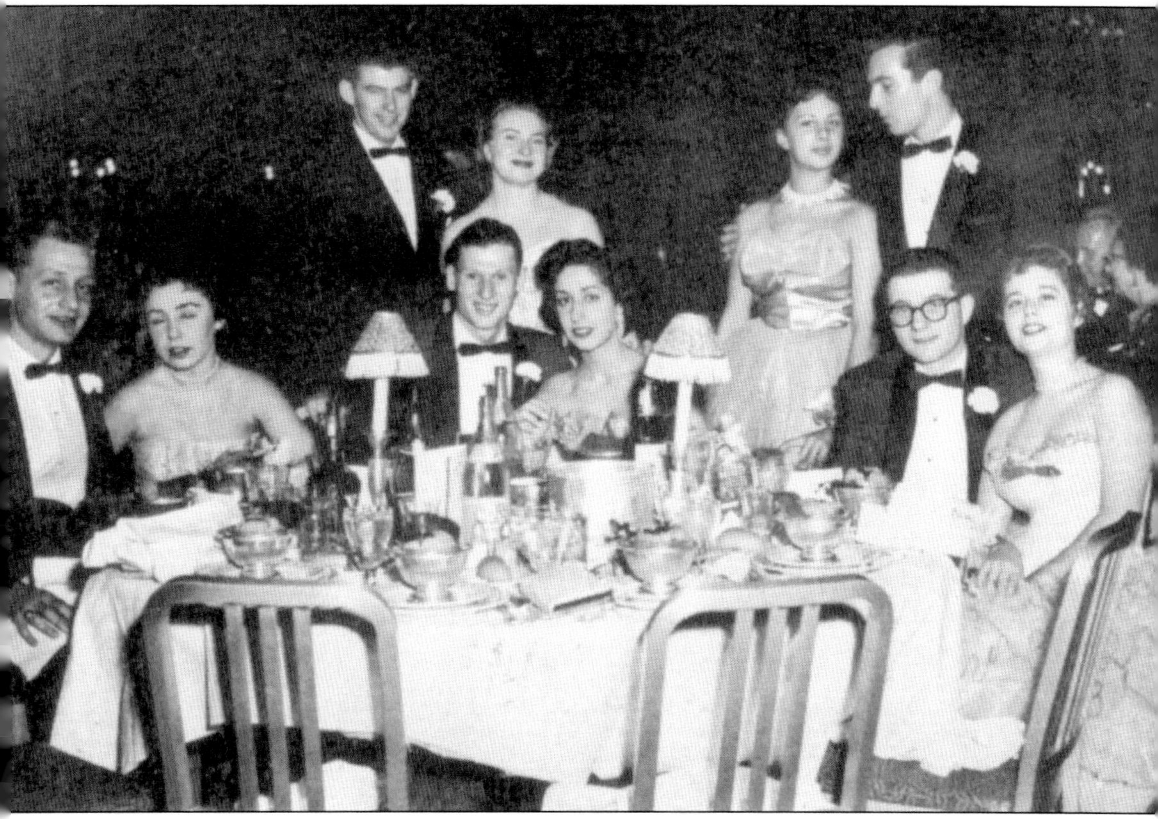

Students of the newly designated Bernard M. Baruch School of Business and Public Administration, named in honor of the distinguished graduate of 1899, celebrated formally at the senior prom held on November 26, 1956, in the Grand Ballroom of the Biltmore Hotel.

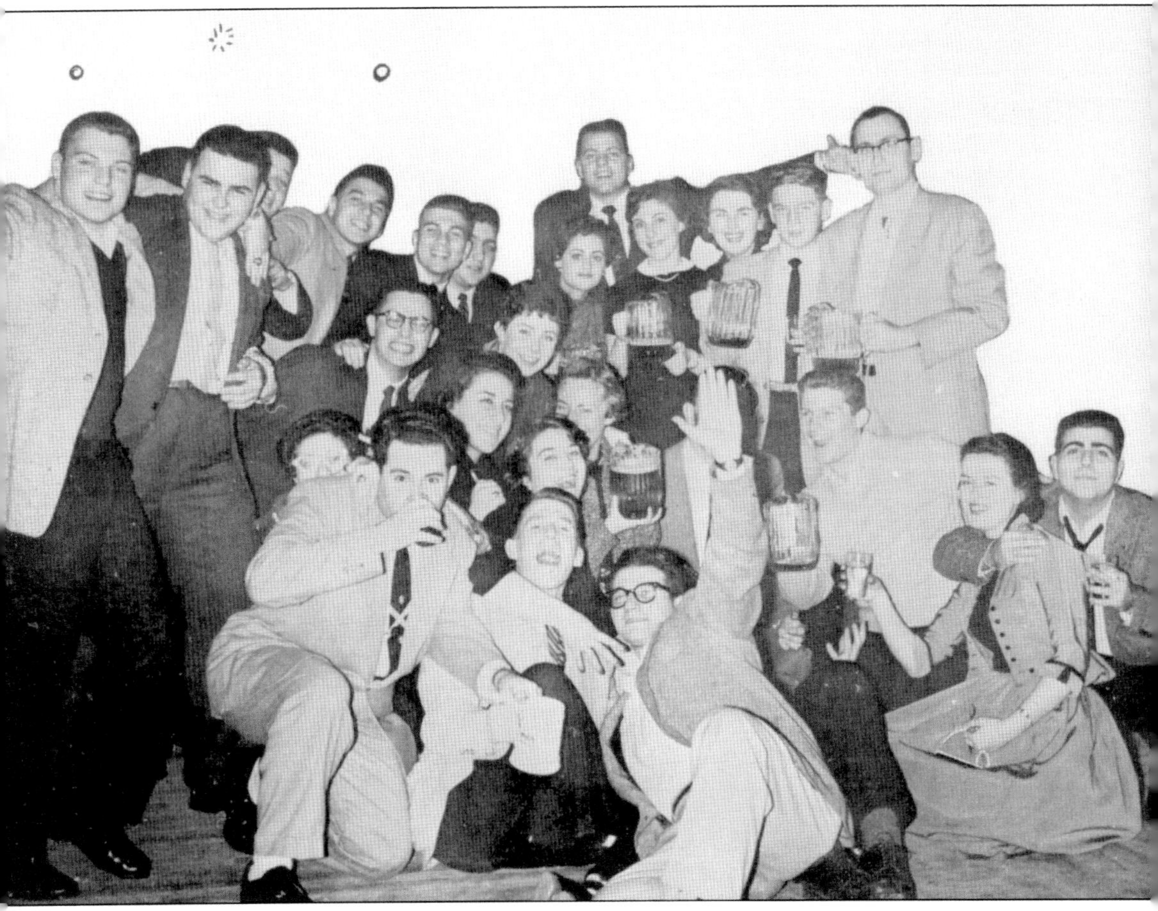

These business school students relax after accounting classes at a "Beer Party." Courses in bookkeeping and phonography or shorthand were part of the first year instruction at the Free Academy.

Four

A Strong Mind

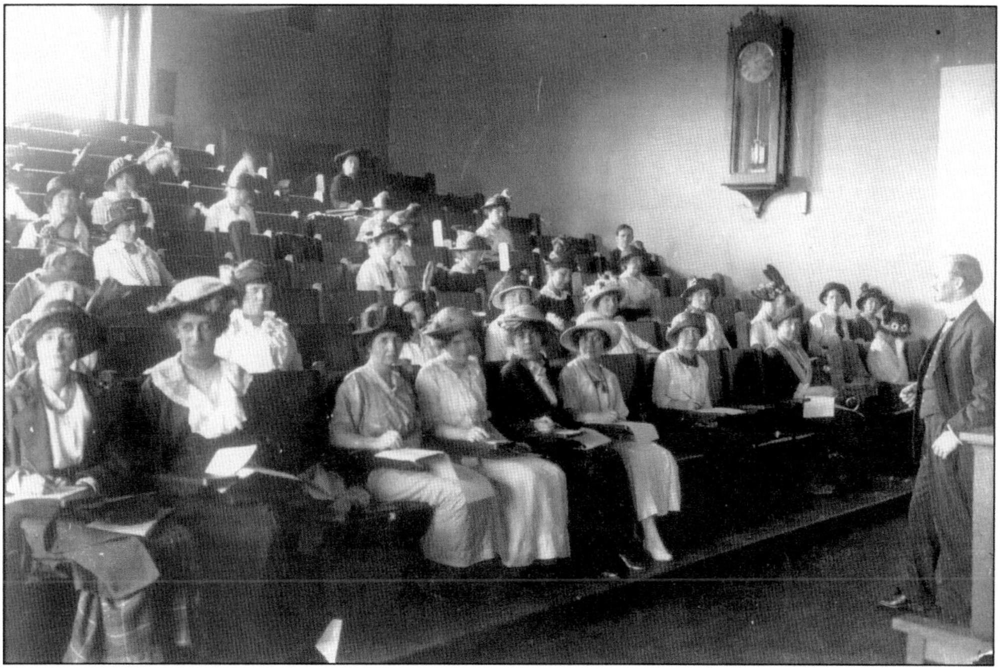

Prof. Frederick Robinson, future president of the college, lectures to education extension students on the art of public speaking in Room 126 of Shepard Hall around 1910. This course, begun in 1910, was taught by some of the college's most distinguished faculty. Classes were conducted in the late afternoon to accommodate teachers and librarians in the public schools—many of whom were women. On September 22, 1913, the *New York Times* printed an article, "30-Hour College Courses" that stated "Prof. Robinson presents another phase of the language in two courses on oral English and methods of teaching reading. The first course will extend over fifteen sessions. The first course presents two branches of oral English; the philosophy of expression and phonetics. The second course treats the history of reading methods and analysis of teaching reading."

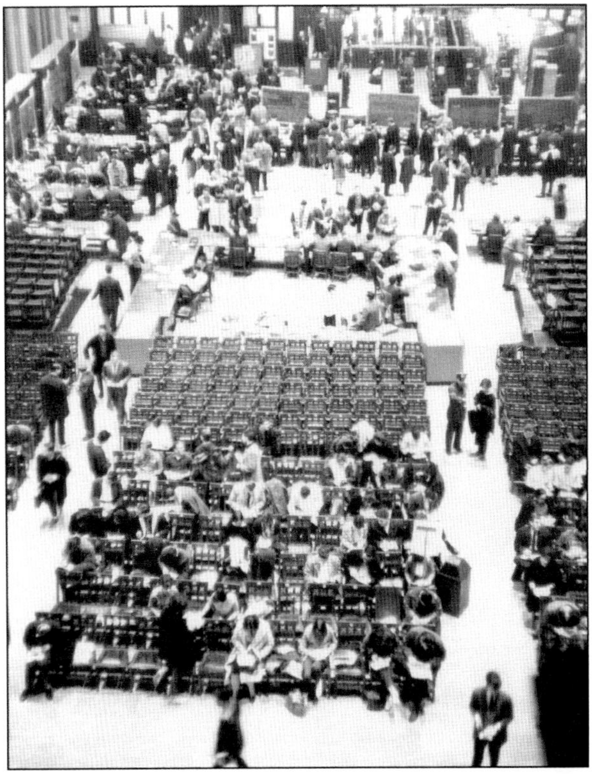

Registration was held in the Great Hall in the early 1960s. There was always a great deal of unease that the course section one wished to choose might be closed.

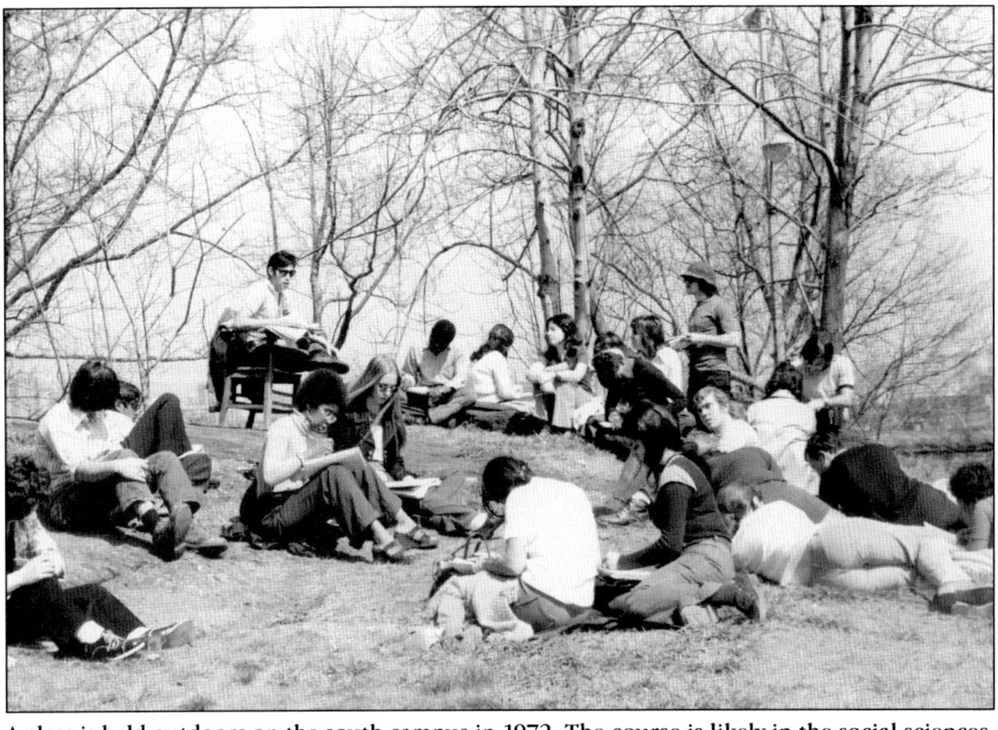

A class is held outdoors on the south campus in 1972. The course is likely in the social sciences, as those programs were located on the south campus.

The senior mechanical class sits on the steps to the chemical laboratory of the Free Academy Building. Prof. William Fox is seated on the lower left, and Prof. Alfred G. Compton is seated on the lower right.

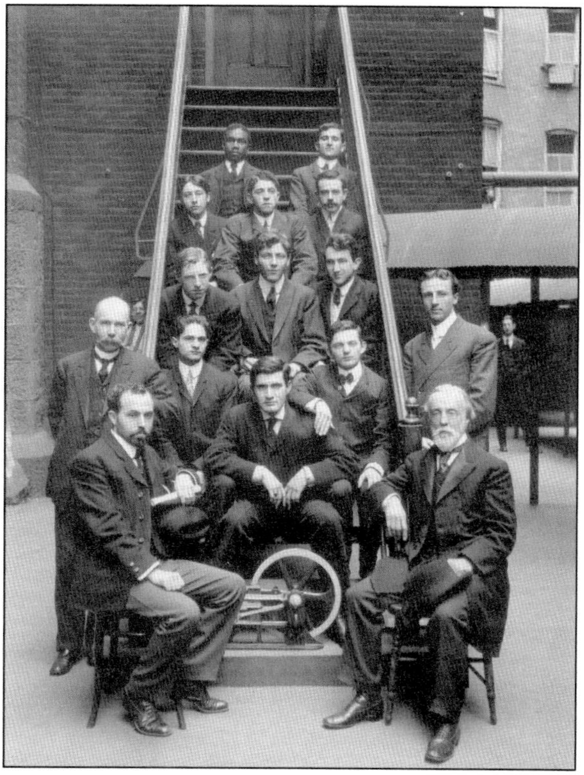

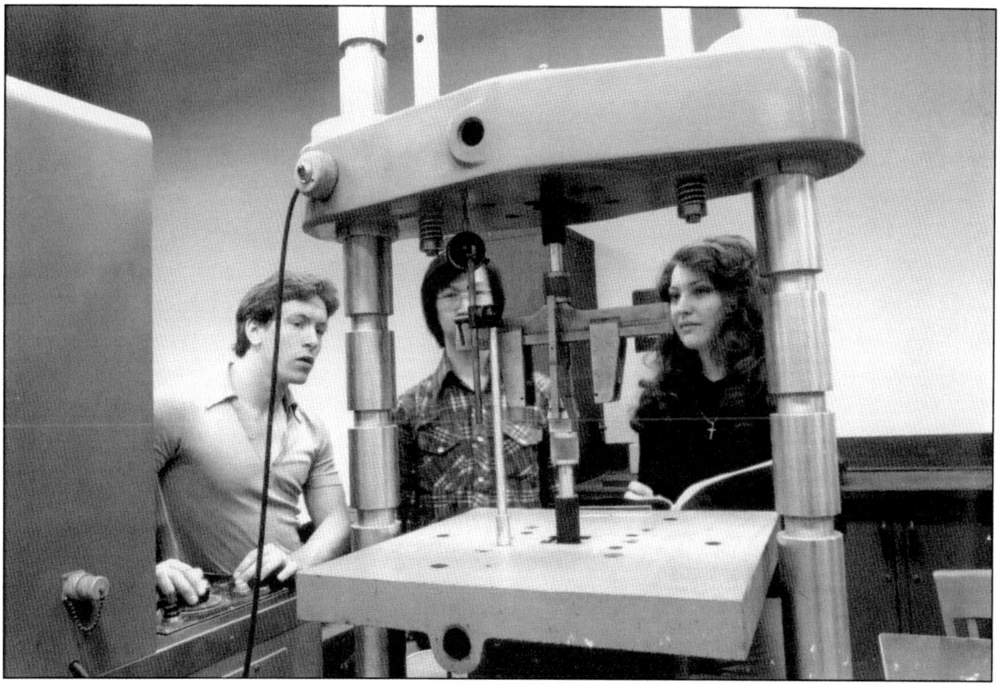

The Grove School of Engineering offers courses in electrical, chemical, mechanical, biomedical, and computer engineering. The tensile strength experiment is discussed during this 1996 mechanical engineering class.

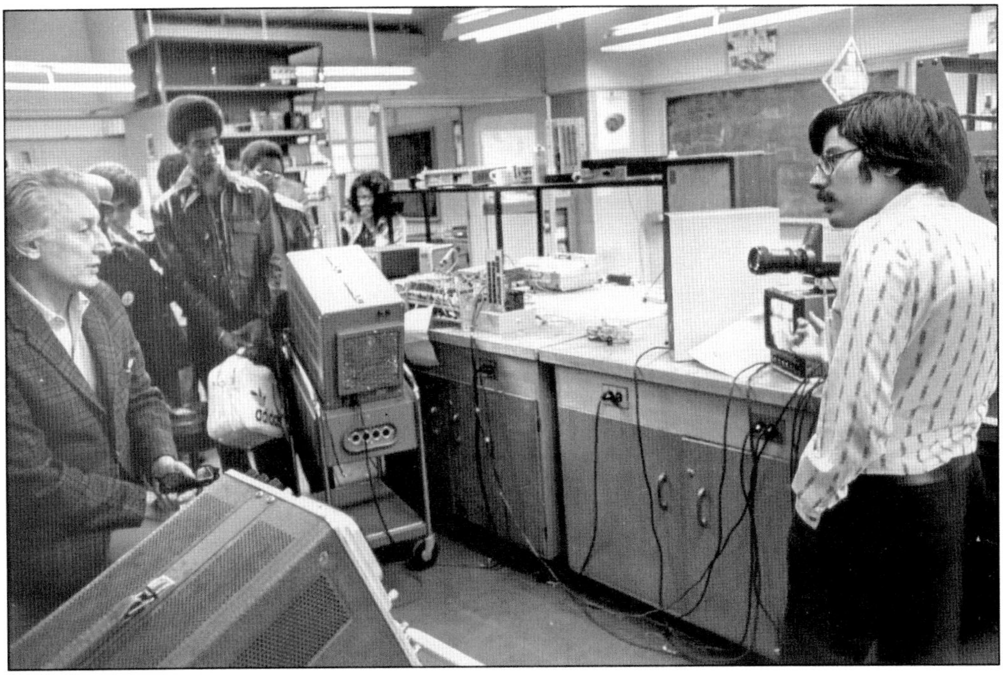

Students discuss an apparatus for a boundary layer experiment in the electrical engineering communications laboratory of the School of Engineering about 1970.

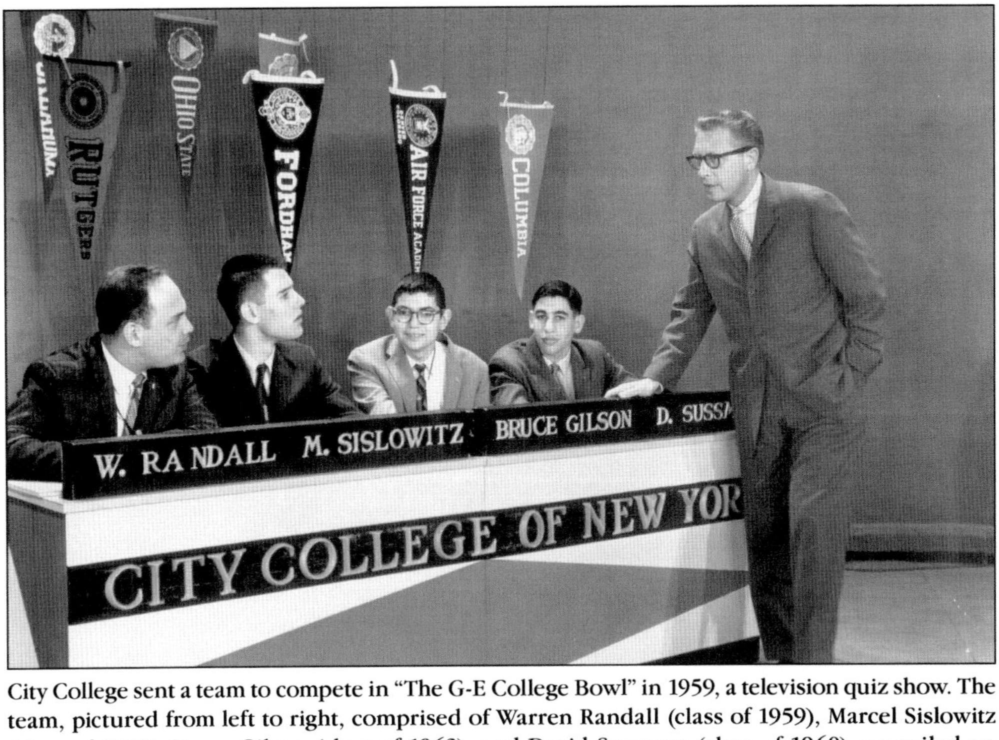

City College sent a team to compete in "The G-E College Bowl" in 1959, a television quiz show. The team, pictured from left to right, comprised of Warren Randall (class of 1959), Marcel Sislowitz (class of 1959), Bruce Gilson (class of 1962), and David Sussman (class of 1960), prevailed on the program for four weeks, defeating teams from Goucher, Syracuse, and Lehigh. Their $5,000 winnings were contributed to the college's scholarship fund.

Cecile Froehlich immigrated to the United States from Europe, where she had been trained in mathematics, pure physics, and philosophy. When she arrived, she found it difficult to obtain a position with a technical firm, so she secured a position teaching in the School of Technology in 1945. The first woman appointed to the faculty of the School of Engineering and Architecture, Froehlich was also the first woman at City College to obtain the rank of full professor in electrical engineering. She was the first woman to be elected chair of any department in the college and the first to head an engineering department anywhere in the country. She retired in 1966.

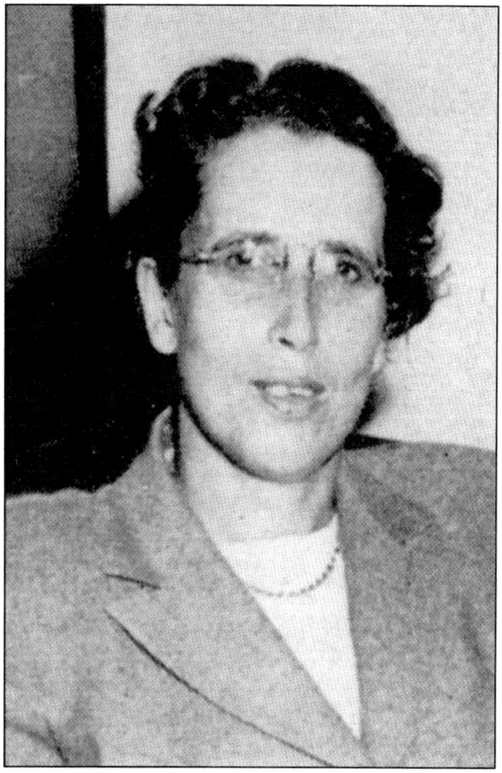

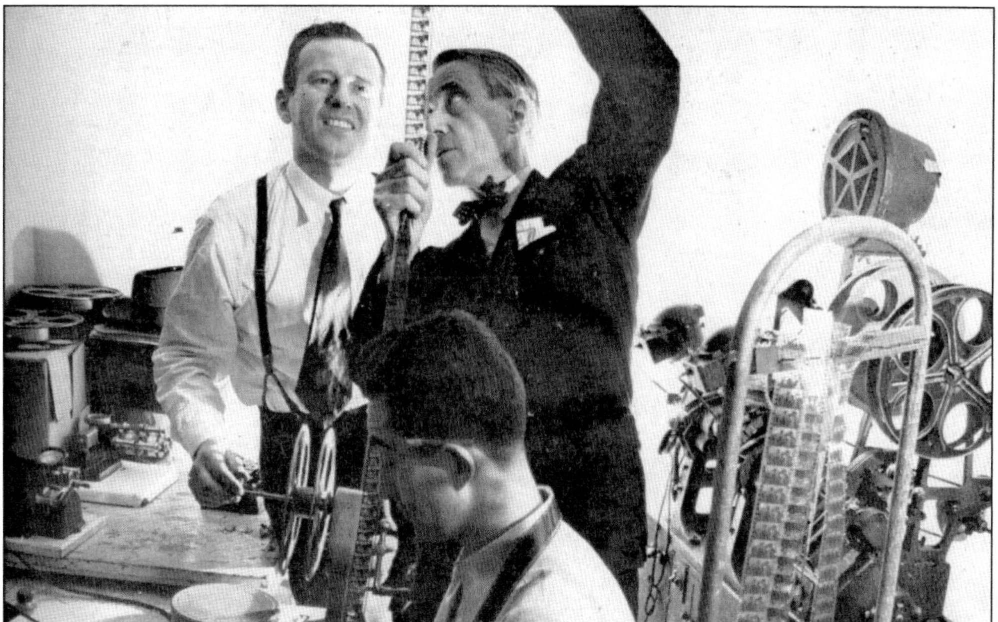

Filmmaker Hans Richter decided to immigrate to the United States after the demise of the Dada movement. Fortunately, this astounding Dadaist found a place at City College as the acting head and later director of the Institute of Film Techniques from 1943 to 1956. He is pictured in the cutting room with students from the City College Institute of Film Technique, holding a strip of film.

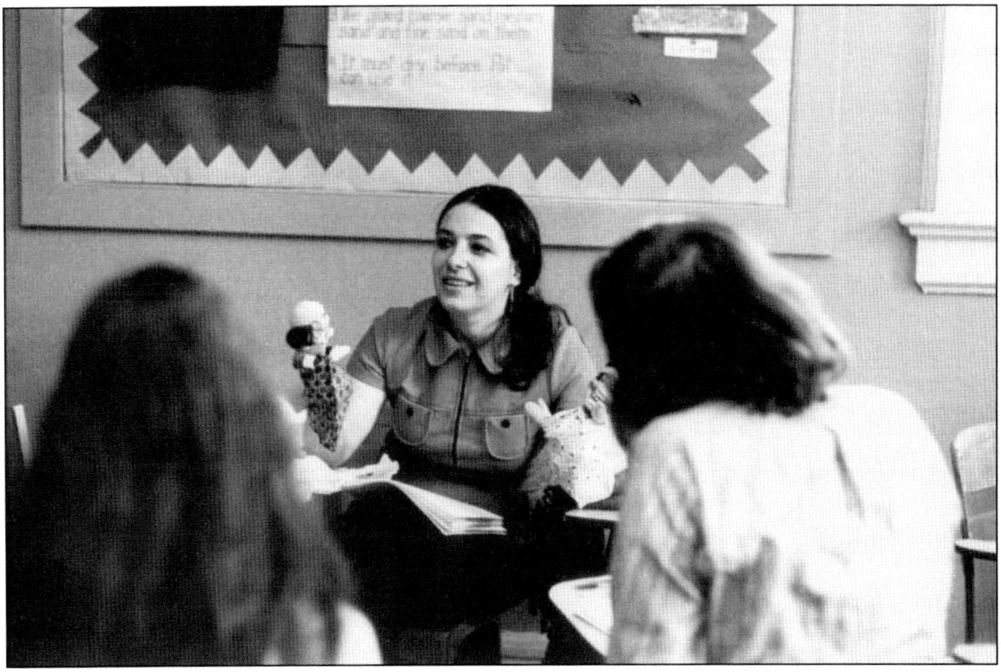

The School of Education began as a sequence of extension course classes for New York schoolteachers. In the 1960s, the school organized the major areas of study into the Departments of Social and Psychological Foundations, Elementary Education, Secondary Education, and School Services. Here, a class discusses political action in relation to education in 1972. (James Shields.)

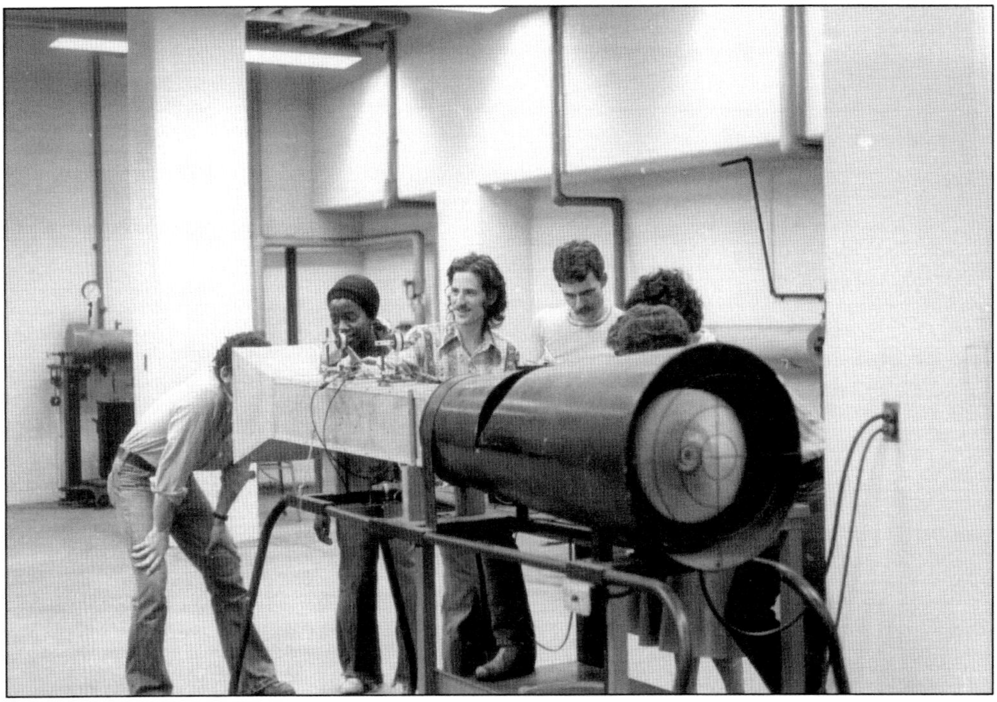

A professor and his students examine a wind tunnel during a mechanical engineering class in the 1970s.

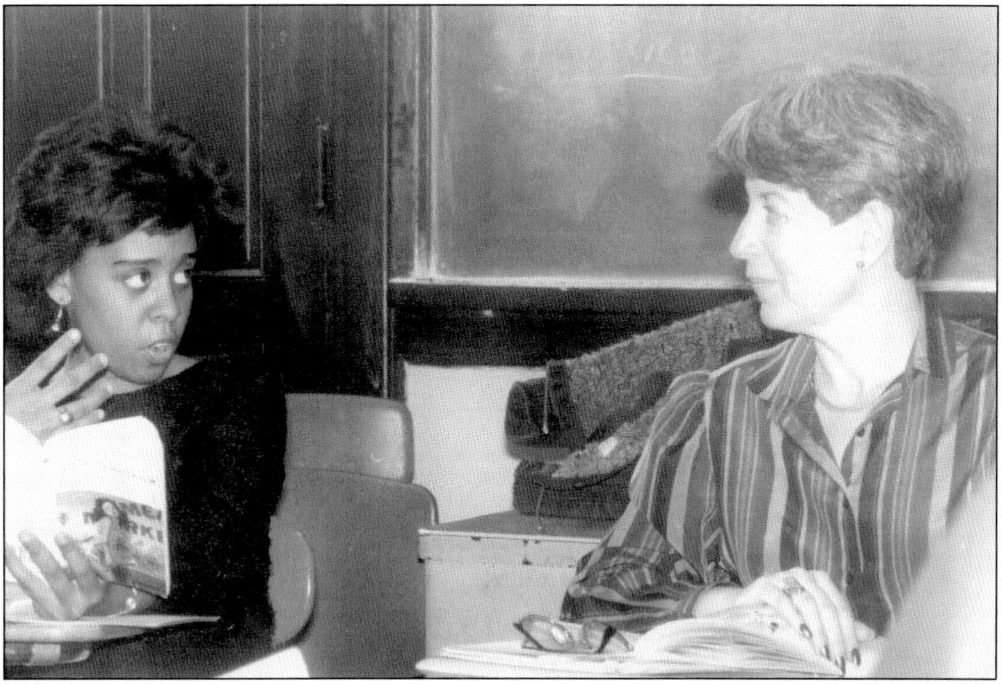

During the 1970s, diversity was not only achieved within the student body, but among the faculty members as well.

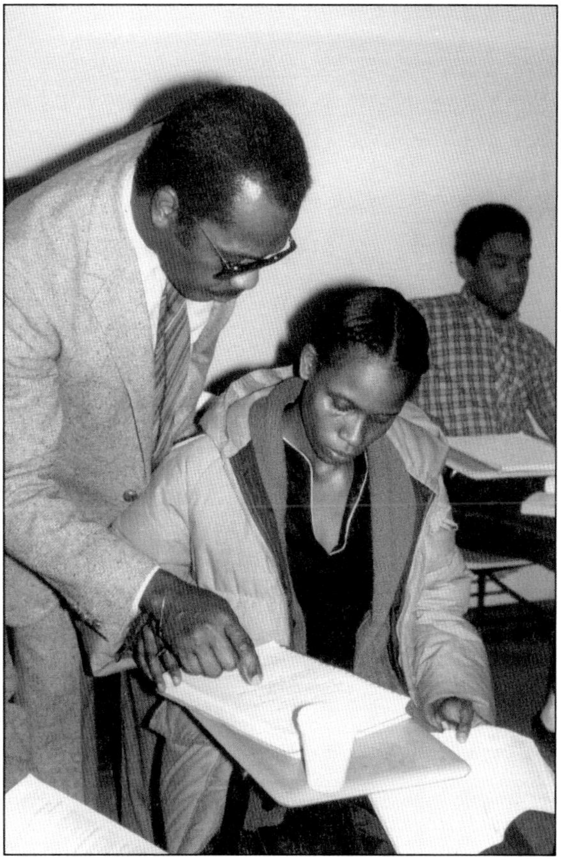

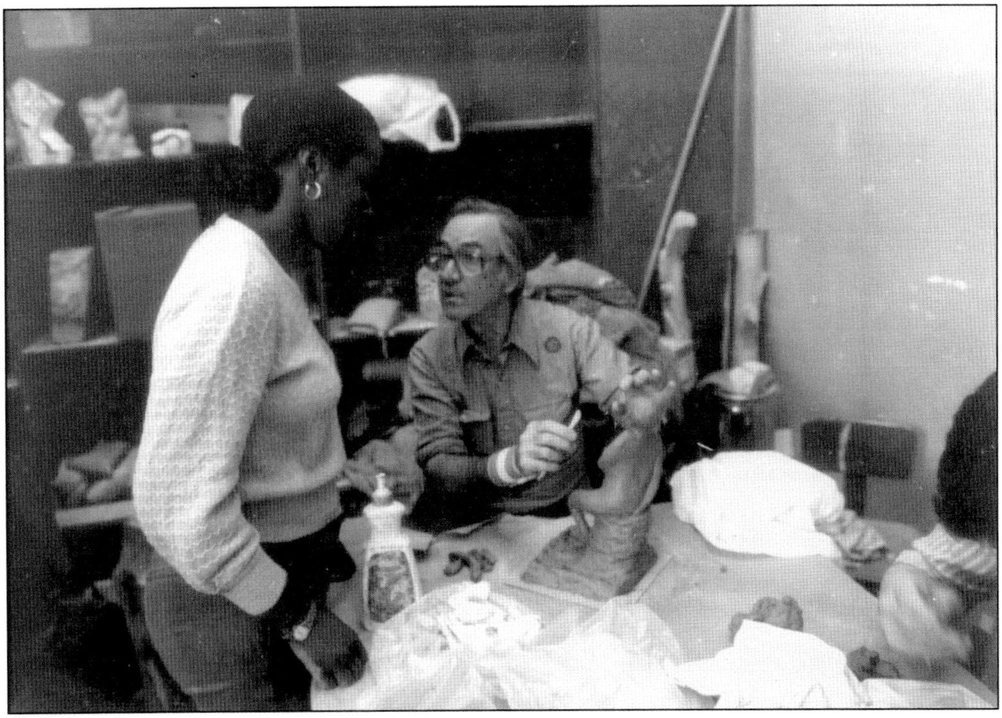

The Department of Art conducts studio art classes in drawing, painting, sculpture, and photography. Here, a 1982 class makes sculptural forms. (Leonard Edmonds.)

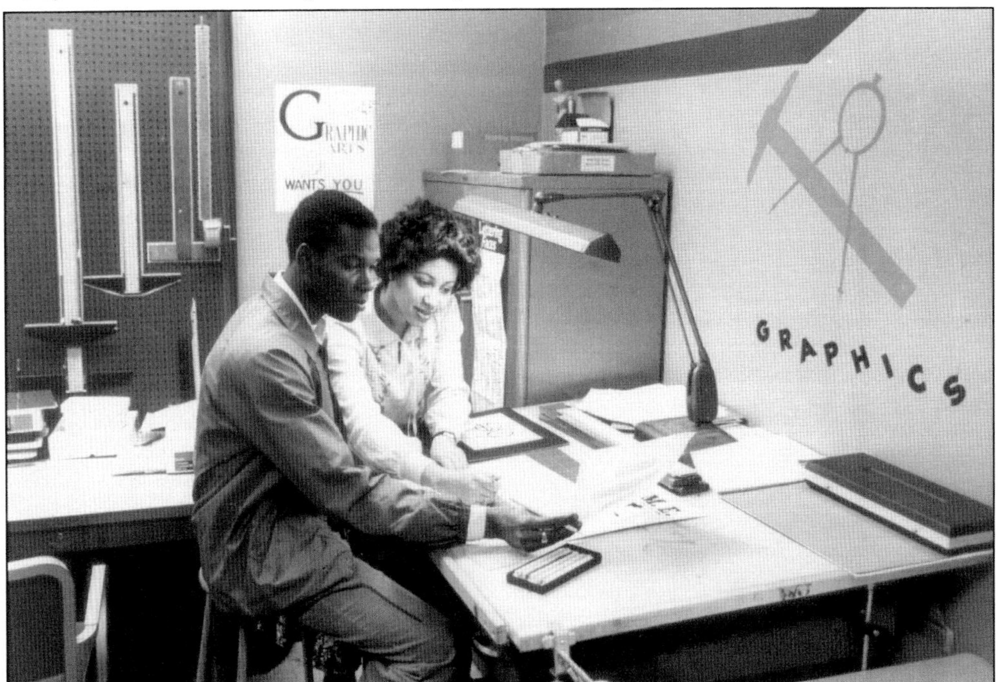

Students interested in studying graphic design can receive training from the Department of Art. A class is seen here in 1982.

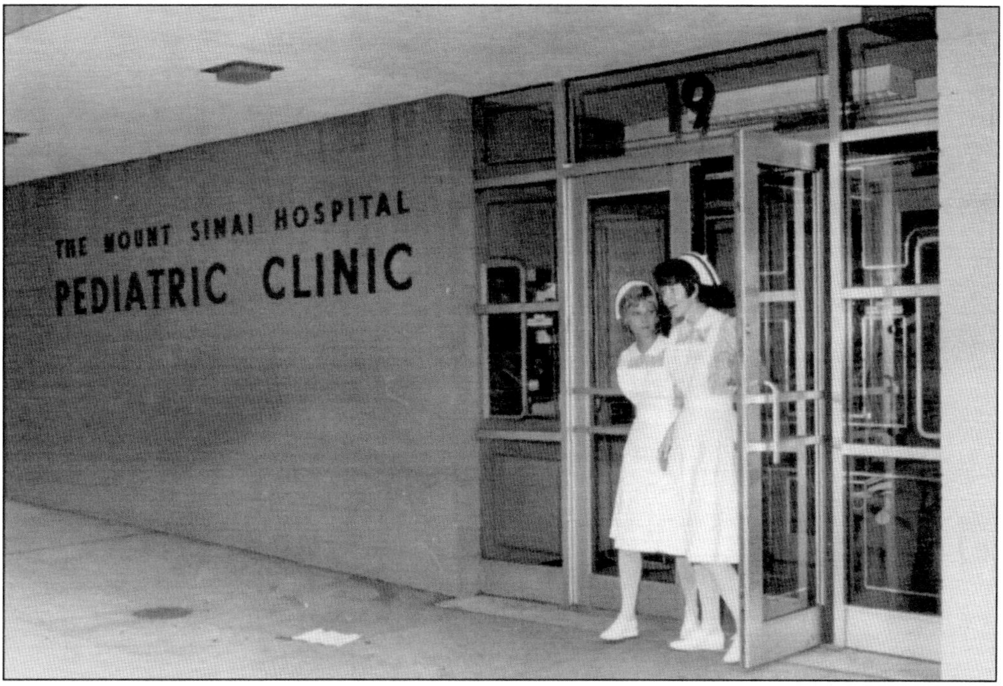

Taken in 1970, these images illustrate the participation of School of Nursing students in the Mount Sinai Pediatric Clinic. Two nursing students leave the clinic (above). Other students incorporate their understanding of the importance of laughter as a healing tool for these young patients (below). The Mount Sinai School of Nursing initially became affiliated with the City University of New York in 1967. Students in the Mount Sinai School of Nursing at City College first began taking classes in 1969. Due to fiscal difficulties, this program was unfortunately closed in 1997.

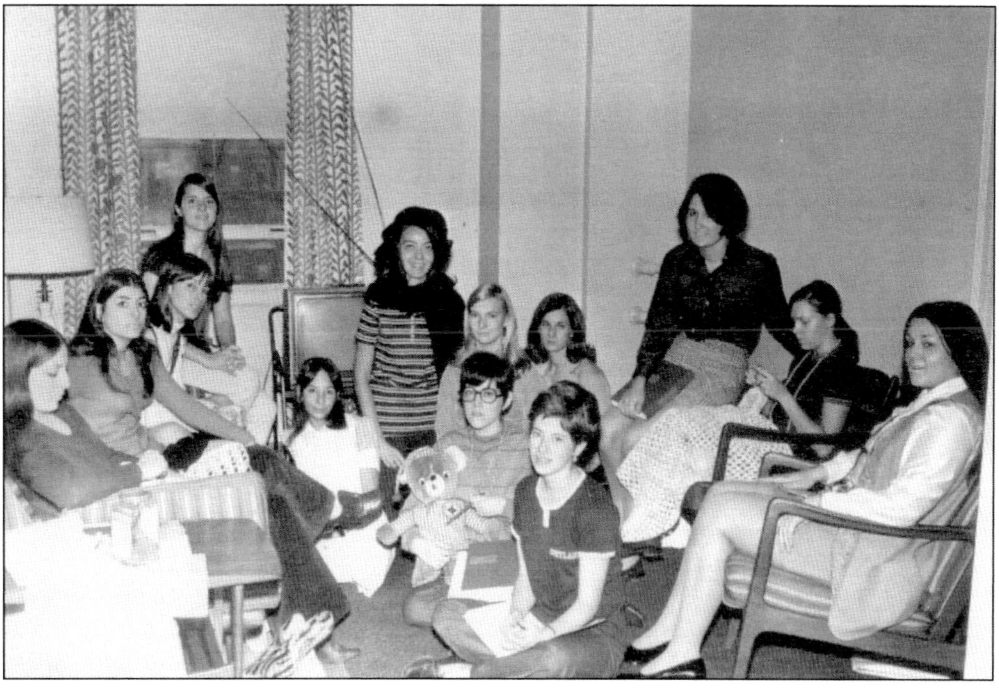

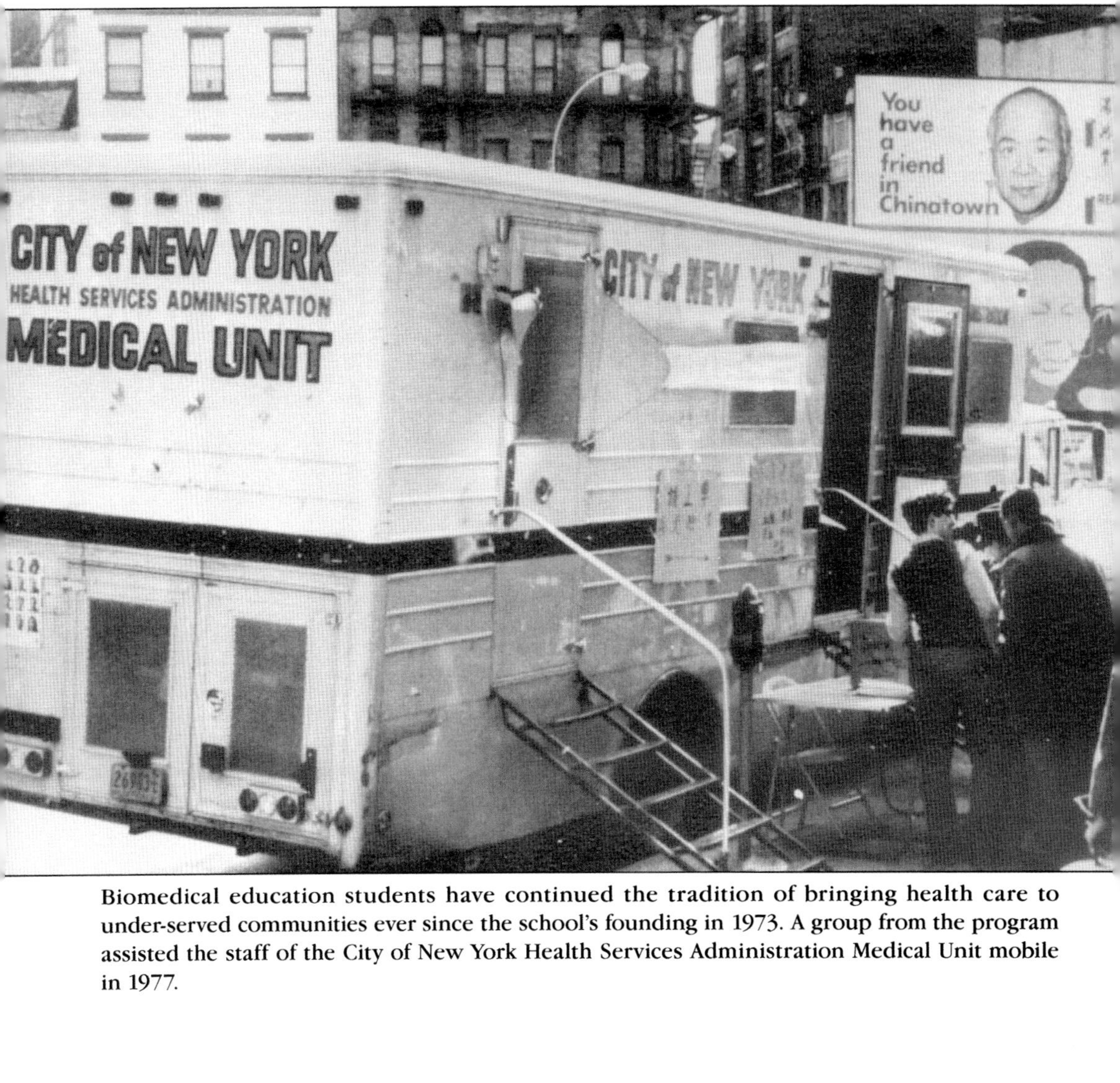

Biomedical education students have continued the tradition of bringing health care to under-served communities ever since the school's founding in 1973. A group from the program assisted the staff of the City of New York Health Services Administration Medical Unit mobile in 1977.

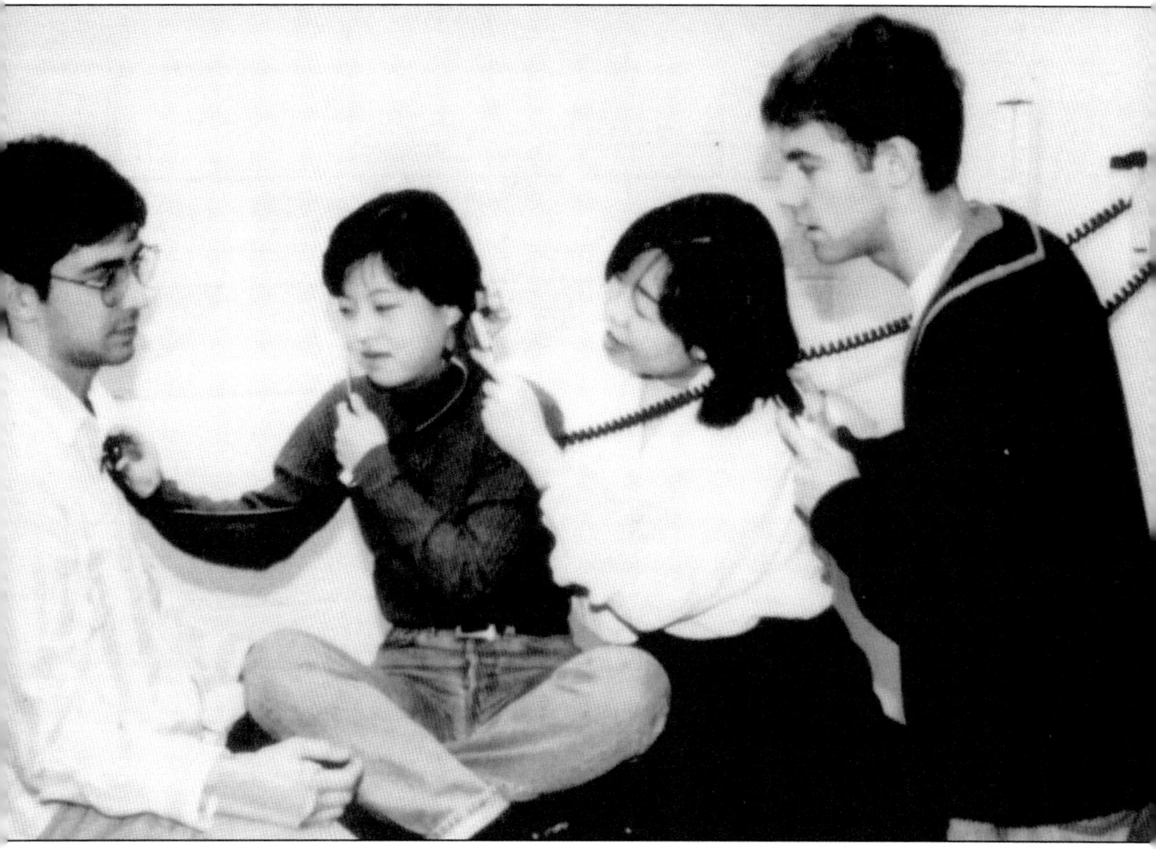

The Sophie Davis School of Biomedical Education prepares ethnically diverse students to become primary health physicians in a seven-year integrated curriculum leading to the bachelor of science and doctor of medicine degrees, with the final two years being taken at a participating medical school. Here, members of the class of 1995 try out their examination technique.

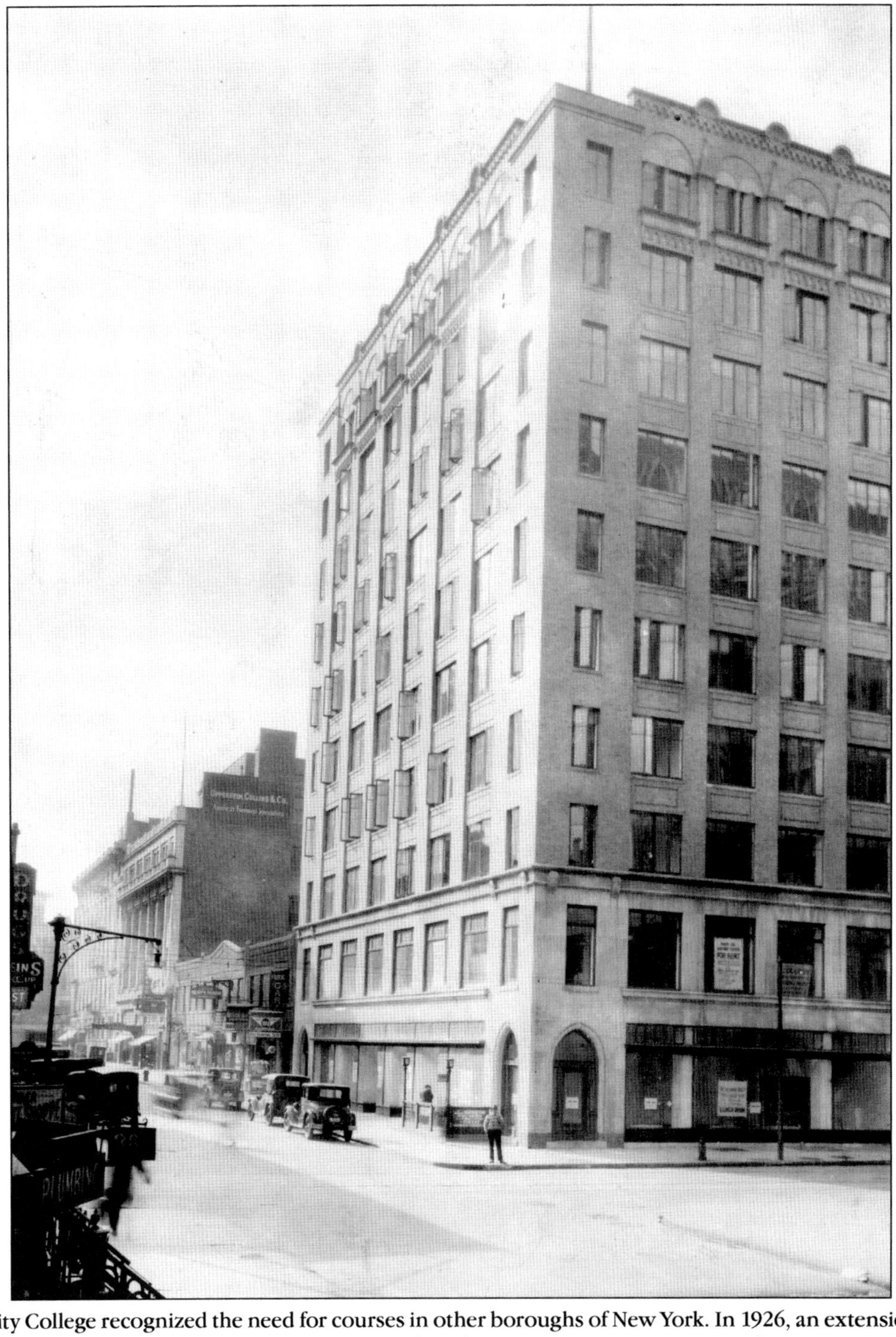

City College recognized the need for courses in other boroughs of New York. In 1926, an extension course campus was opened in Brooklyn, and in the 1930s, a center was opened in Queens. The Brooklyn center, shown here in 1926, was located in the Willoughby Building at the corner of Willoughby and Bridge Streets in downtown Brooklyn. When the City College branch merged with the Brooklyn branch of Hunter College in 1930, the institution became Brooklyn College, the first public coeducational liberal arts college in New York City.

Five

A Strong Body

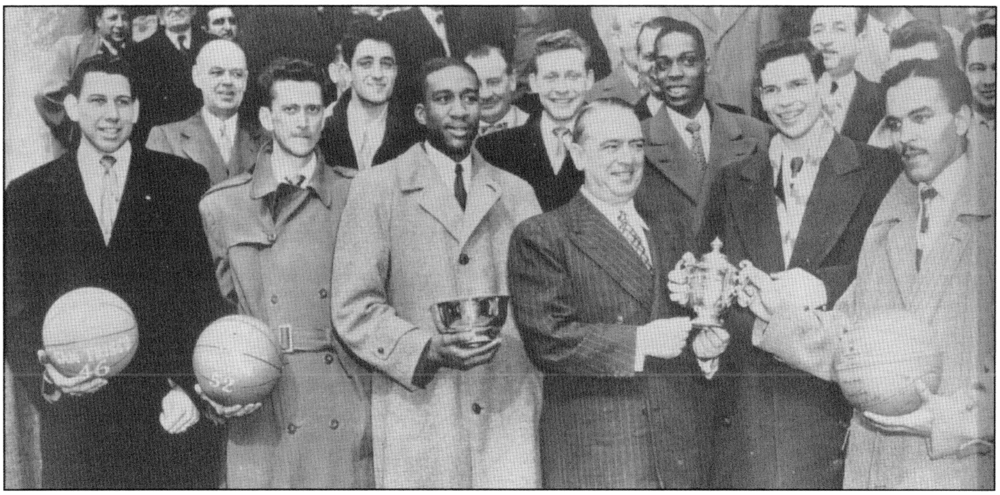

Throughout the 1940s, the City College men's varsity basketball team remained simply average until that magical moment in March 1950 when the team defeated seven opponents in 16 days to win both the NIT and NCAA Tournaments. The starting five consisted of three sophomores and two seniors led by legendary coach Nat Holman. Madison Square Garden was the world's most famous arena, and City College was undeniably the best team in the country. The mayor of New York City, William O'Dwyer, saluted the accomplishment of these hometown heroes when he invited them to city hall, where they posed with the National Invitational Tournament trophy. Such an achievement as the double victories has never been equaled in collegiate basketball.

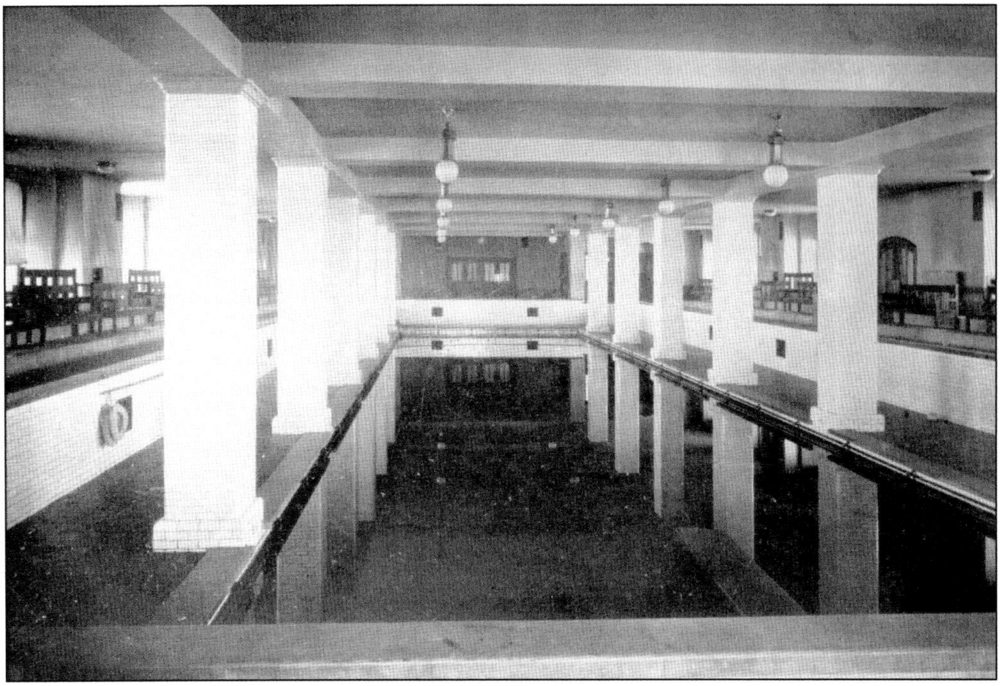

A new campus building (now Wingate Hall) included athletic areas such as a gymnasium and a basement swimming pool. The facilities were enjoyed by these students in 1909 and for many years thereafter.

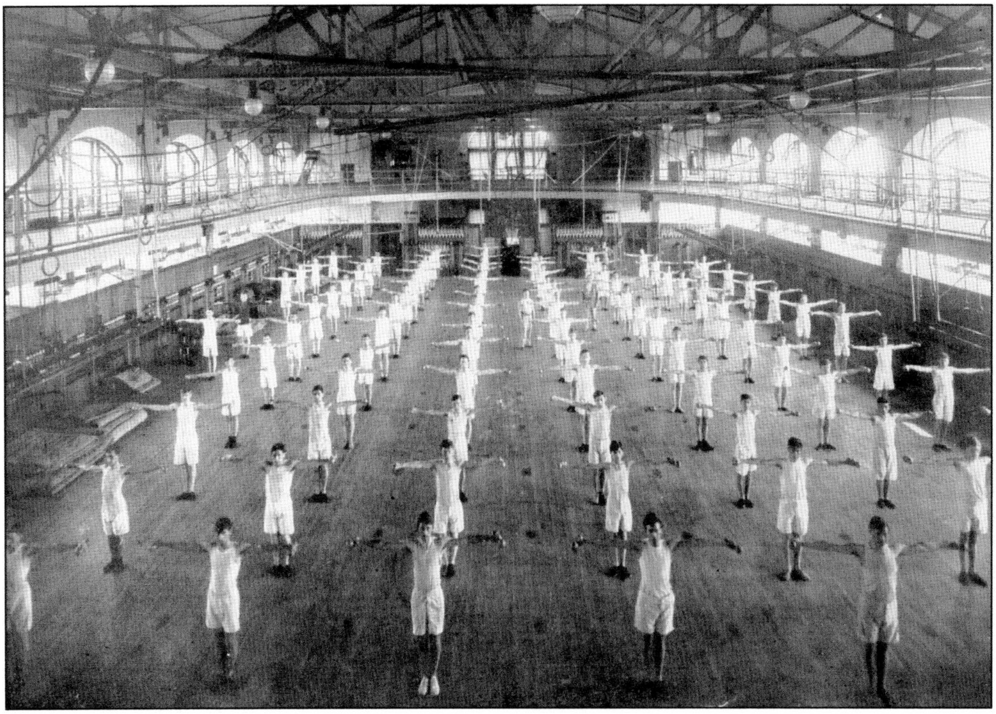

Practice in athletic activities was led by the Department of Physical Instruction and Training. Here, members of the faculty conduct physical training in the gym in 1909.

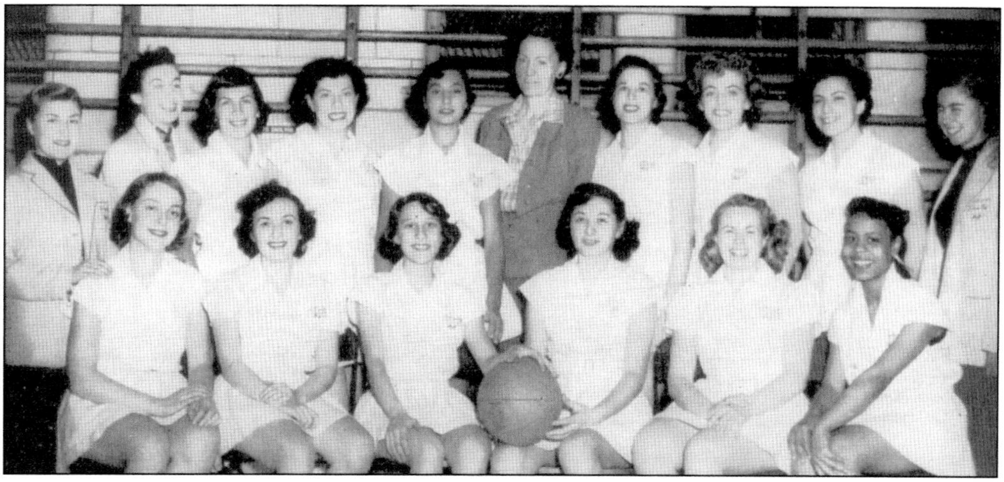

One of the demands made by women advocating for admission to the College of Liberal Arts and Science, which they achieved in 1951, was for equity in the resources available for sports. Female athletes attending other college divisions made efforts between 1947 and 1950 to form a woman's softball and a field hockey team under the direction of Laura C. Ham. However, as of the 1950–1951 season, neither team had gained varsity status. The women's varsity basketball team, or Hoopsterettes, began to build strong teams from 1948 to 1950, incorporating four high scorers. The 1951–1952 team pictured here earned a 6-4 season record. Coach Margeurite Wulfers poses with team members Linda Valentine, Barbara Dette, Judy Levin, B. J. Allen, Phyllis Kaufman, and cocaptains Pearl Zarember and Ann Ulnick, the team high-scorer who posted 23 points against New York University.

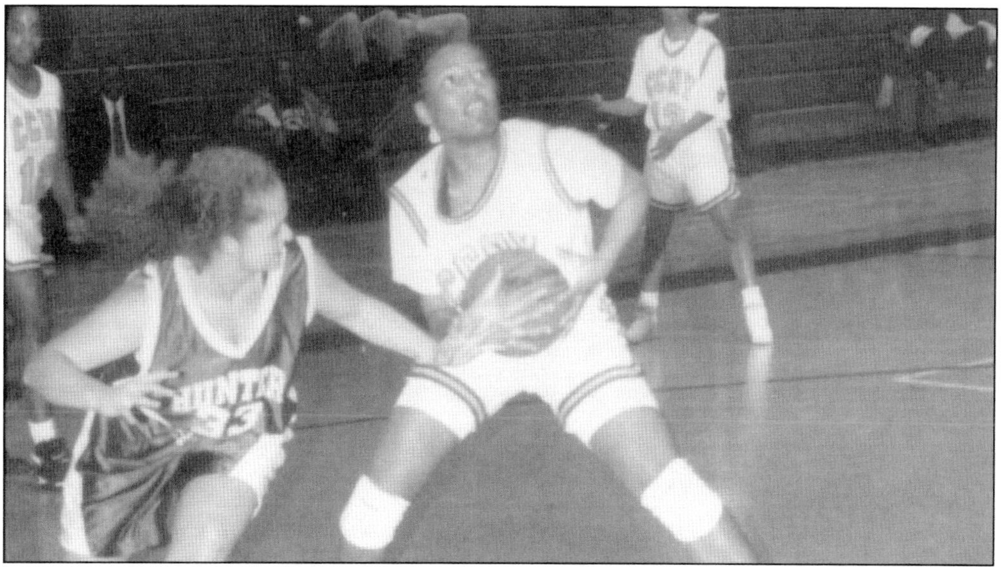

The 1993–1994 women's varsity basketball team is seen playing against Hunter College included coach Stephanie English, assistant coach Larry Lingard, and team members Marcey Brown, Carolyn Isaac, Michelle Lugo, Rhondalyn Mclean, Matseliso Masithela, Julissa Matias, Karyn Morales, Thais Palmer, Ayanna Parker, Edith Pinero, Marcella Wellington, and Christine Woolard. The women's varsity players garnered four straight City University of New York Conference championships, four straight 20-win seasons, three straight Hudson Valley Conference championships, and regional championships in 1987.

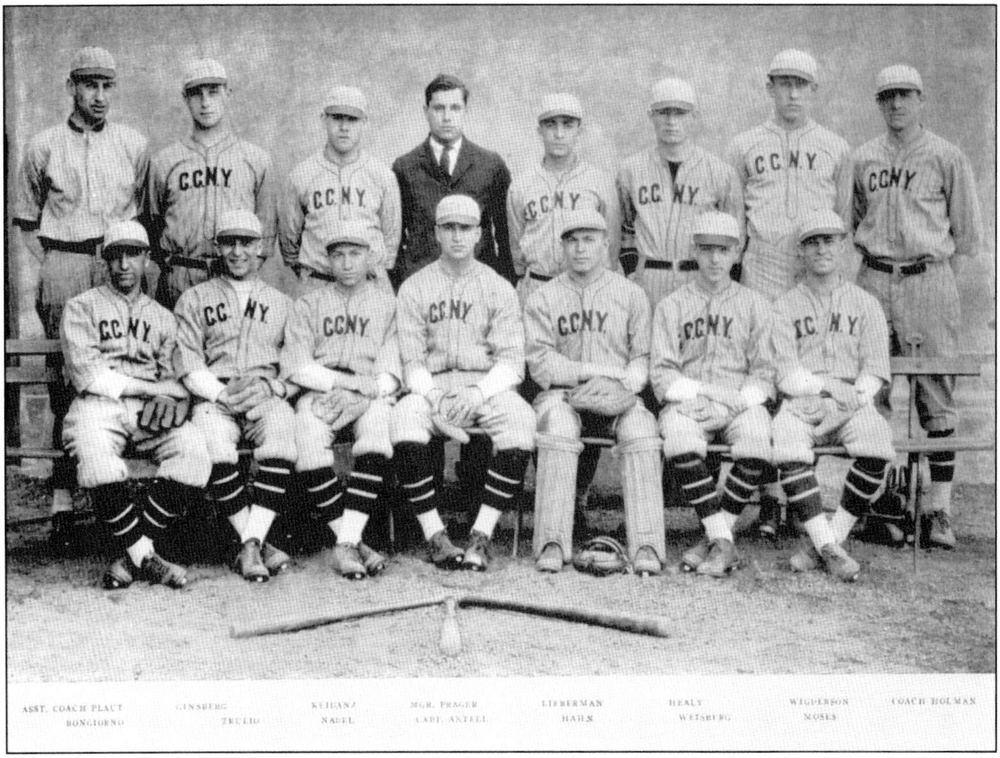

The 1923 City College baseball team is seen here. The coach, Nat Holman, stands on the far right. Holman was responsible for coaching the baseball, basketball, and soccer teams at this time.

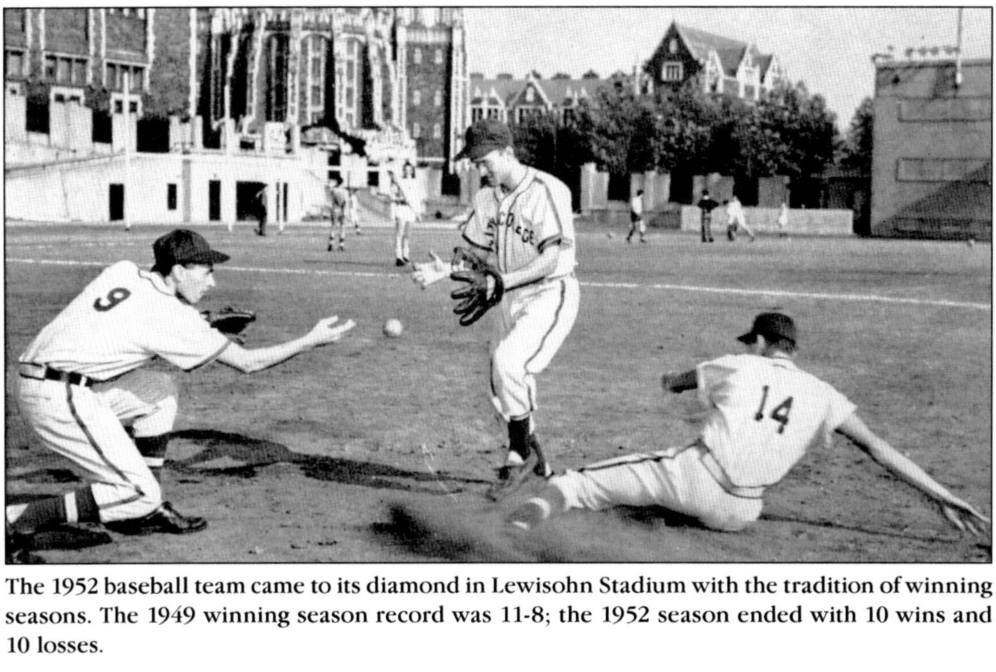

The 1952 baseball team came to its diamond in Lewisohn Stadium with the tradition of winning seasons. The 1949 winning season record was 11-8; the 1952 season ended with 10 wins and 10 losses.

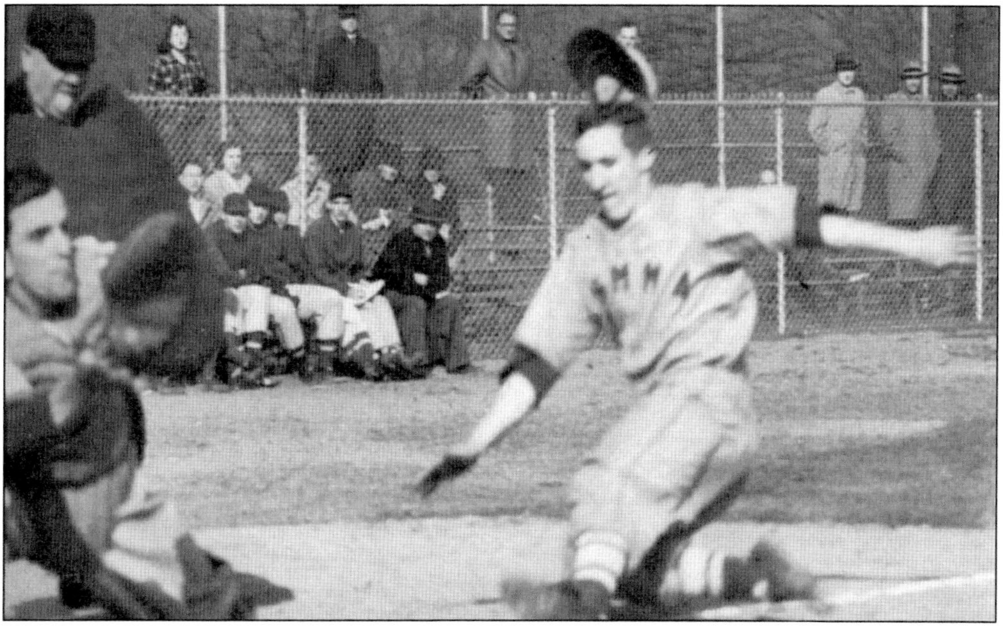

The 1955 baseball team tried its best to uphold the tradition, but finished with an overall season record of 5-9.

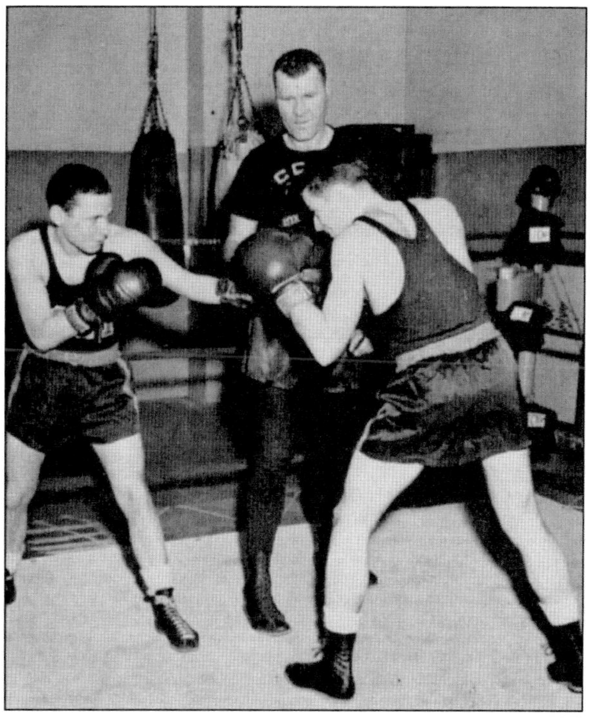

Members of the boxing team had high hopes going into the 1953–1954 season when coach Reich put them through their paces, but they came away with one win and two losses.

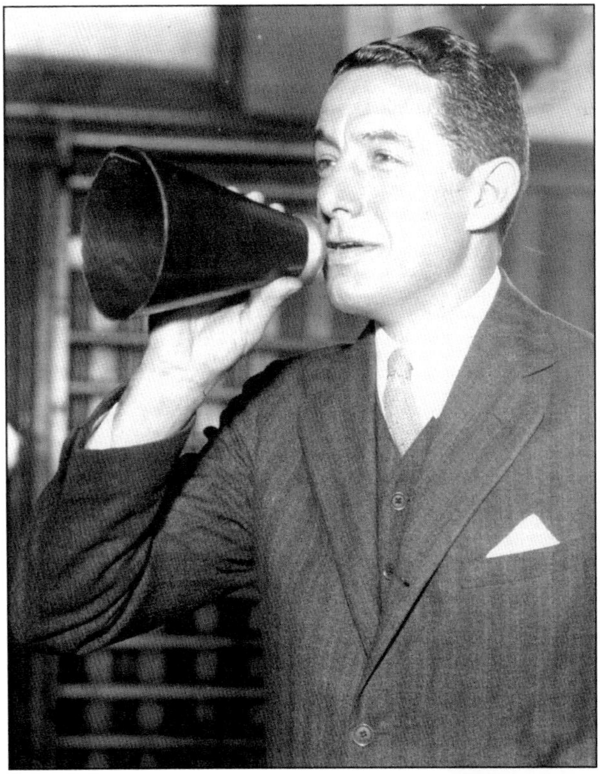

"Kid Holman," "Mr. Basketball," "Old Drill Master," and "the Old Professor" were just a few of the many titles given to basketball's earliest superstar: Nat Holman. Seen here with a megaphone, Holman taught his players to control the ball carefully, to take their time setting up offensive formations, to pass with care, and to shoot only when they had an opening.

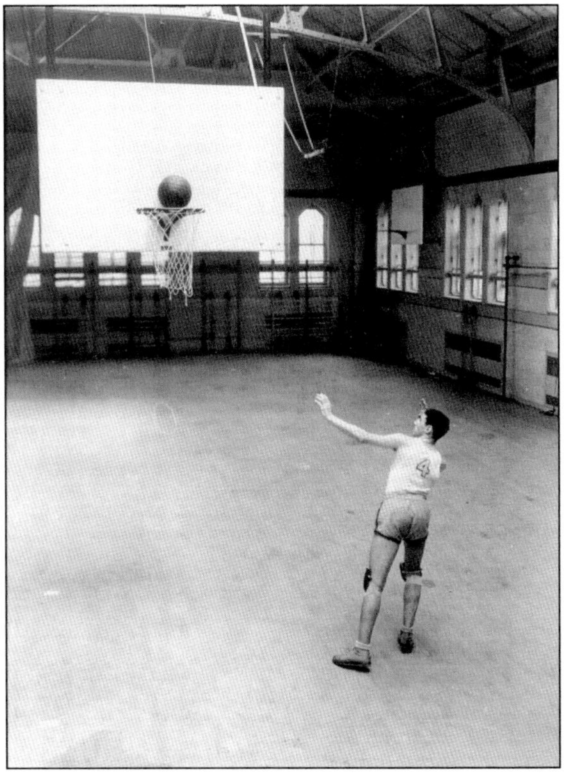

A player shoots a basket in Wingate Hall.

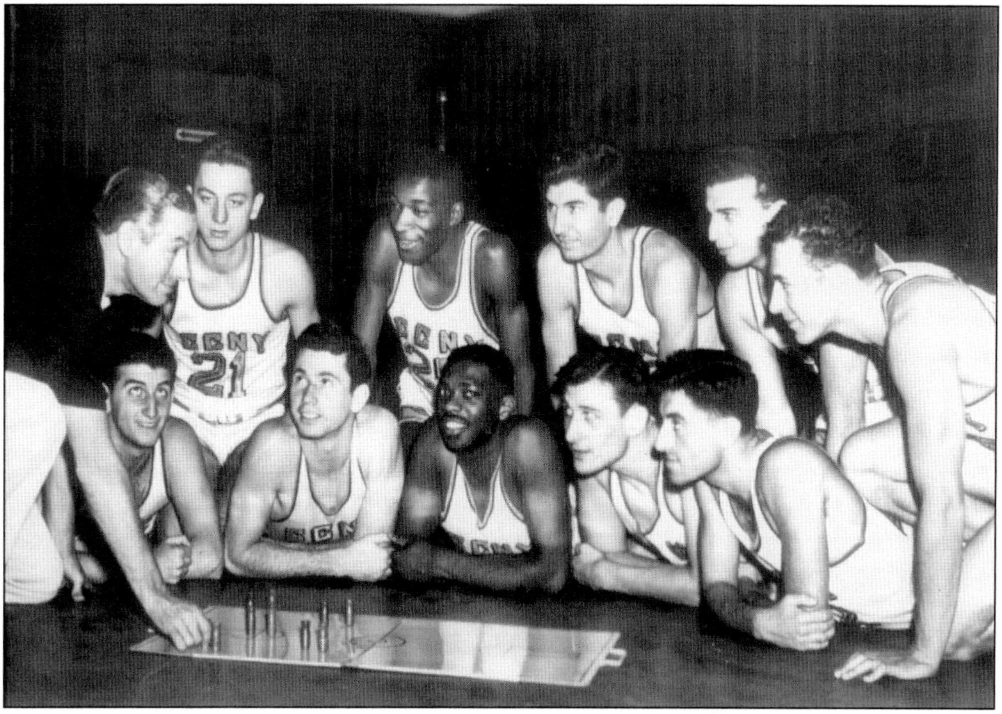

Nat Holman outlines game strategy for the benefit of the new 1951–1952 City College basketball team, which resumed intercollegiate games played in campus arenas.

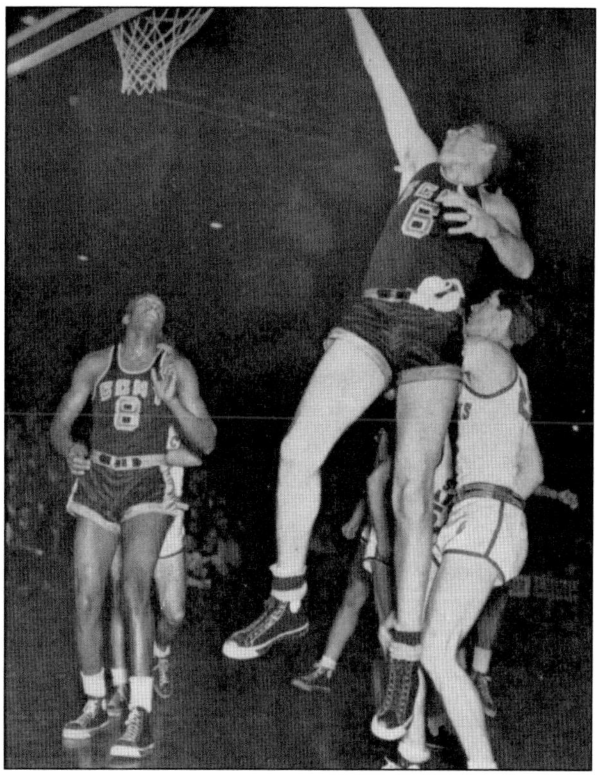

Members of the 1951–1952 City College team display the fast ball handling, speed, and passing game techniques they learned from the Old Professor, coach Nat Holman.

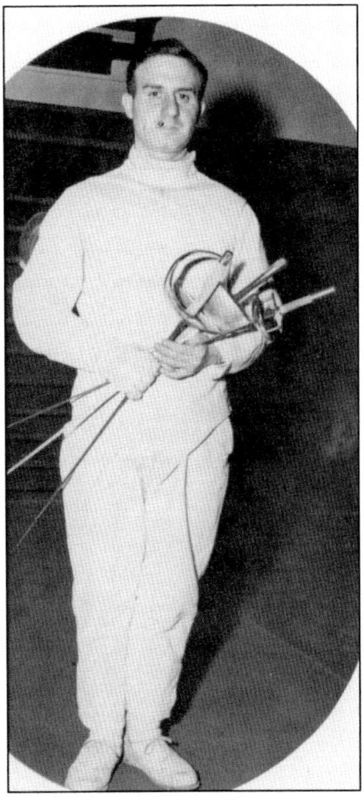

Coach Edward Lucia came from the Baruch center to begin his long association with the City College fencing team. Formerly a national powerhouse in the fencing world, the team reached the highlight of the 1954–1955 season with the capture of the individual saber tourney.

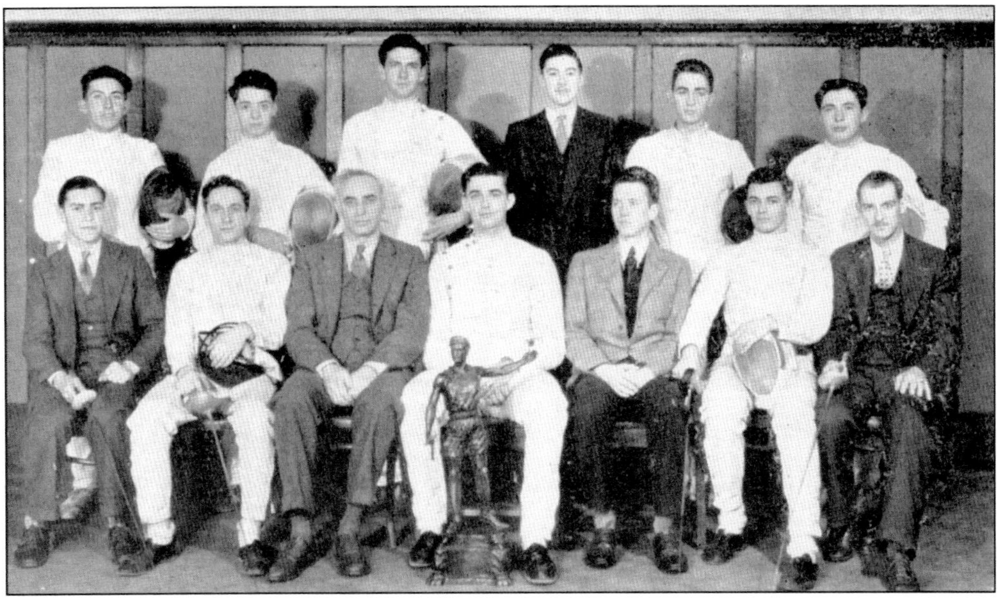

The 1934 fencing team poses with the Little Iron Man trophy they had earned in intercollegiate foil competition. Captain Emil Goldstein led his team members including Bernard Frechtman, Cornel Wilde (seated second from right), and Nathaniel Lubell to this championship. Goldstein was nominated for an Academy Award for his portrayal of Frederic Chopin in the 1945 film *A Song to Remember*. He later directed and starred in the 1966 film *The Naked Prey*.

Charlie Fields made high jumping look easy during the 1949–1950 season. Twice he broke high jump records that had stood at City College for the previous 14 years of track meets with leaps of 6 feet 3 inches and 6 feet 3 and a half inches. He tied for the high jump championship at the May 1950 Metropolitan Intercollegiate Championship. During the indoor season he carried away the Pioneer Club trophy with a mighty leap of 6 feet 5 inches.

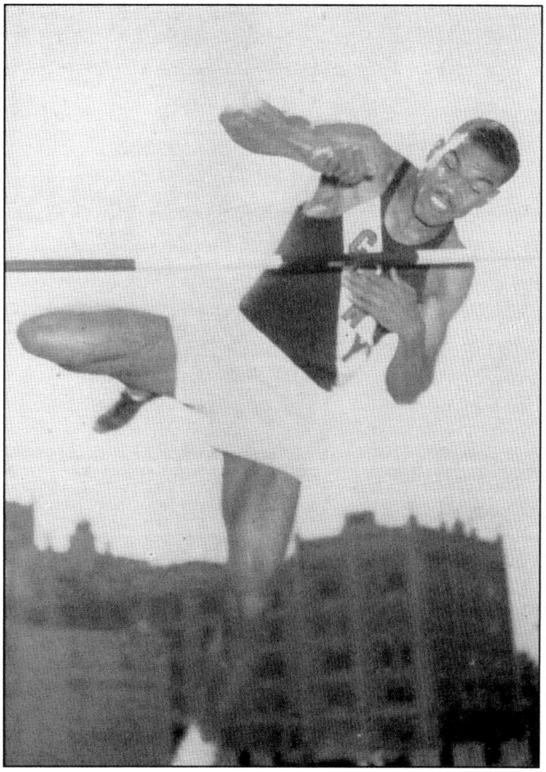

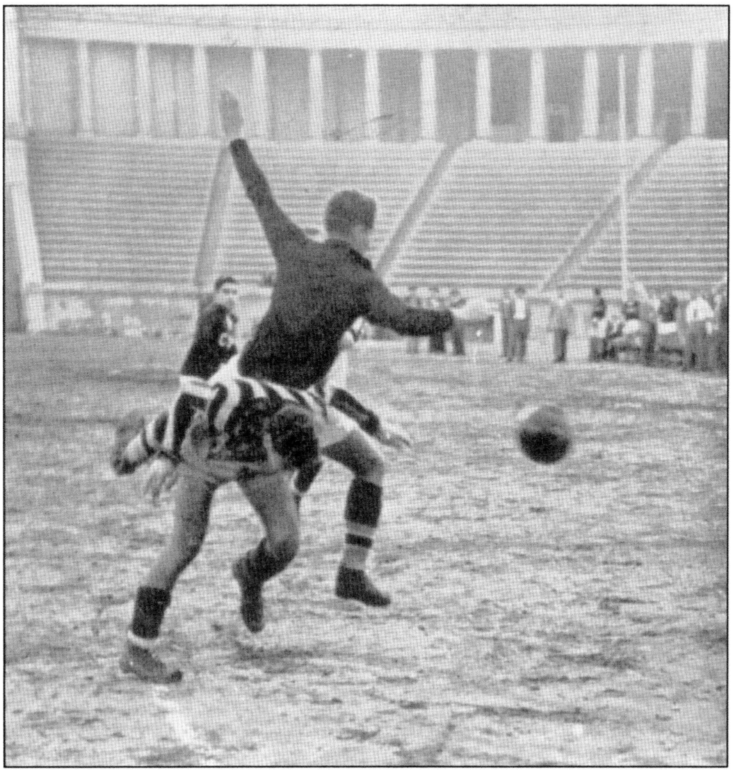

In 1952, the soccer team was at the beginning of a multi-season winning phase. The squad had a lone defeat by Brooklyn College that season before going on to win the next three out of four Metropolitan Conference races.

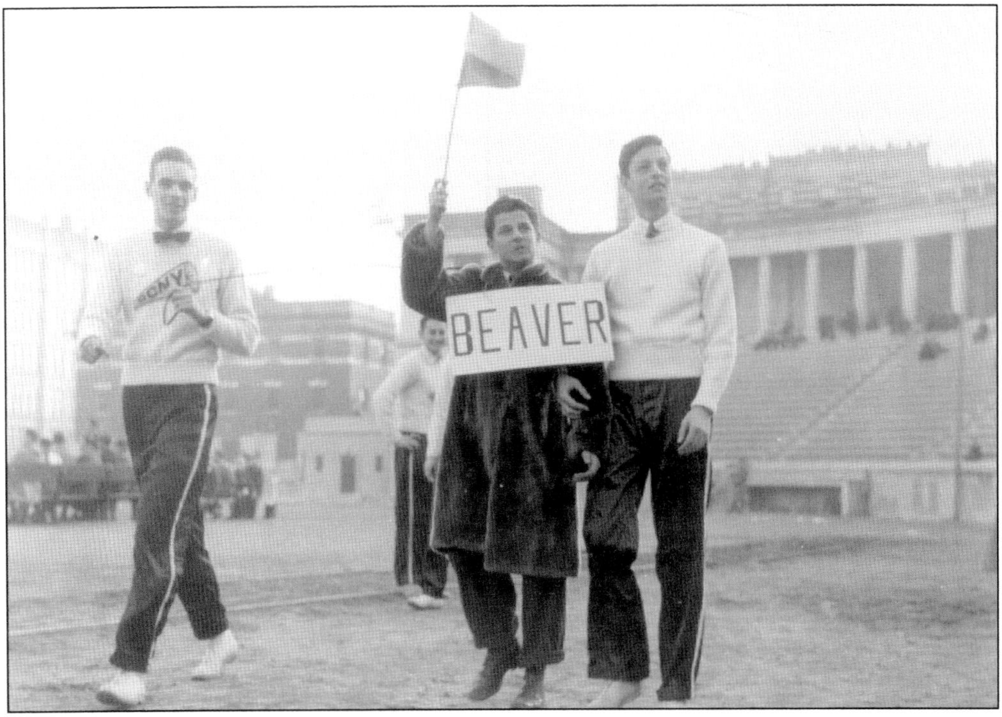

Led by the coaching skills of Benny Friedman, the football team gained a loyal following during the 1930s. Friedman had been a professional player with the New York Giants and an innovator of the forward pass as a genuine offensive weapon.

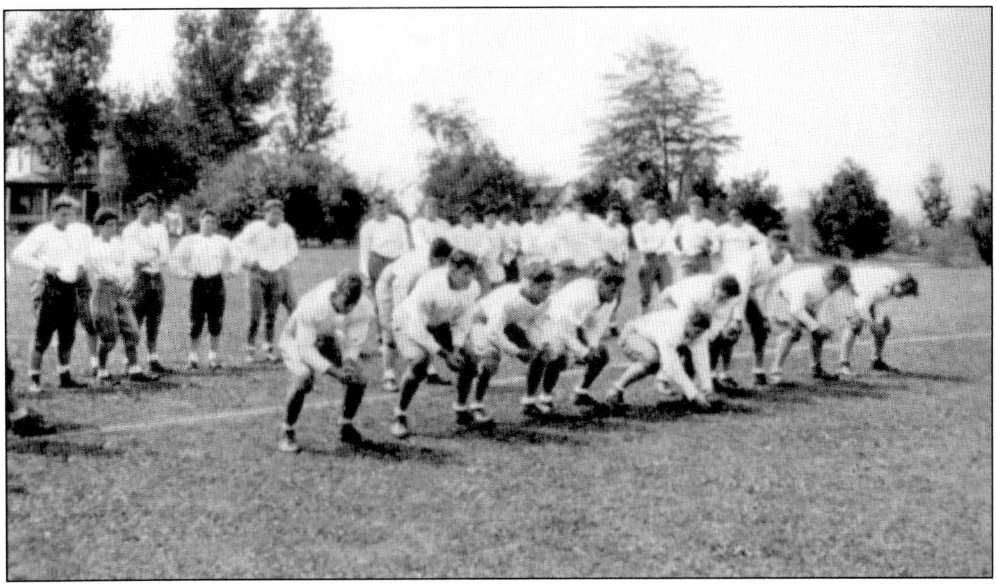

The 1936 Beavers had a winning season under Benny Friedman's leadership.

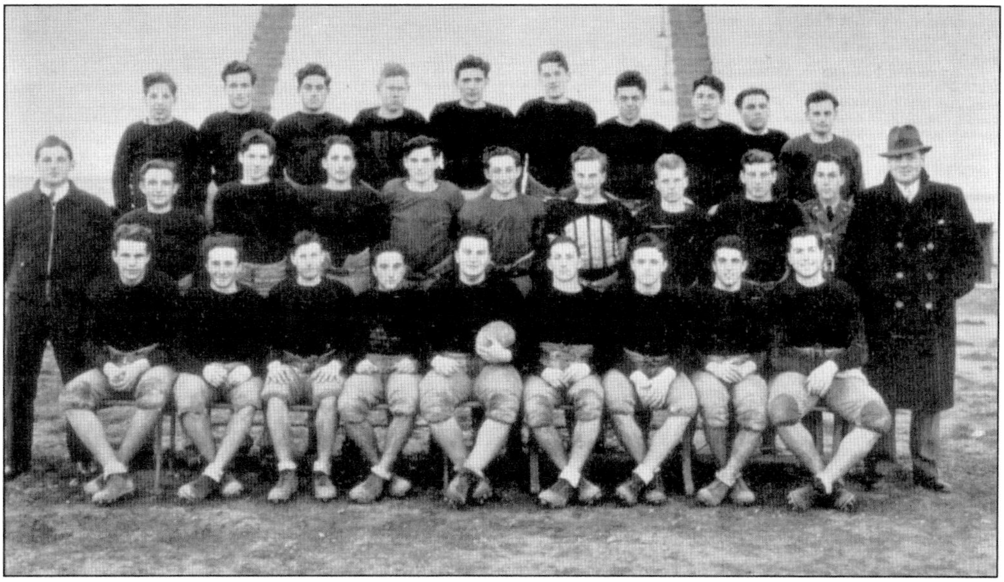

The Beavers gave their opponents pause when they played home games on a dirt field rather than on turf in Lewisohn Stadium.

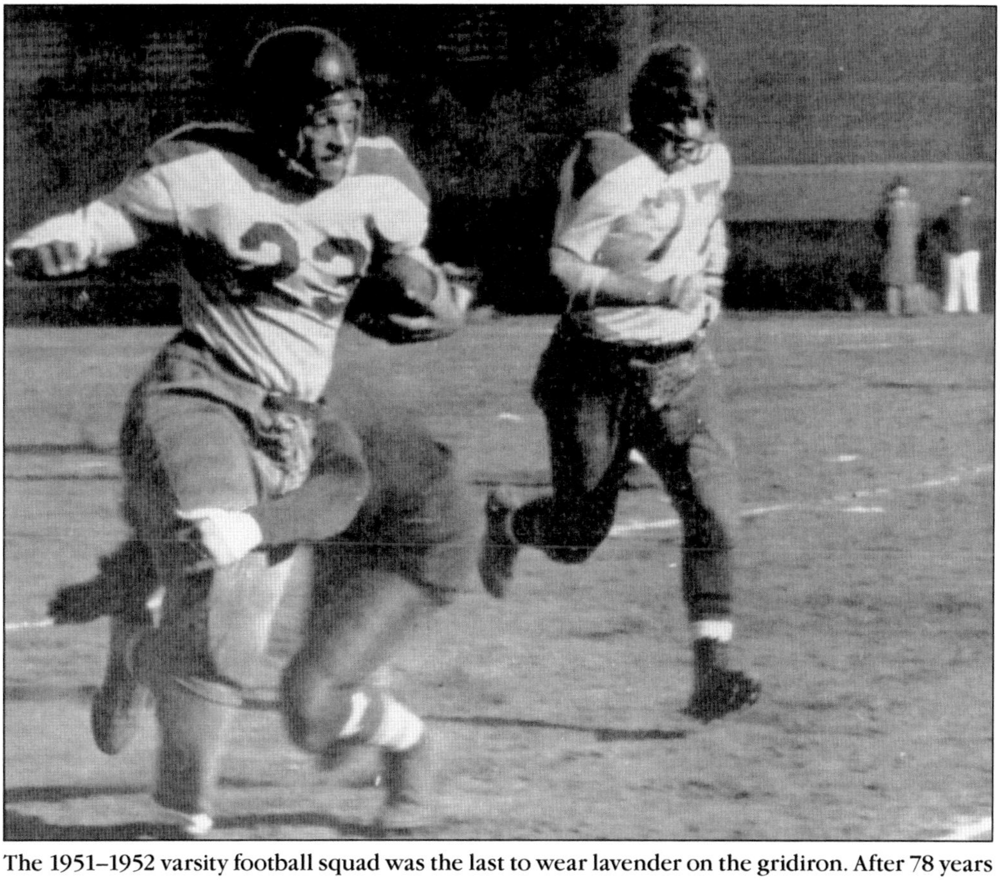

The 1951–1952 varsity football squad was the last to wear lavender on the gridiron. After 78 years of play, football was suspended, partly due to loss of revenue for athletics at City College.

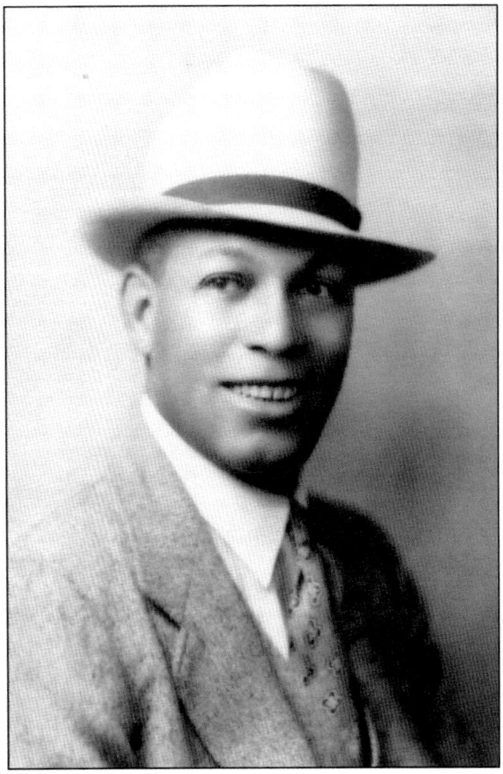

Lacrosse coach Leon "Chief" Miller, also assistant professor of hygiene, was acknowledged as one of the foremost experts on the game. He helped maintain the distinguished tradition of the oldest team sport played by City College students since 1888.

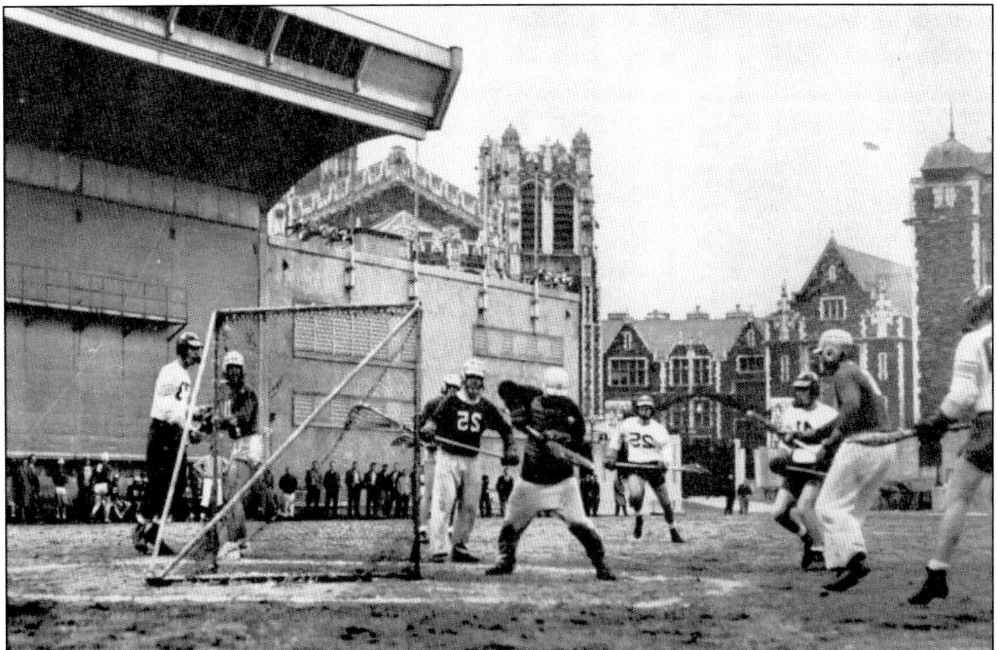

Under the direction of coach Miller, the 1952 lacrosse team had a balance of four wins and four losses, including defeats of powers such as Yale, Army, and Rutgers.

Coach Miller had a turnover of almost half the team members from the prior season. Miller often acted as a referee during practice games. The 1954–1955 season was 3-6 overall.

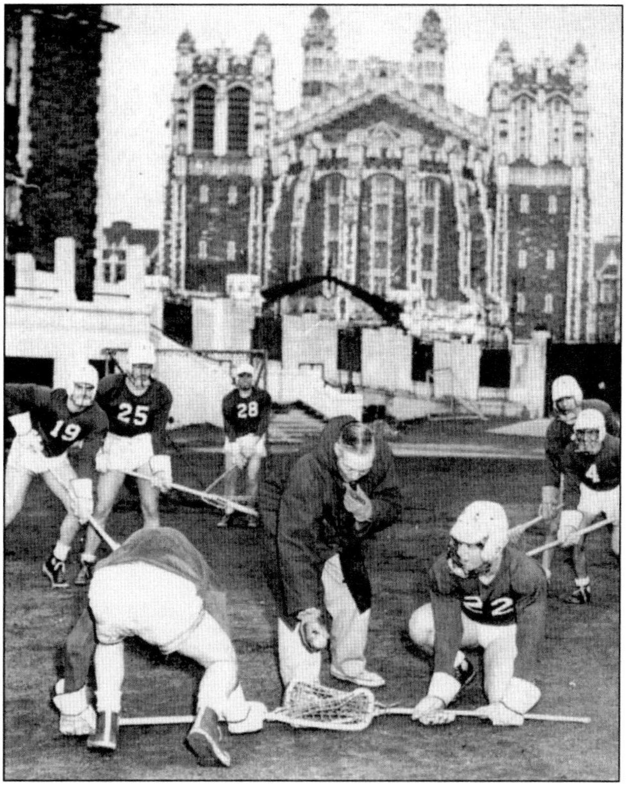

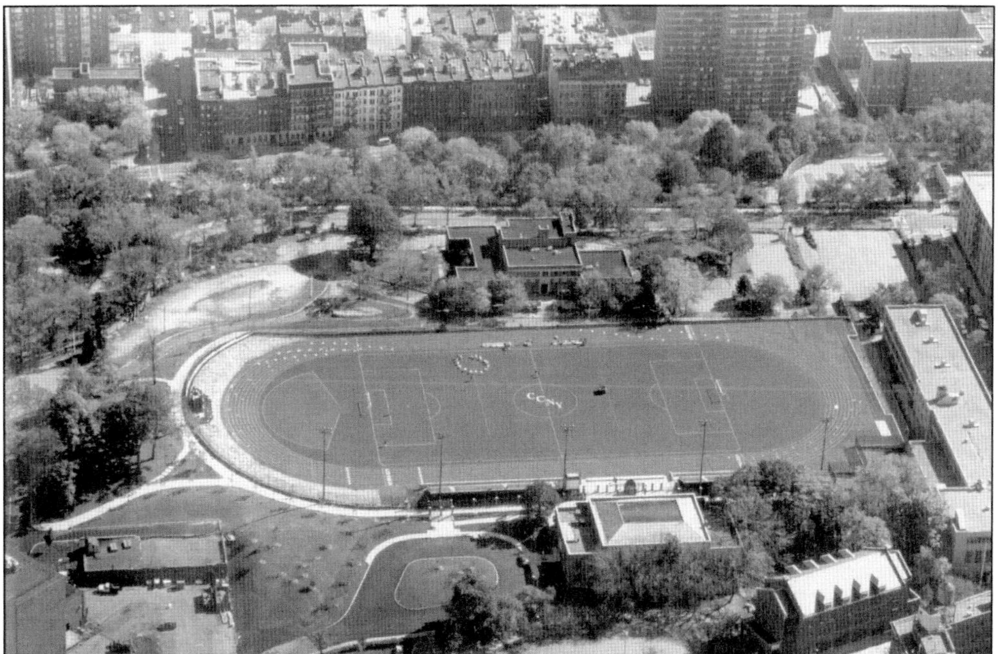

In 1993, the Herman Goldman Field opened on the south campus with a running track and a spacious field for team sports. (Philip J. Carvalho.)

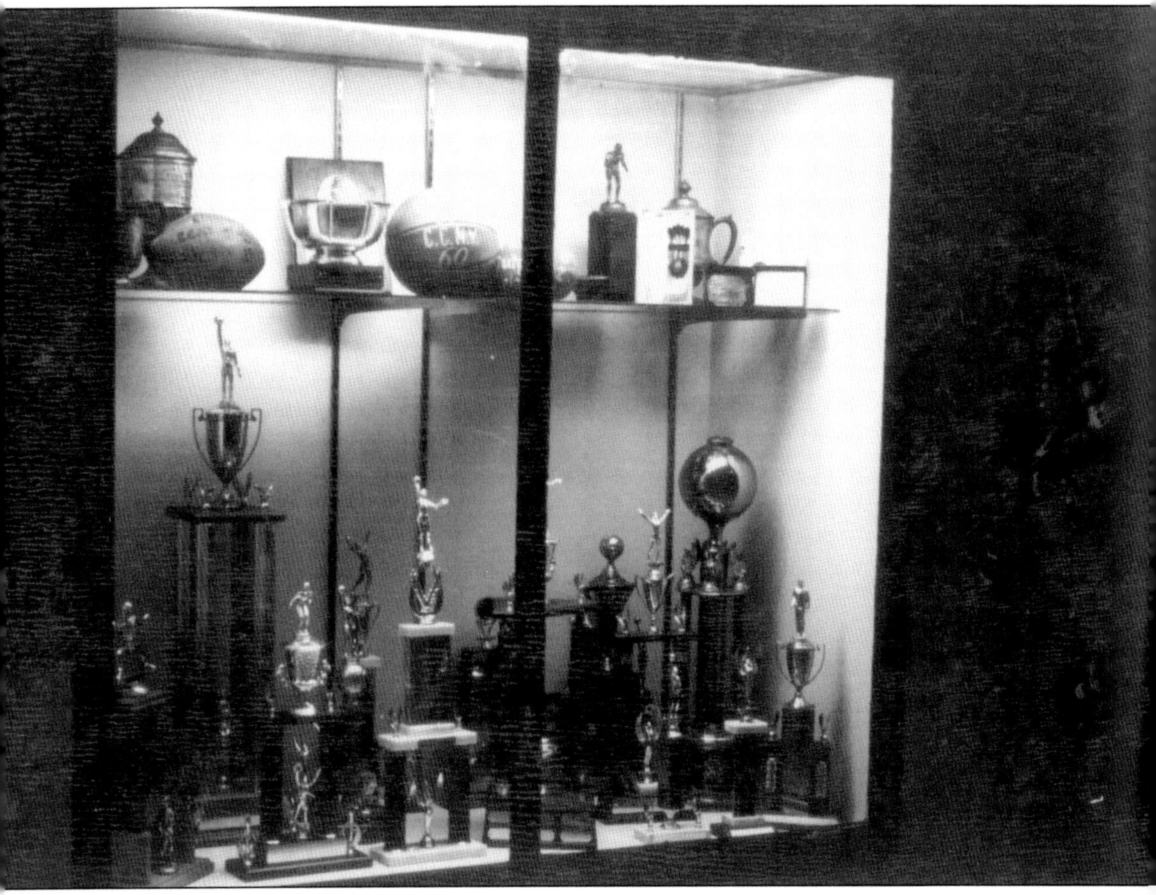

The trophies on display are testimony to the winning seasons of City College teams playing such sports as lacrosse, football, fencing, and basketball.

Six

Local and Global Notable Faces

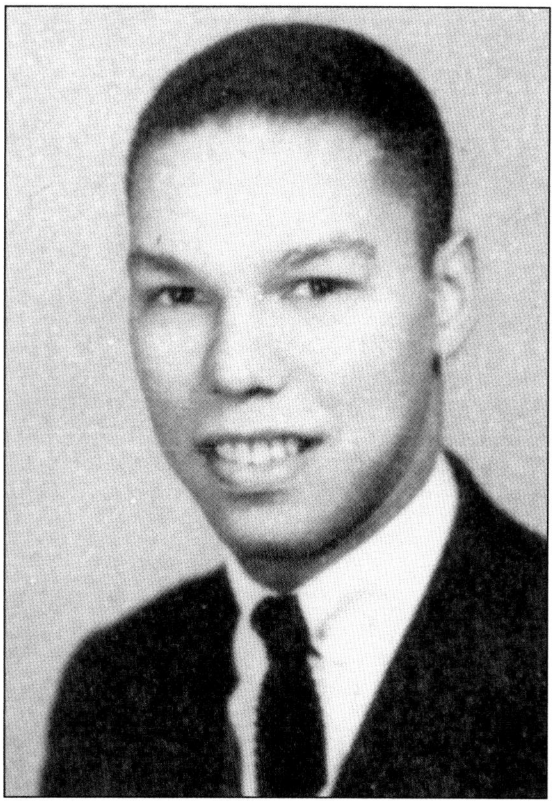

Colin Powell, seen here in his senior portrait from the 1958 *Microcosm*, demonstrated his gift for leadership as a commander in the Pershing Rifles, a fraternity of ROTC members at City College. He began his military career after graduation as a second lieutenant. Further career moves included airborne and ranger schools and the command/general staff and national war colleges. His service as a White House Fellow in the Office of Management and Budget under Nixon prepared him for high posts in the Reagan Administration, including service as the National Security Advisor. Under Pres. George H. W. Bush, Powell was appointed the chairman of the Joint Chiefs of Staff. As a lieutenant general, he achieved the highest military rank ever achieved by a City College graduate. He served as the Secretary of State under Pres. George W. Bush, and since stepping down from that post, he is able to take a greater interest in the Powell Center for Policy Studies at City College.

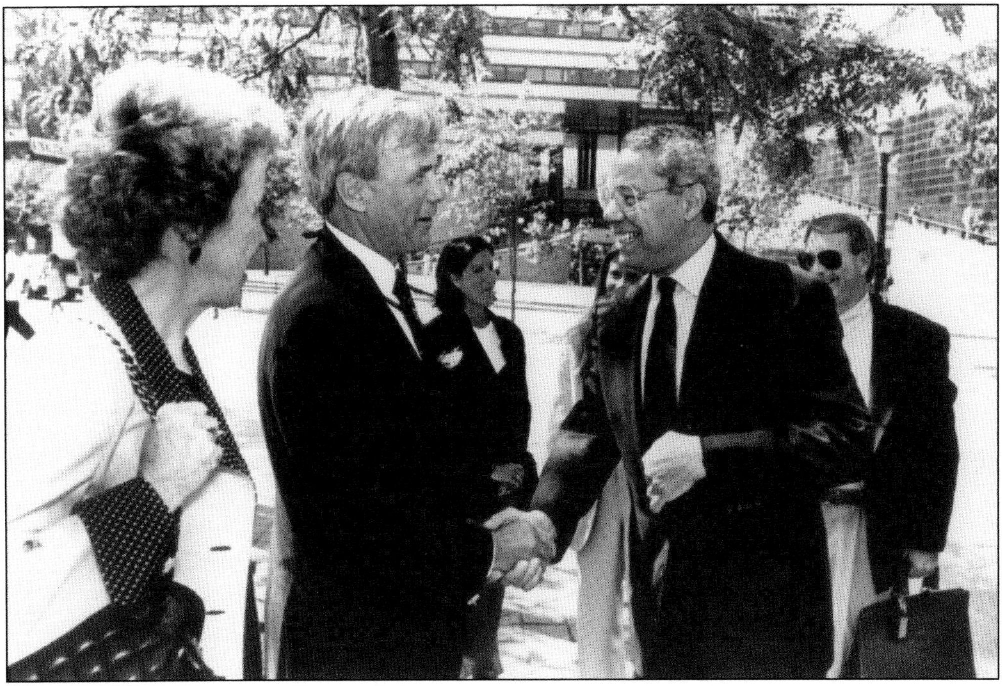

Colin Powell and Tom Brokaw meet at the City College campus in 1995. Brokaw returned to the City College to speak in the Great Hall in December 2005.

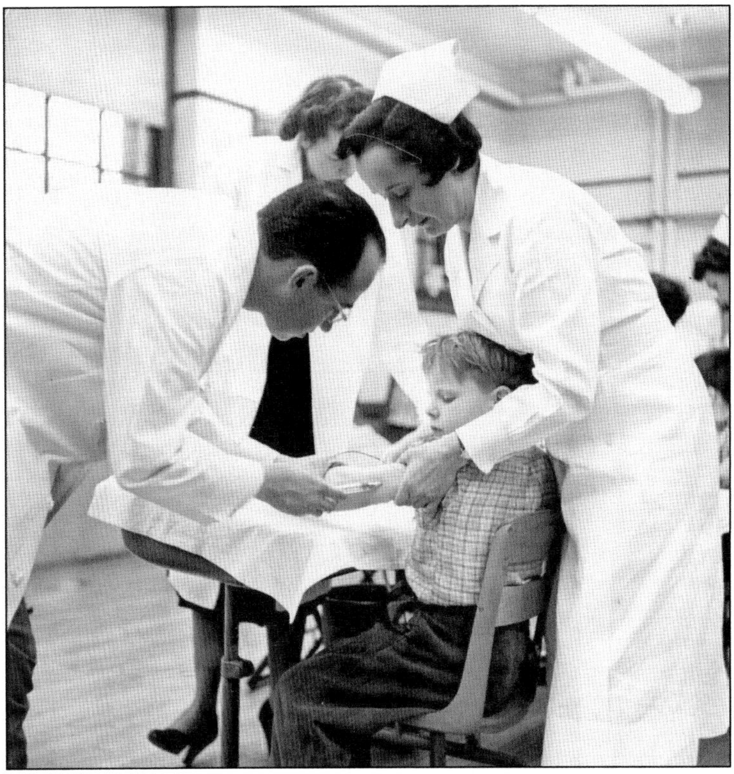

Jonas E. Salk attended Townsend Harris High School prior to City College and medical school. His discovery of a vaccine effective in preventing several strains of Paralytic Polio (poliomyelitis) allayed the fears of parents throughout the country and around the world. Here, a boy in Pittsburgh, Pennsylvania, receives the vaccine from Dr. Salk during a mass inoculation trial in the spring of 1957 that demonstrated the vaccine to be safe and 70 percent effective. (World Health Organization.)

Kenneth Arrow came to City College from the campus preparatory school, Townsend Harris High School. He started as a math major and switched to economics, with an emphasis on statistics. The majority of his work suggests that governments working to redistribute income should interfere only indirectly with the market. As the "economist's economist," he has focused on urban crises, management science, public investment, and economic development. He earned the Nobel Prize for economics in 1972 with John Hicks for "pioneering contributions to general economic equilibrium theory and welfare theory."

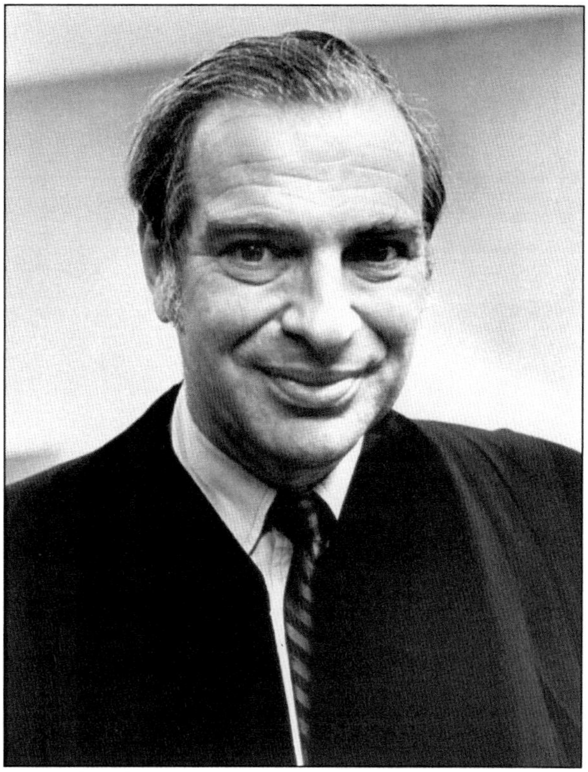

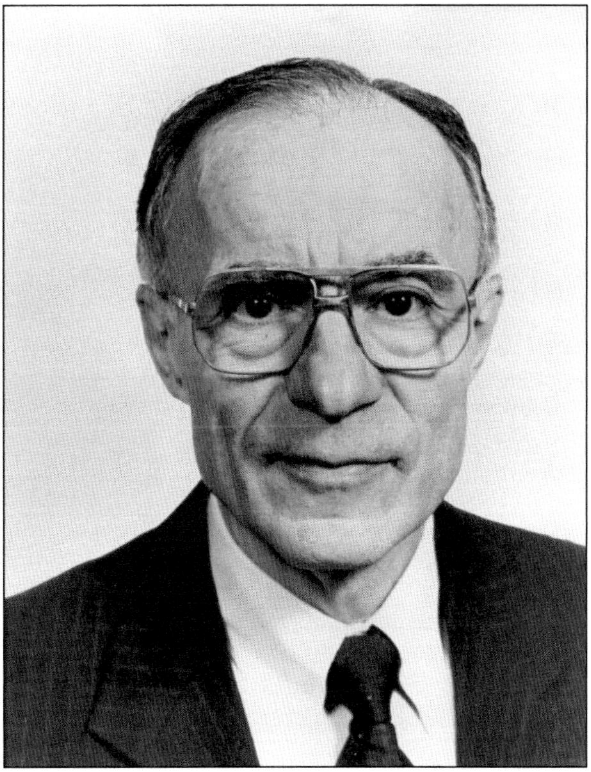

Arno Penzias emigrated with his family from Germany just prior to World War II. As a freshman, he changed majors from chemical engineering to physics with the assurance that he could earn a living in that field. He joined the Physics Society and ROTC. He became a radar officer in the Army Signal Corps. In 1963, while working with Robert W. Wilson, he began converting a horn antenna into a precisely calibrated antenna with a sensitive amplifier enabling the two researchers to measure the intensities of several extraterrestrial radio sources. Penzias and Wilson were jointly awarded the Nobel Prize in physics in 1978 "for their discovery of cosmic microwave background radiation."

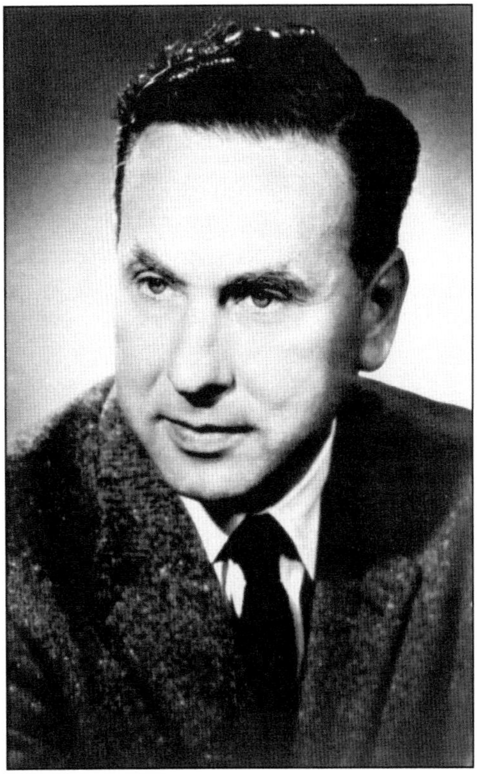

In 1935, Robert Hofstadter graduated with high honors as a double major in mathematics and physics and received the Kenyon Prize in those fields. He returned in 1941 to teach physics. Hofstadter discovered that the density of all nuclei is about the same; further experimentation demonstrated that the nucleus is not simply a hard-edged sphere, but bears a soft skin whose thickness is the same regardless of size. His Nobel Prize for physics in 1961 with Rudolf Mossbauer was given for Hofstadter's "pioneering studies of electron scattering in atomic nuclei and for his thereby-achieved discoveries concerning the structure of the nucleons."

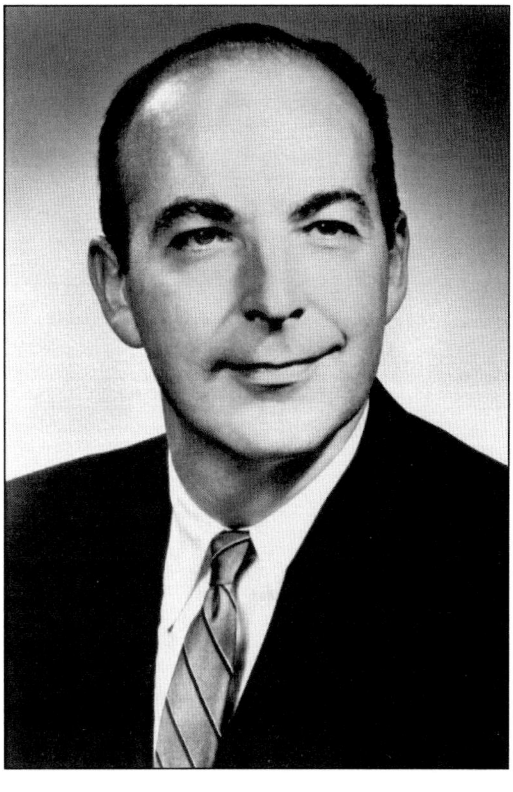

Arthur Kornberg enrolled in City College at age 15, studying biology and chemistry with the aim to practice medicine. He served as secretary of the school's Biology and Physics Societies. After medical school, he became a biochemical researcher focused on enzymes and metabolism. Kornberg isolated the enzyme responsible for the synthesis of DNA. In 1959, he received the Nobel Prize for physiology with Severo Ocha "for their discovery of the mechanics in the biological synthesis of ribonucleic acid and deoxyribonucleic acid." The discovery of these mechanisms led to new research in biochemistry and genetics.

Jerome Karle earned the top academic prize from the natural science department. He also served as a research assistant on the Manhattan Project. Karle and his City College classmate Herbert Hauptman began collaborating in 1947 on the development of interpreting three-dimensional molecular structure by X-ray crystallography. A major barrier to the application of this research was that most chemists did not understand the mathematics involved and did not utilize the direct-method system. In 1985, the two shared the Nobel Prize in chemistry for "their outstanding achievements in the development of direct methods for the determination of crystal structures."

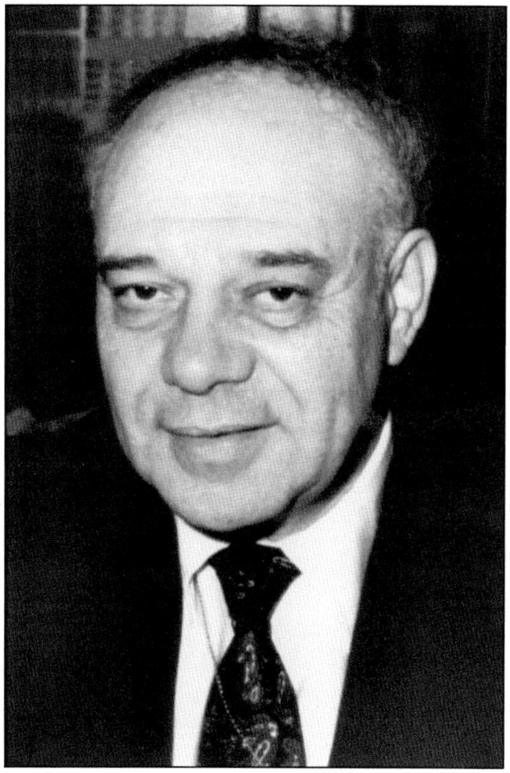

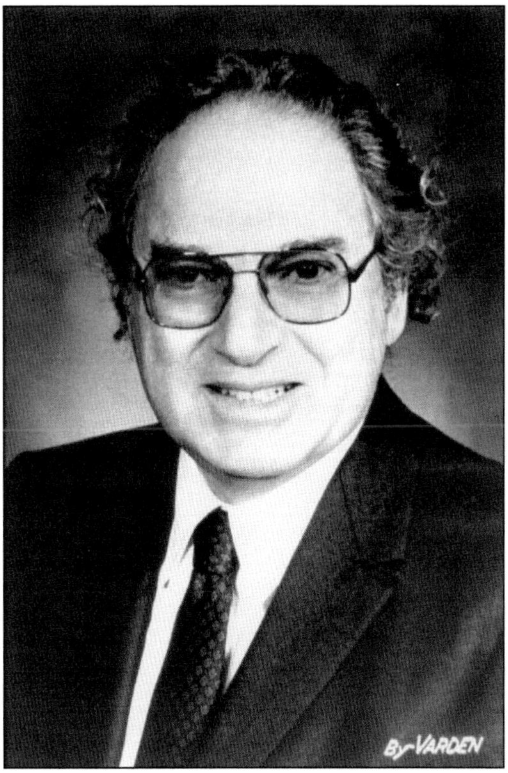

Herbert Hauptman was a product of the rigorous Townsend Harris High School who went on to study mathematics at City College, graduating with the top mathematics prize. At the Naval Research Laboratory, Hauptman reunited with former City College classmate Jerome Karle and embarked on developing direct methods of interpretation of X-ray crystallography, resulting in a complex mathematical structural model for antibiotics, vitamins, and hormones. Hauptman and Karle earned the 1985 Nobel Prize in chemistry.

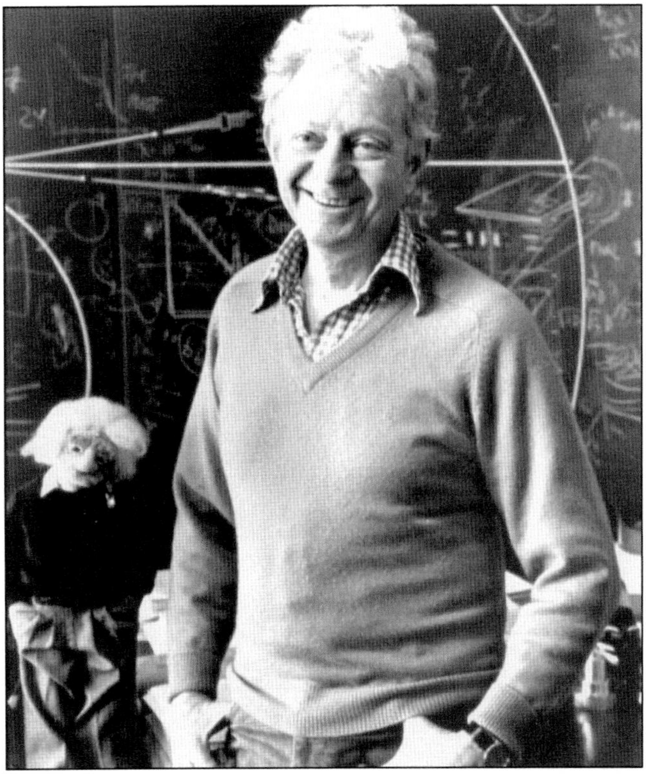

As a chemistry major and member of the Physics Society, Leon Lederman was inspired by "outstanding teachers" and "outstanding contemporaries." In addition to his seminal contributions to the analysis of the innermost structure and dynamics of matter (for example, the discovery of the long-lived neutral K-meson particle in 1956) he has mentored the careers of numerous students at every level, including over 50 doctoral students. His discovery of the muon neutrino proved that there was more than one type of neutrino and garnered the Nobel Prize in physics in 1988.

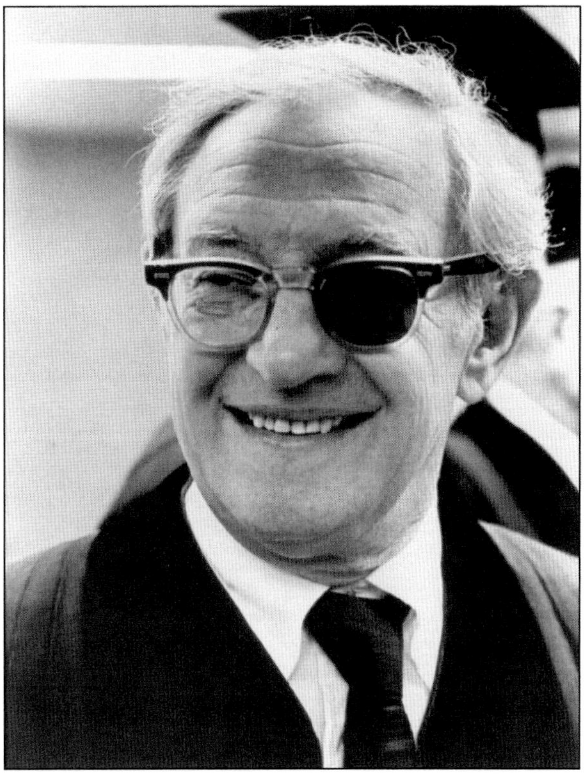

Julius Axelrod enrolled at City College, majoring in biology and minoring in chemistry, and conducted graduate research in drug biochemistry, particularly metabolism. He became a recognized pharmacology expert in the early 1950s, when his research revealed a great deal about the degradation and metabolism of amphetamines. In the 1960s, his experimentation focused on hormone-neurotransmitter relationships, and the links between these and the pineal and adrenal glands. He shared the 1970 Nobel Prize for physiology (medicine) with Bernard Katz and Ulf von Euler for "discoveries concerning the humoral transmitters in the nerve terminals and the mechanism for their storage, release, and inactivation."

Robert Aumann (class of 1950) majored in mathematics at City College and went on to graduate studies at the Massachusetts Institute of Technology. He once taught at the University of Maryland and now teaches at the Center for Rationality at the Hebrew University of Jerusalem. He shared a 2005 Nobel Prize in economics with Thomas C. Shelling "for having enhanced our understanding of conflict and cooperation through game-theory analysis," according to the Royal Swedish Academy of Science.

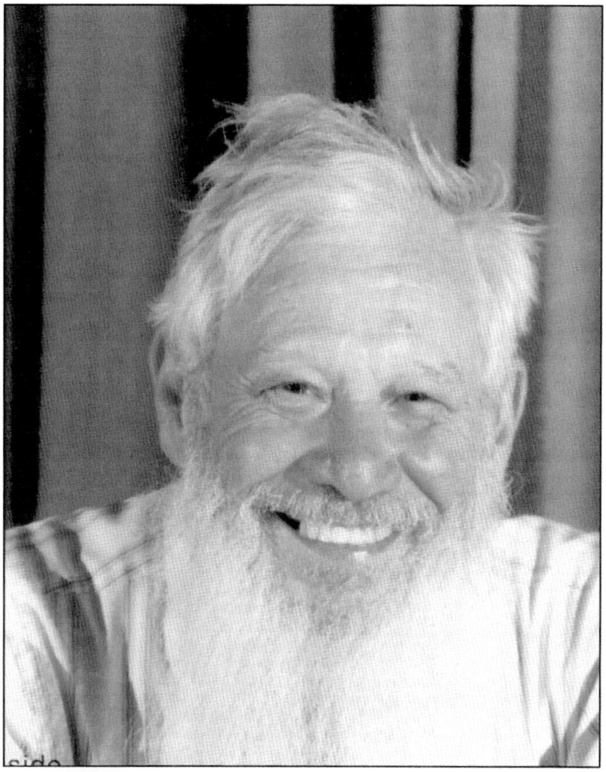

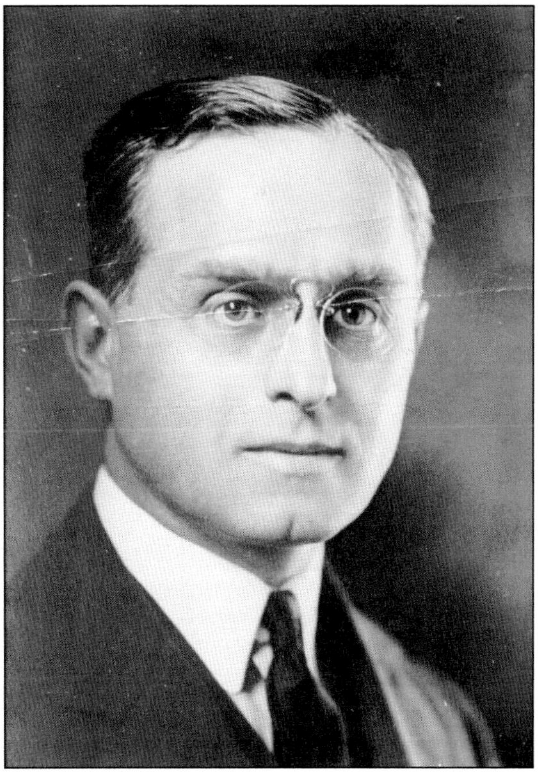

Born in Austria, Felix Frankfurter (class of 1902) joined a number of remarkable contemporaries in the corridors of the Free Academy Building seeking an education at the close of the 19th century. A legal scholar and professor of law at Harvard University, he championed due process. Frankfurter was a figure worthy of public trust who constantly rejected offers to seek public office. He upheld that trust as chairman of the war policies board of World War I and particularly as a U.S. Supreme Court justice from 1939 to 1962.

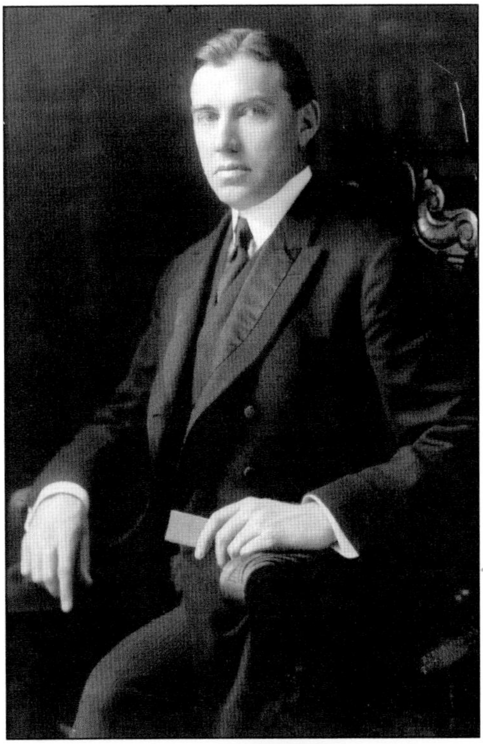

John Huston Finley served as the third president of the college from 1903 to 1913. Growing up in Illinois, he graduated from Knox College and then enrolled in graduate studies at Johns Hopkins University, where he became a close friend of Woodrow Wilson. Their paths crossed again at Princeton University when Wilson was president and Finley became a professor of political science. Wilson supported his friend by attending the inauguration ceremony at Carnegie Hall on September 29, 1903, when Finley was installed as the president of a growing public educational institution. The elective system was introduced into the curriculum during Finley's tenure, while the demerit system and military atmosphere were abolished. The college moved from the cramped 23rd Street building to the open spaces of Hamilton Heights in 1907. Following his days as City College president, Finley became the New York State commissioner of education from 1913 to 1921 and then editor of the *New York Times* from 1921 to 1938.

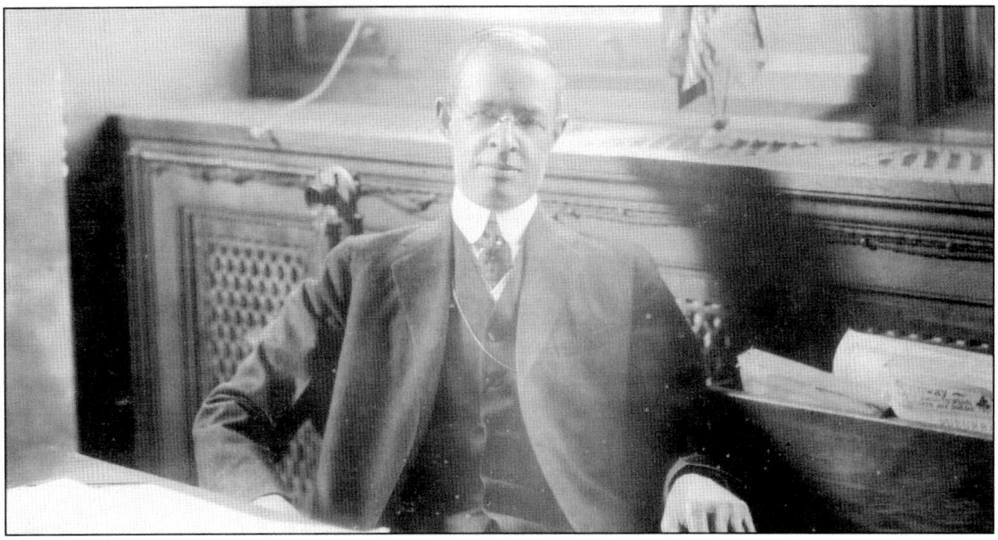

The son of a Spanish family in California, Sidney Edward Mezes was educated at the University of California and Harvard University. He had prior experience as an administrator at the University of Texas, where he served as dean and then president in 1908. Although he was suffering from tuberculosis, he devoted his energy to administration, and during his tenure as president of City College beginning in 1914, he saw the growth of the college with the establishment of the Schools of Education (1921), Business (now Baruch College, 1919), and Technology (now Engineering, 1919). A military training course was established in 1916 and maintained at the college as ROTC until 1972. The Summer Session opened in June 1917 under Prof. Frederick Robinson, who would become the college's next president in 1927.

Frederick Bertrand Robinson (class of 1904) was the first graduate and former faculty member to become president of the college. He earned a doctorate from New York University and displayed artistic flair by playing the cello, etching, and sculpting. His 1927 inauguration ceremony in Lewisohn Stadium included a platform party of 250 people, a huge academic procession, and the attendance of the entire student body. Under his presidency, the School of Business building opened, replacing the original Renwick-designed edifice at Lexington Avenue and 23rd Street. During this time, there were numerous student protests against fascism in Europe and Depression conditions in America. President Robinson suspended or expelled some of the protestors. He resigned from the presidency in 1938.

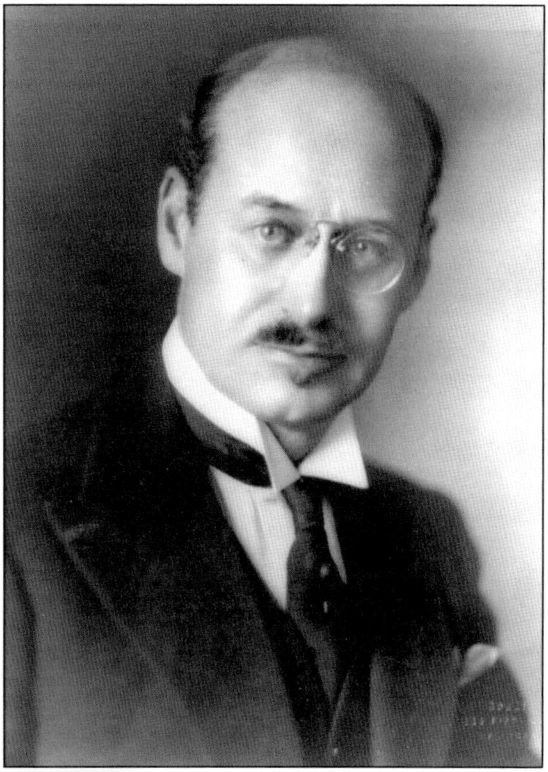

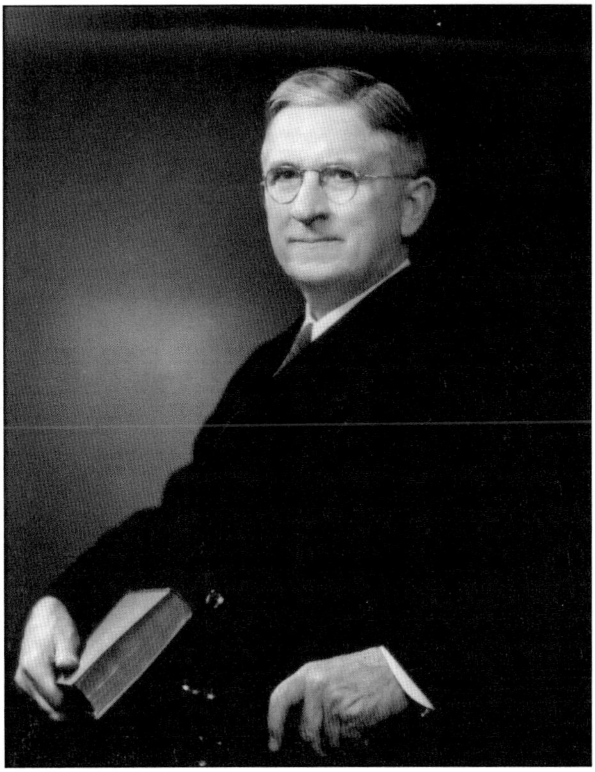

Harry Noble Wright began as a professor of mathematics at the college in 1931 and directed the Evening Session. Asked to serve as acting president in January 1941, he was inaugurated in the Great Hall on September 30, 1942, during the somber atmosphere of World War II. The new president stated, "higher education is a common bond which unites free scholars, in free institutions, in a free country in a common loyalty." During the decade of his presidency, the college participated in the Army Specialized Training Program, teaching engineering, mathematics, and languages to thousands of enlisted men. The Manhattanville College grounds were acquired, extending the campus south from 135th Street to 130th Street. The college also celebrated its centennial in 1947.

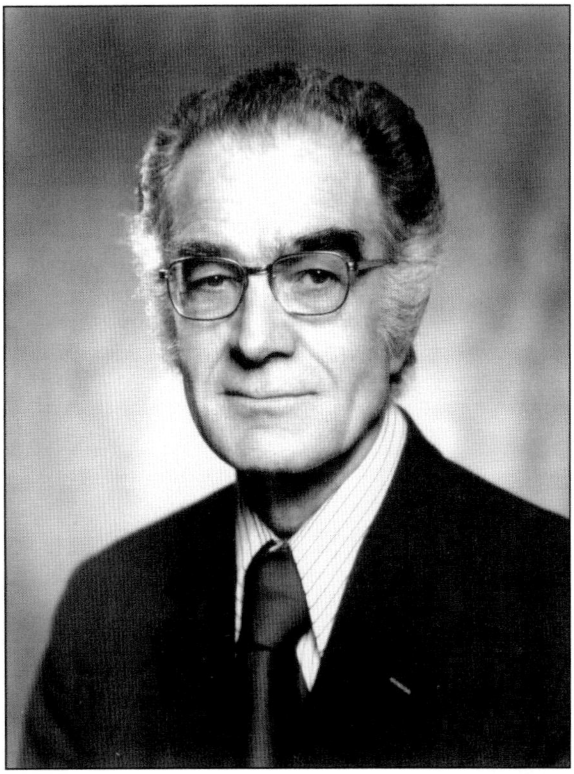

Buell Gordon Gallagher was a Congregational Church minister and former assistant commissioner for higher education in the U.S. Office of Education. In his inaugural address, delivered on February 19, 1953, he discussed the threats to intellectual freedom from both the right and the left. "This institution is a microcosm of American democracy. All the problems and all the hopes of a great nation converge within its sometimes turbulent and always exhilarating life." Gallagher's administration saw the construction of the new home for the Grove School of Engineering in Steinman Hall. The Schools of Nursing and Architecture were created. Massive student protests in the late 1960s opposed the war in Vietnam and called for curriculum reforms and admission policy changes. These protests triggered a series of events that led to President Gallagher's resignation in May 1969.

Robert Eugene Marshak was a Bronx native who attended Columbia College and earned his doctorate in physics at Cornell University. During World War II, while on a leave of absence from the University of Rochester, he became the chief deputy in theoretical physics at the Los Alamos, New Mexico, laboratory for the government's atomic bomb project under J. Robert Oppenheimer. While there, he developed a theory of shock waves that became known as the Marshak Wave. He served as president of City College from 1970 to 1979. In 1970, the college (and the entire City University System) instituted the open enrollment policy allowing admission to any graduate of a New York City high school into the university. Tuition fees were implemented in 1976. Despite these difficulties, new curricula were developed in virtually every division of the college.

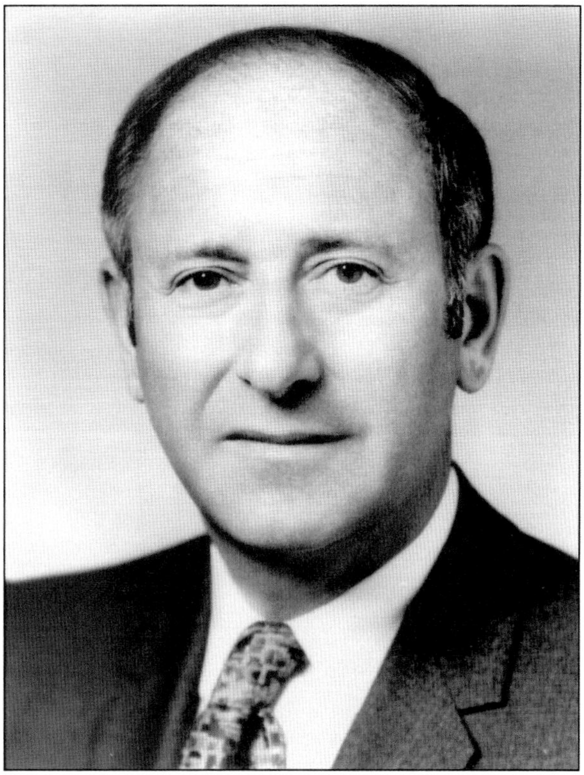

Prior to assuming the post of City College president in 1981, Bernard Warren Harleston received academic training in experimental psychology and served as the dean of the Faculty of Arts and Sciences at Tufts University. In his inaugural address delivered in the Great Hall, he articulated the importance of the liberal arts in teaching "that the price of freedom of choice is personal accountability." During his tenure, extensive international student and faculty exchanges were developed with several foreign nations. Construction of the Herman Goldman Sports and Recreation Center on the south campus began; it was completed in 1993, a year after President Harleston stepped down from the presidency.

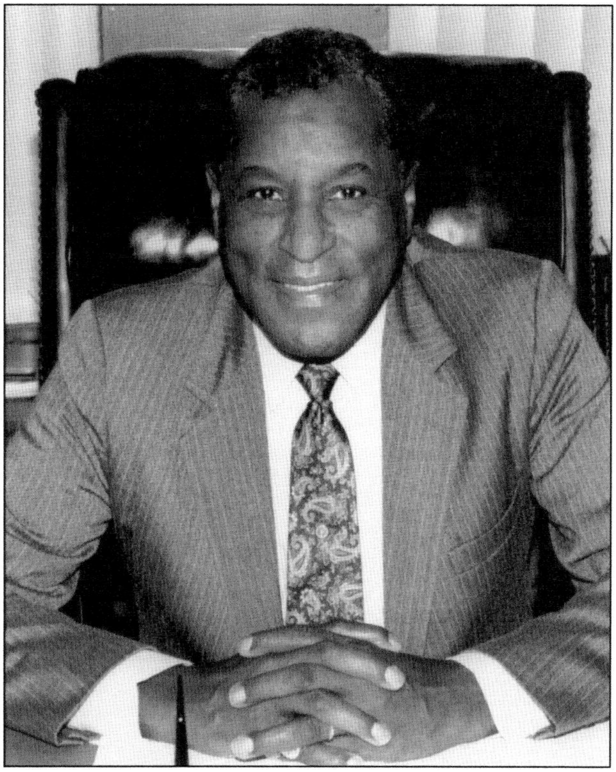

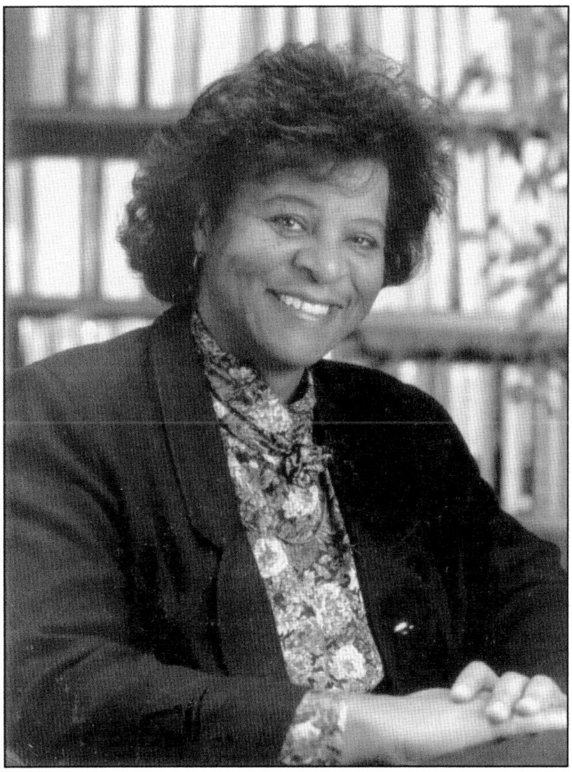

Yolanda Theresa Moses received her bachelor's degree from California State College–San Bernardino and her master's and doctorate from the University of California at Riverside. She then held the position of vice president for academic affairs and professor of anthropology at California State University–Dominquez Hills. Her inauguration ceremony in 1993 was combined with the New Student Convocation. Under President Moses's leadership, City College played a leading role in launching a national higher education diversity initiative in cooperation with the Association of American Colleges and Universities. She was a member of the Ford Foundation's board of trustees. Moses resigned in 1999 after serving as the first female president of the college.

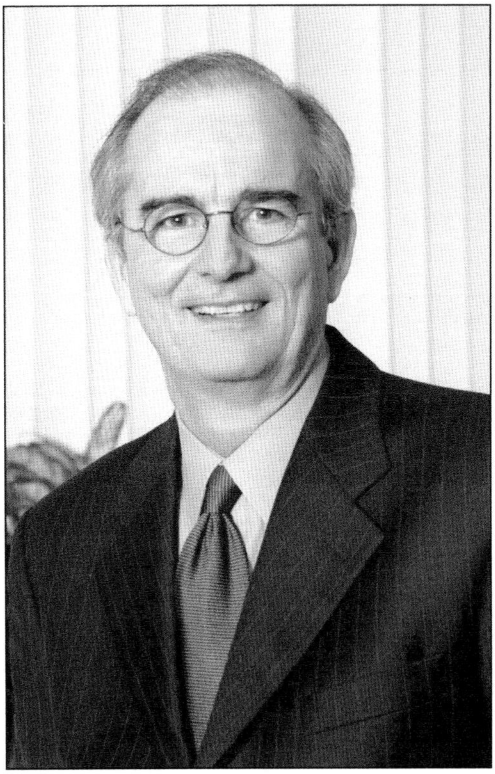

Gregory Williams, the 11th president of City College, served as dean of the law school and Carter C. Kissell Professor of Law at Ohio State University prior to arriving on campus in August 2001. He holds two graduate degrees from Washington University—a doctor of law and a doctor of philosophy—as well as three honorary doctorates. Under his leadership, the college has gained greater national recognition and increased student enrollment in a single year by 15 percent. Williams is the author of three books, including *Life on the Color Line: The True Story of a White Boy Who Discovered He Was Black*, which recounts his days growing up in Muncie, Indiana. President Williams is the recipient of numerous awards such as the Austrian Cross of Honor in Science and Art, First Class, in 2006.

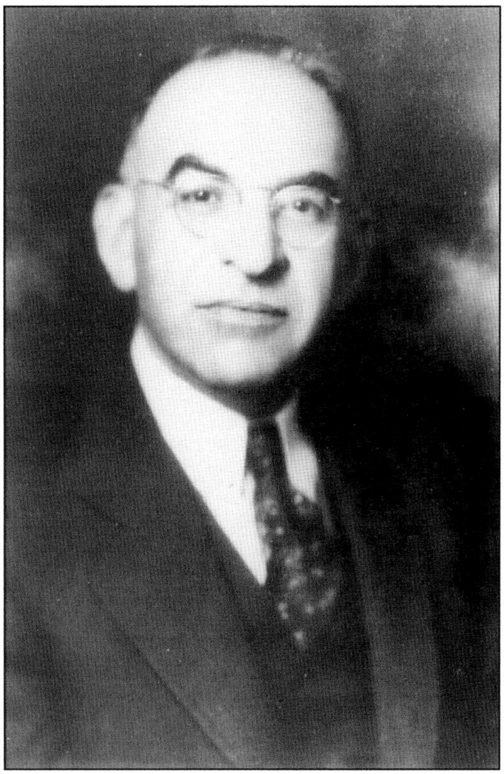

Paul Klapper's days at City College included active participation in the Civic Club and the Debating Society. He stayed as a teacher, rising through the ranks in three years to professor of education. The department, which had begun as a sequence of extension courses for teachers in the New York City school system, became the fourth school created by City College in 1921. Klapper served as dean of the School of Education from 1922 to 1937. He left the Sr. Nicholas Heights campus in 1938 to become the first president of Queens College. Klapper worked as a consultant over the years in educational finance and curriculum.

The first City College graduate to venture into space, Mario Runco Jr. realized his boyhood dream as a veteran of several missions. He prepared by majoring in meteorology and physical oceanography at the college and qualified in 1988 as an astronaut mission specialist for the National Aeronautics and Space Administration. During his first mission aboard the *Atlantis* in 1991, Runco displayed a City College medallion and pennant, and on his next mission on the *Endeavor*, he walked in space.

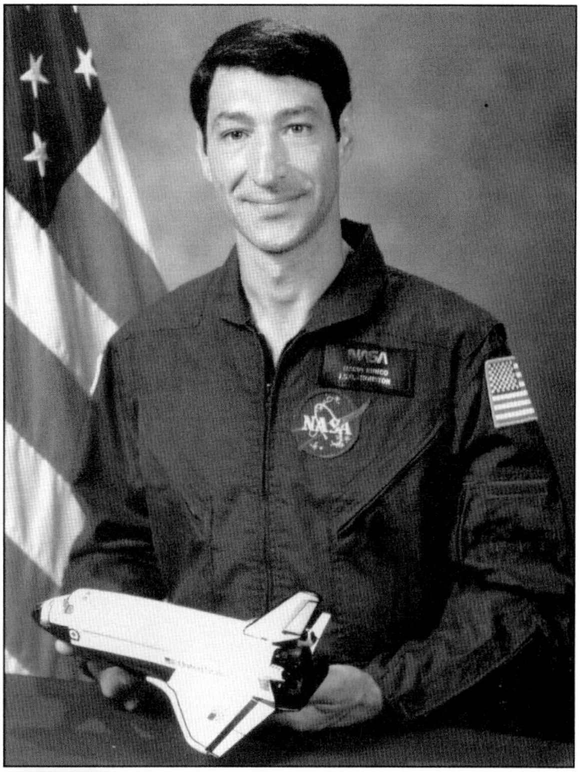

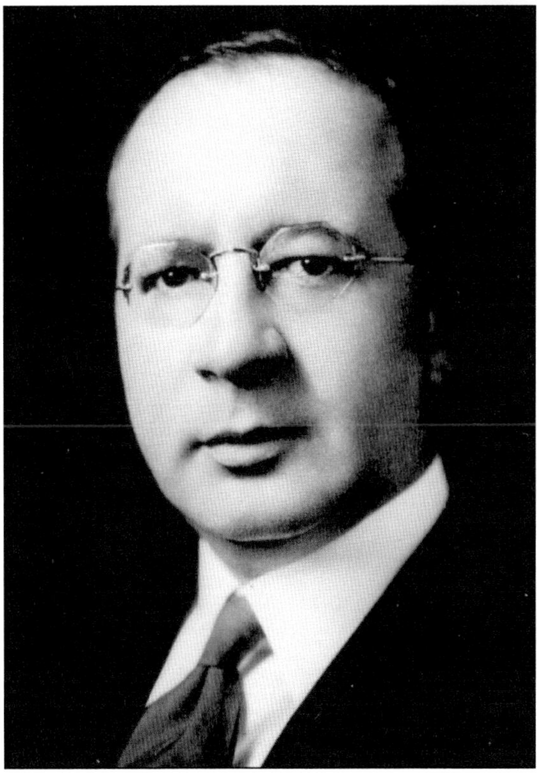

When David B. Steinman graduated from City College, he originally intended to become a teacher, but a fortuitous scholarship allowed him to pursue graduate studies at Columbia University and embark on a career in civil engineering. One of the distinguishing achievements of his career was the designing and supervision of the construction of the Mackinac Bridge connecting the lower portion to the Upper Peninsula of Michigan. Closer to his alma mater, two spans in the Hudson River Valley that can be credited to him are the Henry Hudson and the Kingston-Rhinecliff Bridges. Steinman Hall, home of the City College Grove School of Engineering, was named in his honor.

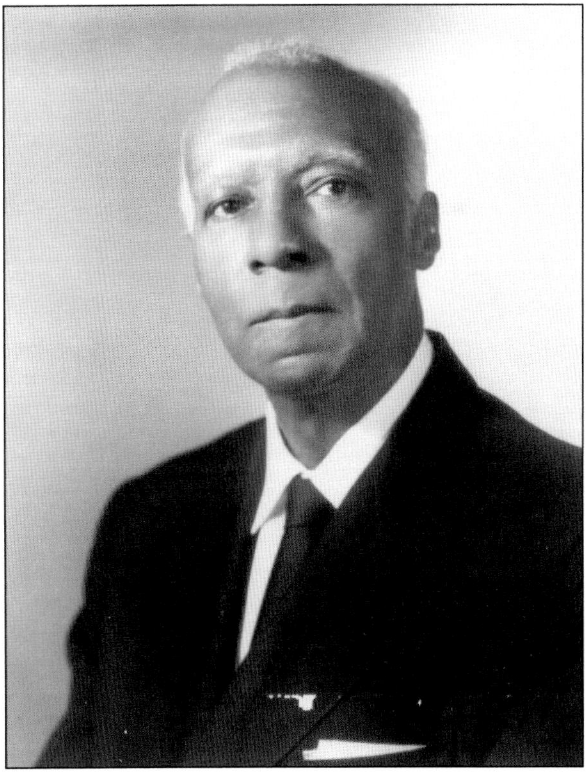

As the founder of the *Messenger* in 1915, A. Philip Randolph provided a forum for social and economic reforms, particularly through his voice of moderation and decency in contrast to the violence experienced for over half a century. His labor movement activities began in 1925 with his founding and leadership of the International Brotherhood of Sleeping Car Porters. He was the principal lobbyist for the establishment of the Federal Employment Practices Commission and a potent force in ending armed forces racial discrimination in America.

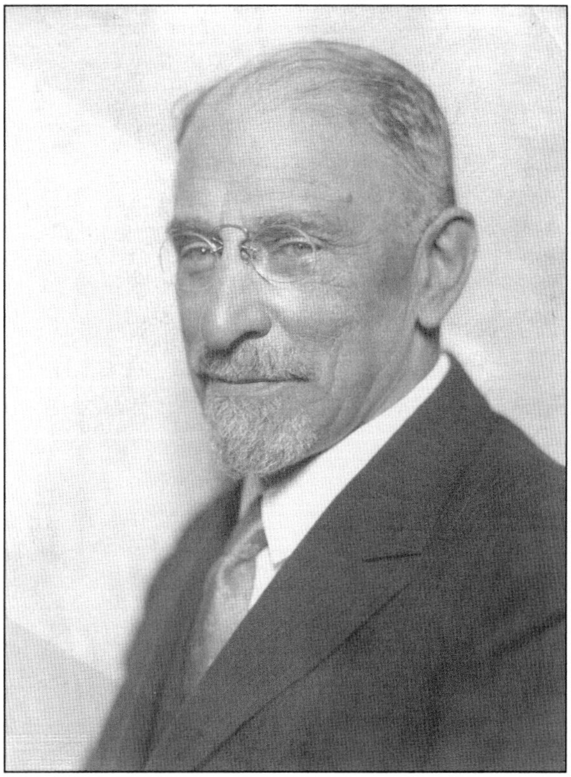

Henry Morgenthau was a distinguished businessman, attorney, and diplomat. He administered his own law firm and directed the Equitable Life Assurance Society. He not only served as ambassador to Turkey, but also as chairman of the Greek Refugee Settlement Commission, created in 1923 by the League of Nations, and as technical advisor to the Monetary and Economic Conference in 1933. Morgenthau was one of the founders of the American Red Cross.

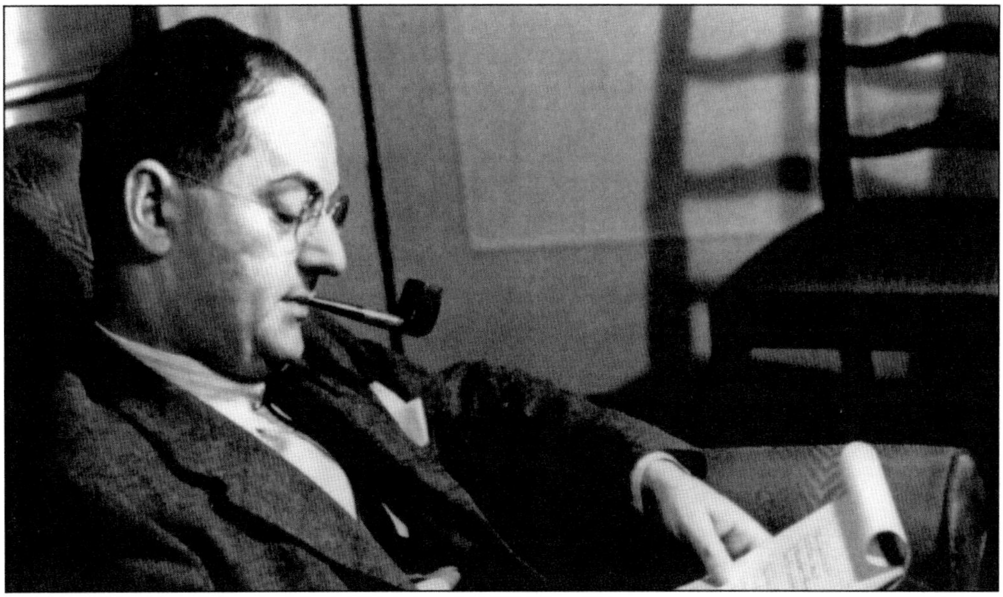

Born in New York's Lower East Side, Ira Gershwin attended the preparatory high school before entering City College. His sense of humor is evident in the stories appearing in issues of *Mercury*, sometimes jointly with his friend and classmate E. Y. "Yip" Harburg. Gershwin is most widely known for the collaboration with his brother in the 1920s, in which he wrote the lyrics set to the haunting melodies composed by George. He once described his craft as "fitting words mosaicly to music" for such works as "It Ain't Necessarily So" and "Summertime" in *Porgy and Bess*, a masterwork of the American theater. His film musicals include *A Star Is Born* and *An American in Paris*.

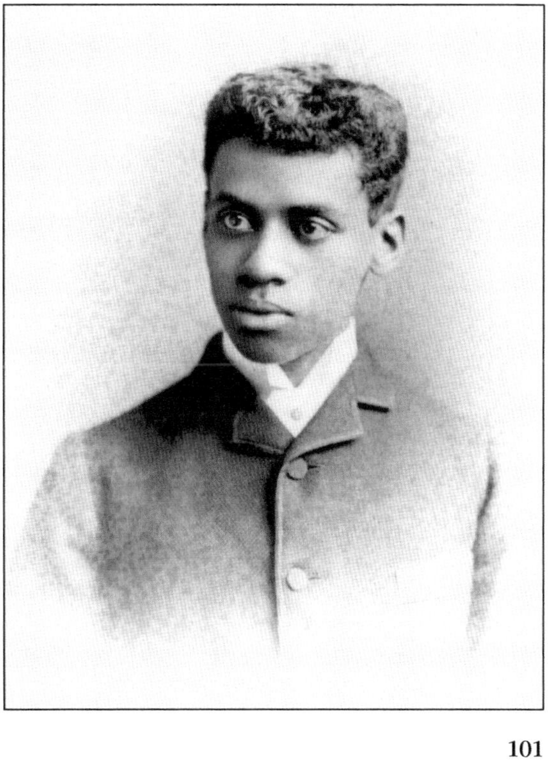

William Hallett Green (class of 1884), the first known African American graduate of City College, served in the U.S. Signal Service.

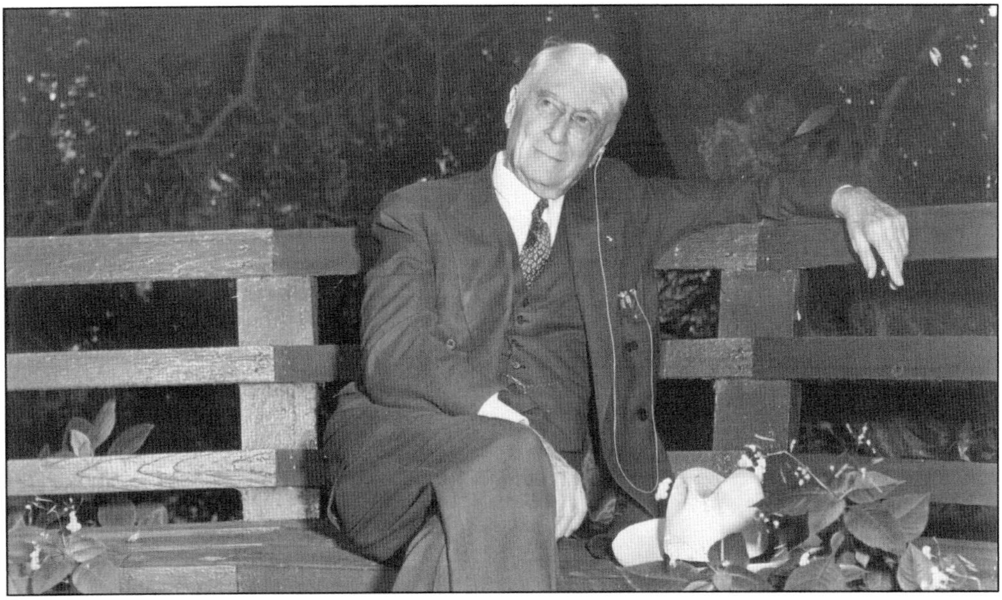

Bernard M. Baruch (class of 1899) sits on a bench in Washington's Lafayette Park, his favorite site for a conference due to the privacy and relaxed atmosphere with which to greet government officials including six American presidents. His trademark hat lies nearby. The "Park Bench Statesman" began to learn the brokerage business after graduating from City College and earned enough to purchase a seat on the New York Stock Exchange. His success on Wall Street brought him to the notice of Pres. Woodrow Wilson for the chairmanship of the War Industries Board.

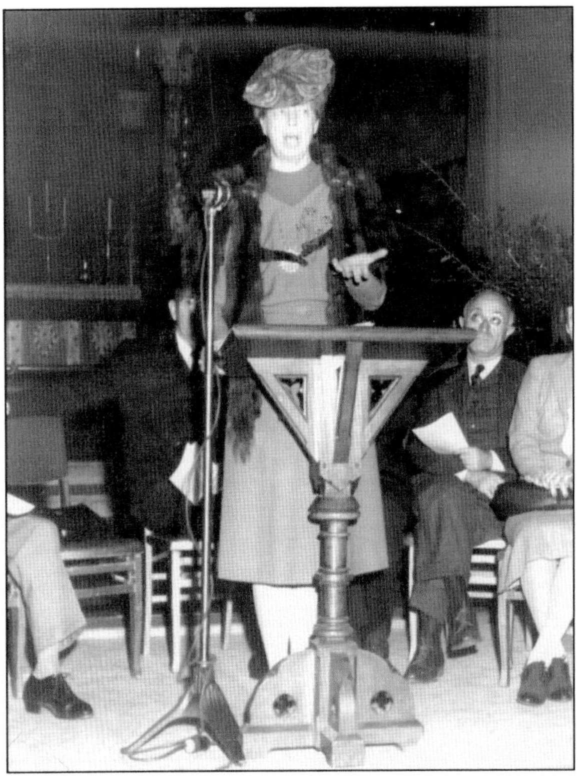

Eleanor Roosevelt spoke at the invitation of the Hillel in 1945. She visited City College a few times during her years of social policy advocacy, meeting with the Education Society on a separate occasion in 1953. Her husband, Franklin D. Roosevelt, came to City College in 1929 while he was governor of New York State and gave a speech in the Great Hall during his campaign for the vice presidency.

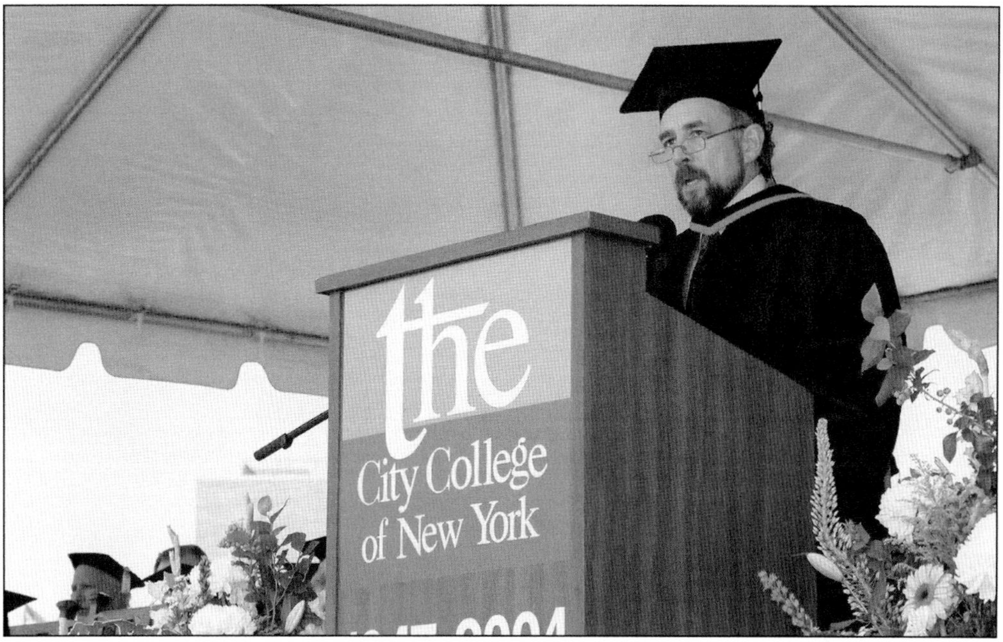

After Richard Schiff (class of 1983) founded the Manhattan Repertory Theater, he continued his career in Los Angeles acting on the stage and in over 40 films. He was awarded an Emmy for his role in the television series *The West Wing*. His ability to inhabit so completely the great characters of stage and screen continues to intrigue and entertain the world. (3D Studios.)

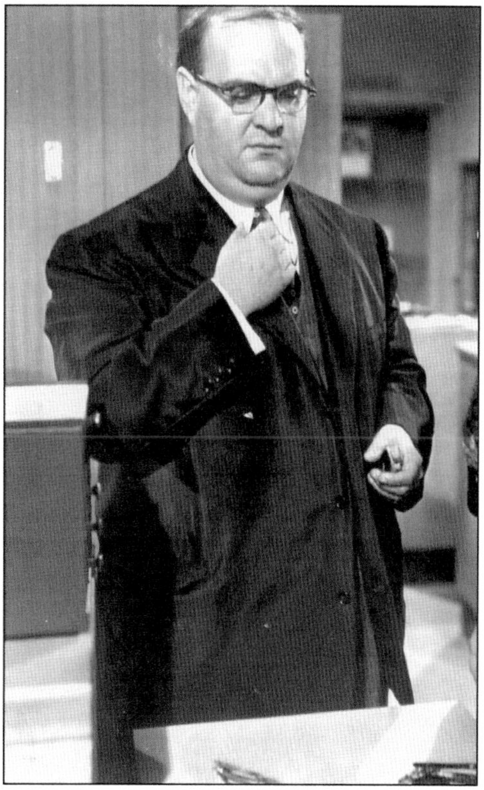

Samuel "Zero" Joel Mostel took art classes as a young man before attending City College. Although he entered a master's program in art at New York University, he did not complete the degree; instead, he began to teach art to young people in a Works Progress Administration program. When discussing art at galleries grew too dull, he began telling jokes, which led to a career in show business as a comic, mime, and tragedian on the stage, and in nightclubs and films. His roles in *A Funny Thing Happened on the Way to the Forum* and *Fiddler on the Roof* earned him two of the three Tony Awards of his career. Mostel continued to pursue his interest in painting throughout his life.

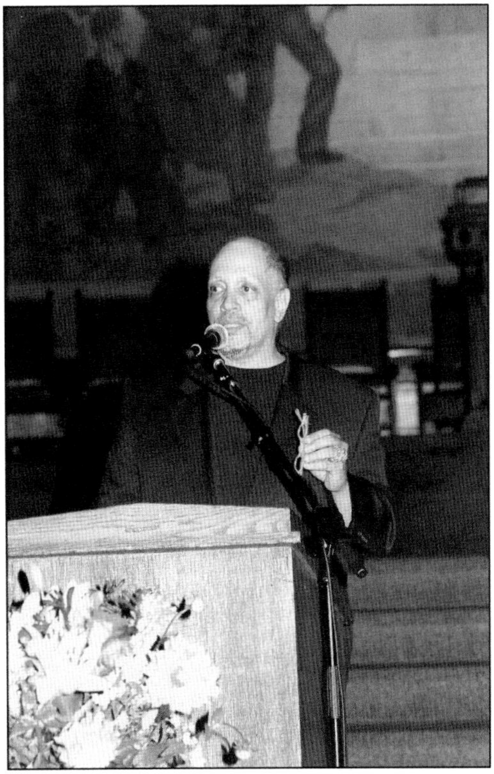

Walter Mosley sought out the creative writing program at City College in order to "be in the company of other writers," as he puts it. He remembers, "The atmosphere at City was so diverse, and even within the program was more so than in most other schools, so I never felt like a fish out of water. Neither did the other people of color there." His series of mysteries about detective Easy Rawlins has been widely reviewed, translated into many languages, and transposed to the big screen following the popular film adaptation of the first novel, *Devil in a Blue Dress*. Mosley continues to create new characters and new themes, such as the world of blues musicians in *RL's Dream*. (3D Studios)

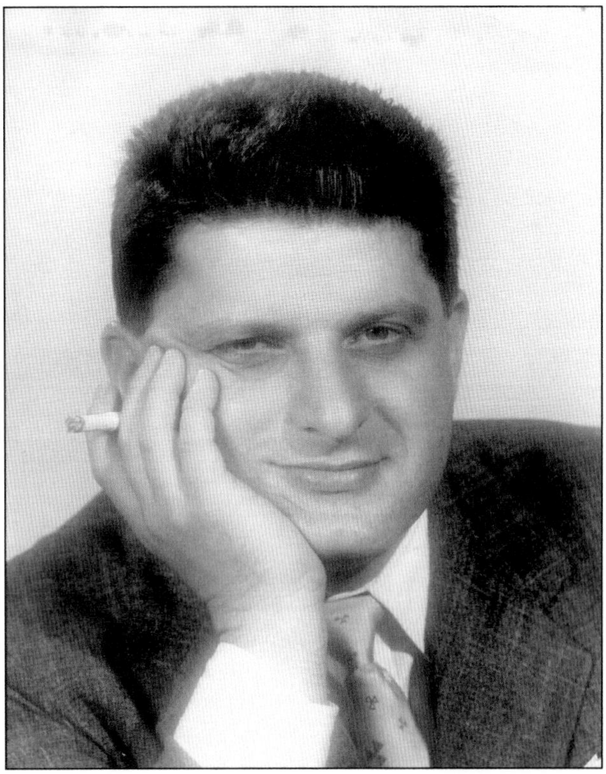

Sidney "Paddy" Chayefsky developed his interest in writing at City College. He turned to script writing during World War II, which is also when he acquired his nickname. Perhaps the most articulate spokesperson of the fears and aspirations of the common man in the confusing 1950s, he created the character Marty, who debuted in 1953 as one of the most enduring characters in television history. Chayefsky continued to explore characters who confronted the modern world—Dr. Herbert Bock sustaining rationality in the irrational urban environment of *The Hospital*, and Howard Beale expressing assertion in the line that became the hallmark of the film *Network*: "I'm mad as hell and I'm not going to take it any more." Chayefsky received an Academy Award for each of these films.

Majoring in physical education, Jane Katz joined the school's Physical Education and Modern Dance Societies and later served as president of the synchronized swimming team, foreshadowing her future achievements as teacher, athlete, and author. A member of several U.S. All-American swimming teams, including the Synchronized Performance Team at the 1963 Olympics, she has written books on swimming and physical fitness and presented "Swim Basics" on video. Katz has been a consultant for the President's Council on Physical Fitness and has joined the faculty of the John Jay College of Criminal Justice of City University as a professor of physical education.

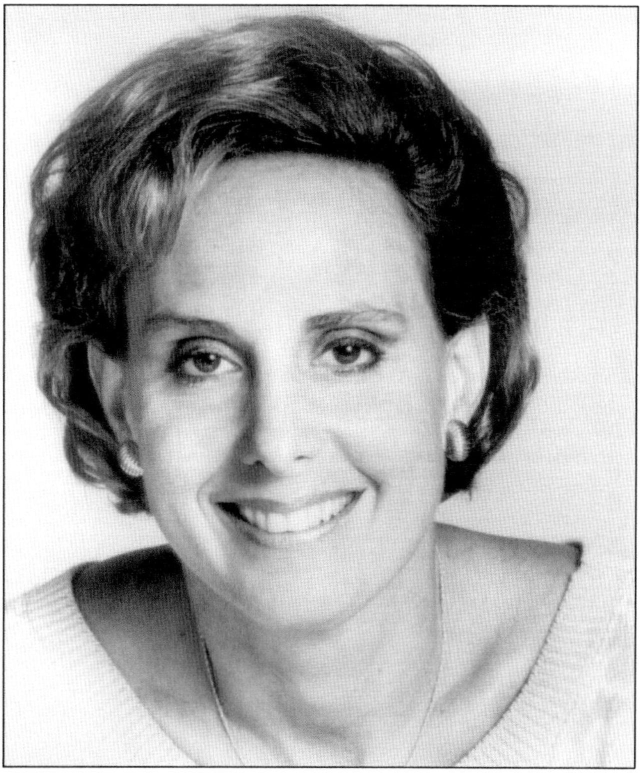

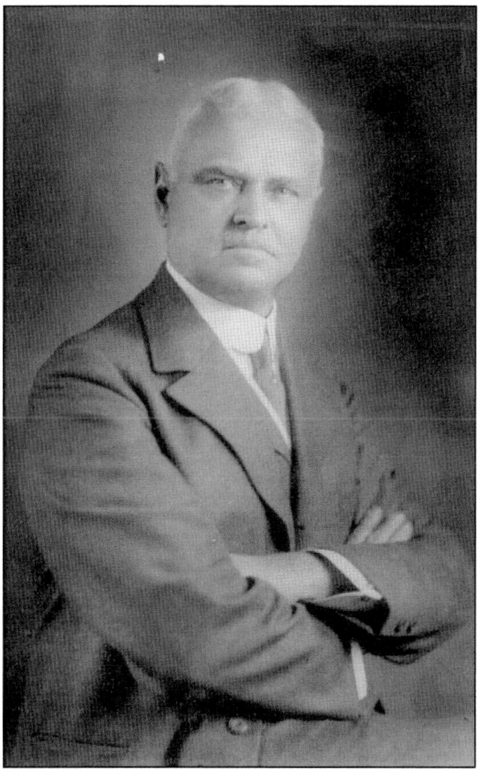

George W. Goethals (class of 1877) would have been familiar with the U.S. Military Academy's emphasis on class recitation because these expressions of memorized lessons were a common feature of the curriculum at City College, his alma mater. He earned the rank of major general and served as chief engineer for the construction of the Muscle Shoals Canal in Tennessee. After overseeing the awesome effort to build the Panama Canal, Goethals then served as first civil governor of the Panama Canal Zone.

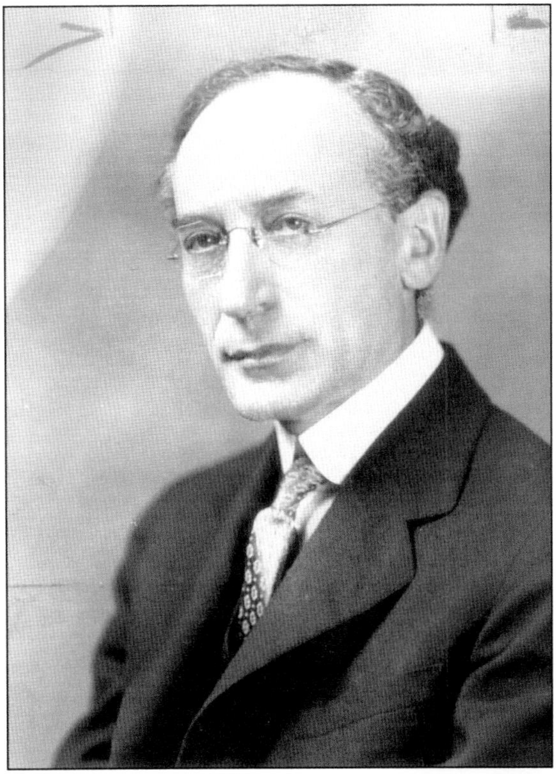

Morris Raphael Cohen (class of 1900) began teaching at the college in 1902 while a graduate student and then as an instructor in 1906 following completion of his doctorate in philosophy from Harvard University. He was one member of the faculty noted for serious scholarship, and in particular for his writing on philosophy that made him the most quoted philosopher in the country. In recognition of Cohen's 32 years of service and his scholarship, the main research library of the college was named in his honor.

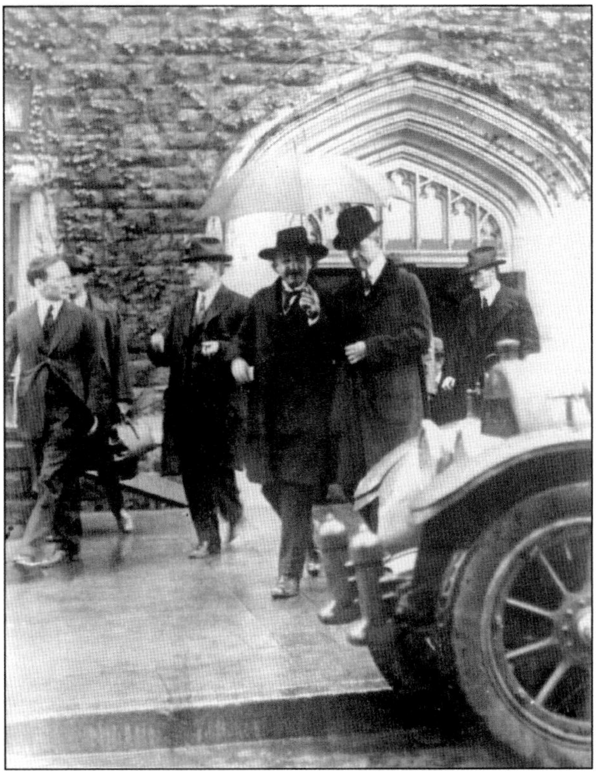

Albert Einstein gave a series of lectures at City College during his first visit to America in April 1921. Here, he leaves Shepard Hall with Pres. Sidney E. Mezes, who holds an umbrella. To their immediate left is Prof. Rheinhard A. Wetzel, and to the far left is Prof. Morris R. Cohen.

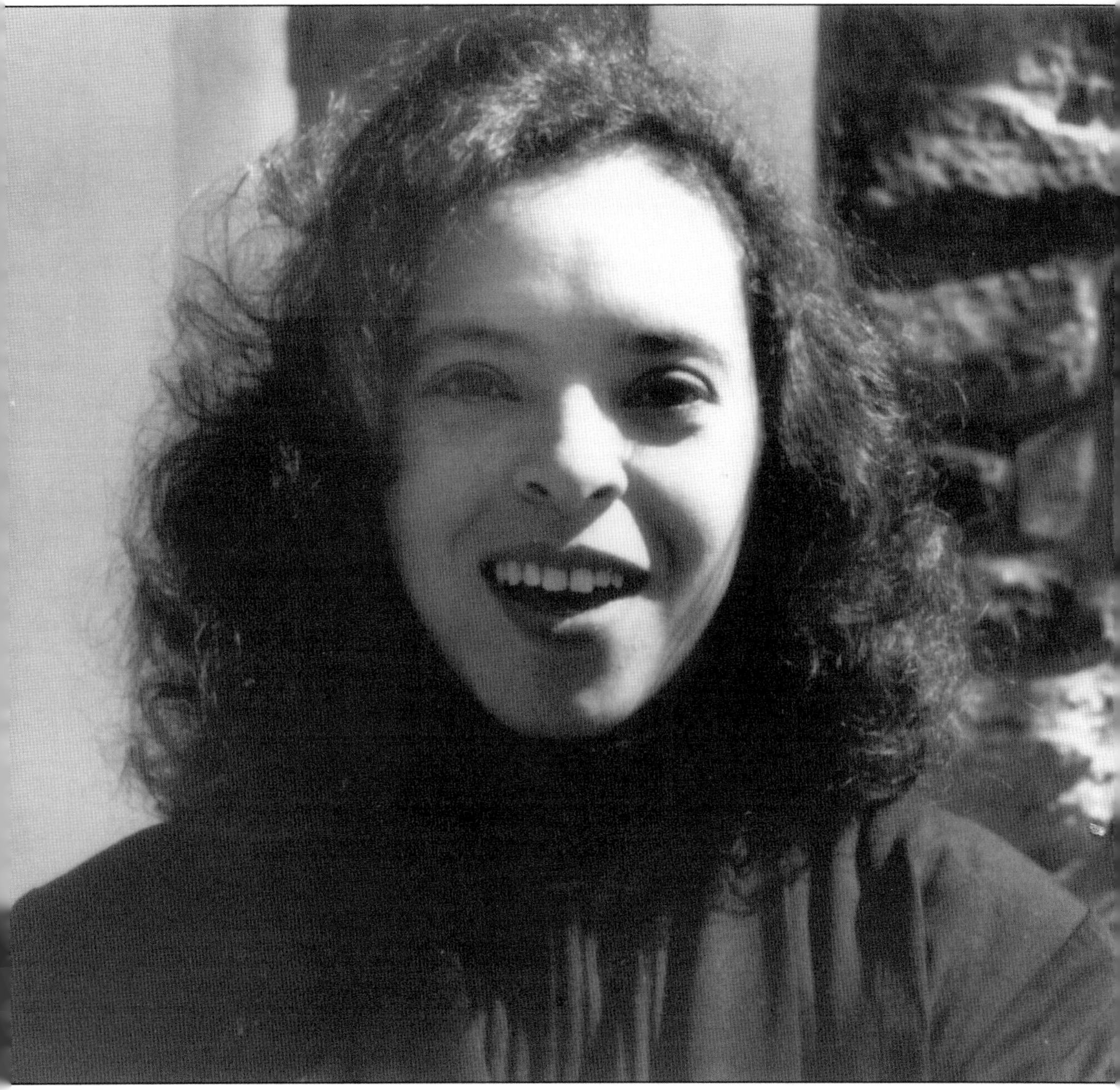

Vera Grant, a member of the class of 1995, was the first City College undergraduate to win a prestigious Fulbright Fellowship for Study Abroad in 1996–1997. A history major, she spent a year studying and conducting research at the University of Mainz, Germany. Grant went on to receive a master's degree from Stanford University in 2000 and is currently an adjunct associate professor in the German department of Wesleyan University.

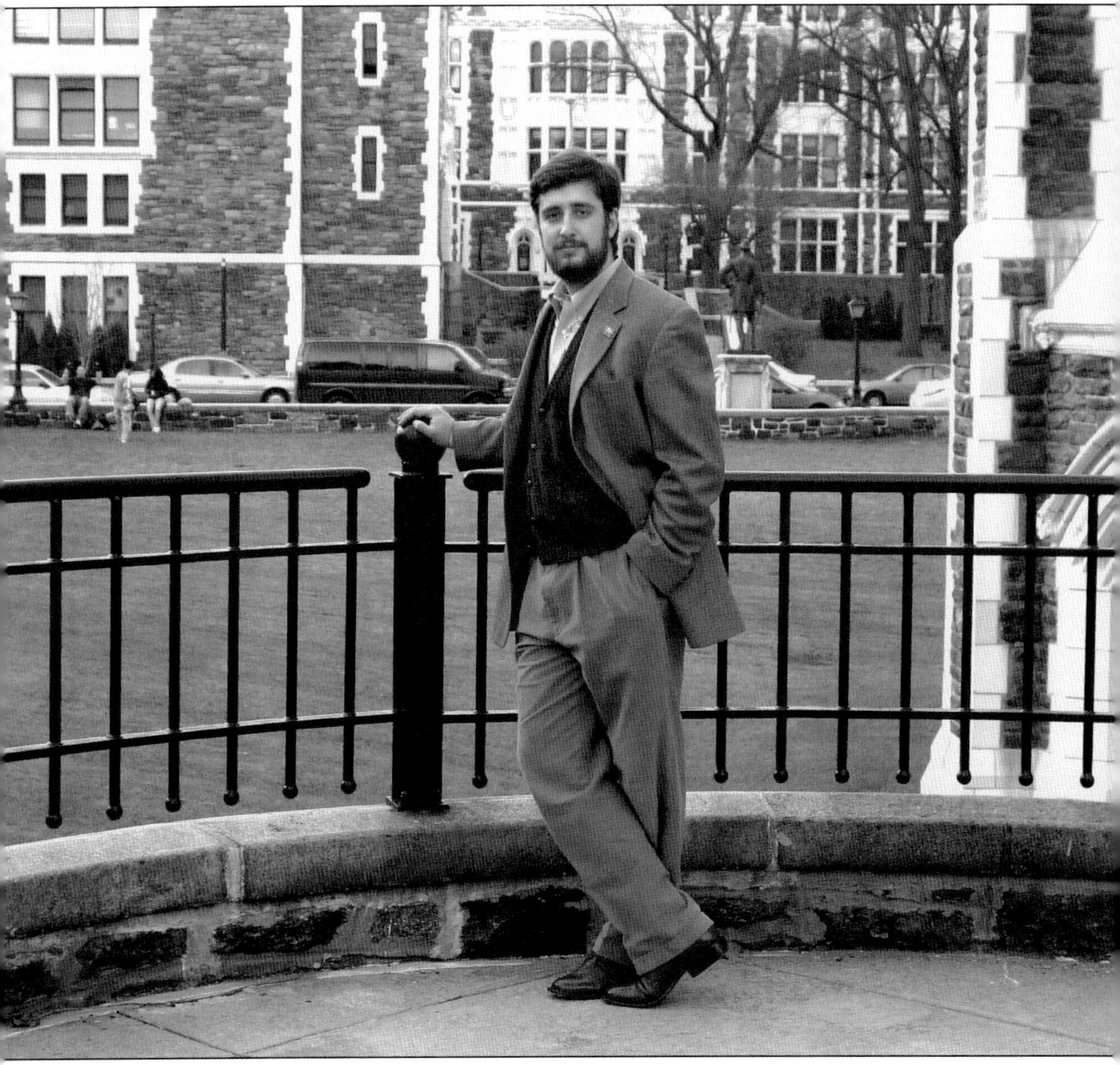

Lev Sviridov (class of 2005) is the second student from City College to be awarded a Rhodes Scholarship. He came to the United States in 1993 with his mother and worked at a variety of jobs to earn his way through City College as a chemistry major. Sviridov is pursueing his interest in environmental research and science policy. The first recipient of this scholarship from City College was Robert T. Malloy, class of 1938. (Bill Summers.)

Seven

Celebrations and Ceremonies

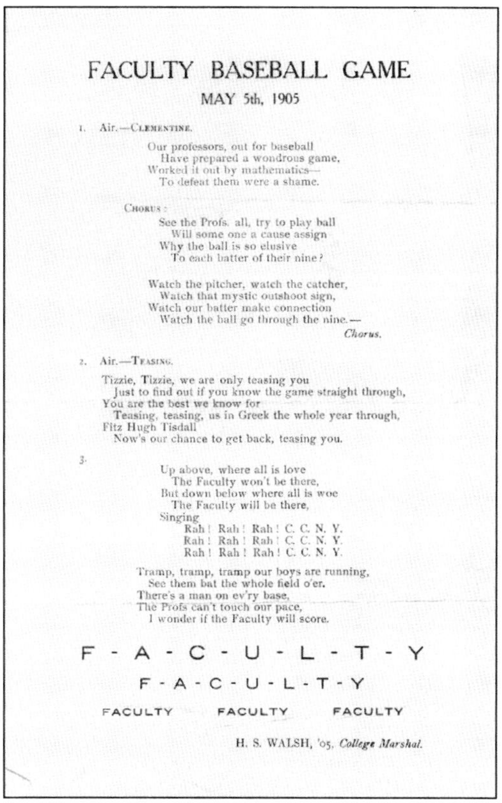

FACULTY BASEBALL GAME

MAY 5th, 1905

1. Air.—Clementine.

Our professors, out for baseball
Have prepared a wondrous game,
Worked it out by mathematics—
To defeat them were a shame.

Chorus:

See the Profs. all, try to play ball
Will some one a cause assign
Why the ball is so elusive
To each batter of their nine?

Watch the pitcher, watch the catcher,
Watch that mystic outshoot sign,
Watch our batter make connection
Watch the ball go through the nine.—
Chorus.

2. Air.—Teasing.

Tizzie, Tizzie, we are only teasing you
Just to find out if you know the game straight through,
You are the best we know for
Teasing, teasing, us in Greek the whole year through,
Fitz Hugh Tisdall
Now's our chance to get back, teasing you.

3.

Up above, where all is love
The Faculty won't be there,
But down below where all is woe
The Faculty will be there,
Singing
Rah! Rah! Rah! C. C. N. Y.
Rah! Rah! Rah! C. C. N. Y.
Rah! Rah! Rah! C. C. N. Y.

Tramp, tramp, tramp our boys are running,
See them bat the whole field o'er.
There's a man on ev'ry base,
The Profs can't touch our pace,
I wonder if the Faculty will score.

F - A - C - U - L - T - Y

F - A - C - U - L - T - Y

FACULTY FACULTY FACULTY

H. S. WALSH, '05, *College Marshal.*

In 1905, Pres. John Huston Finley began the custom of celebrating the college's birthday with appropriate exercises. He designated May 5 as Charter Day to commemorate the date when both bills had been reconciled and passed both houses of the New York State legislature, authorizing the expenditure of the Literature Fund with approval on May 7, 1847, "to establish a free academy in the city of New-York." On the first Charter Day, assemblies were held both in the chapel of the old Free Academy Building and on the grounds of the new campus under construction in Hamilton Heights. A copy of a program from the first Charter Day is seen here. Speakers generally included the president of the college, class officers, and sometimes trustees. Classes were cancelled, allowing members of the community to attend the opening festivities held in the Great Hall, a gathering place meant to echo the Free Academy Chapel. During the afternoon, the faculty-student softball game was a highlight of the day.

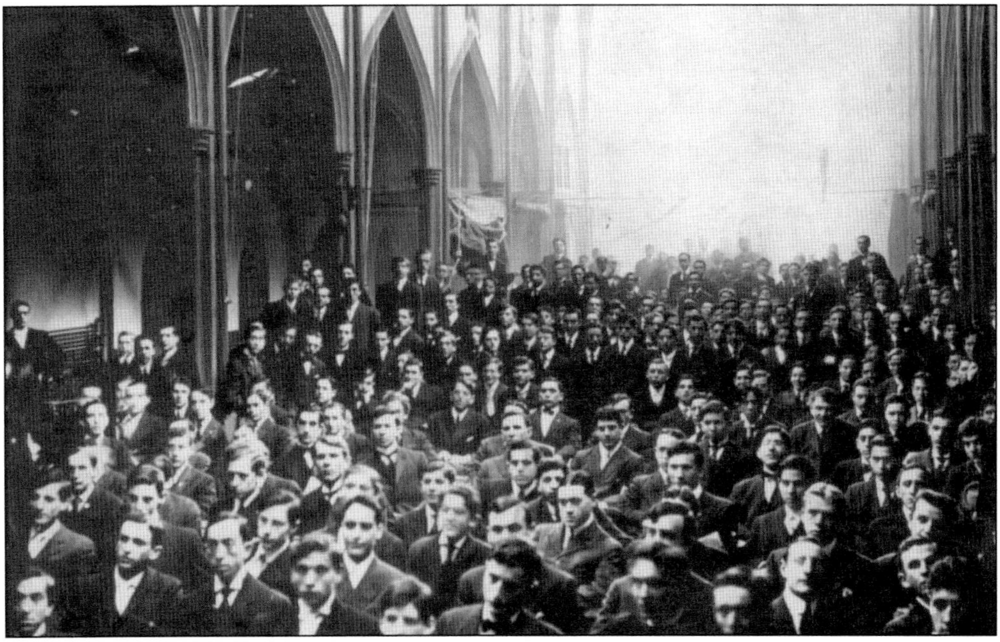

The 1907 Charter Day was the last in which festivities took place at the old location on 23rd Street. Here, students are assembled in the chapel of the Renwick building on the third Charter Day celebration. A silk American flag made for Townsend Harris in Japan in 1857 was displayed in the chapel.

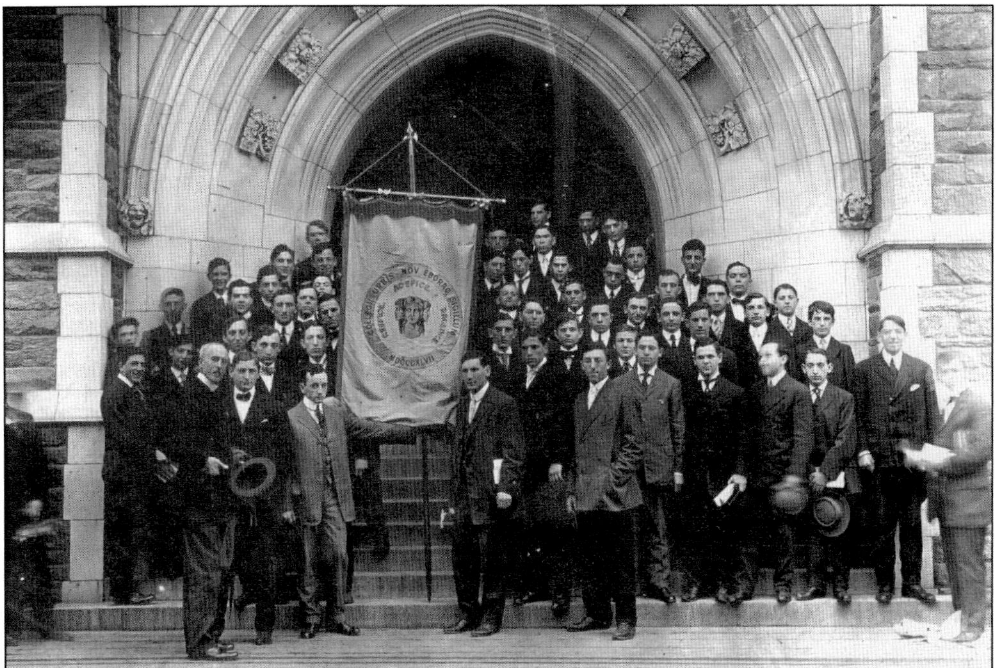

A contingent of students displays the City College banner on the steps of Harris Hall during Charter Day in 1907, the year that the festivities were scheduled on both campuses. This building on the new campus had been completed the previous fall.

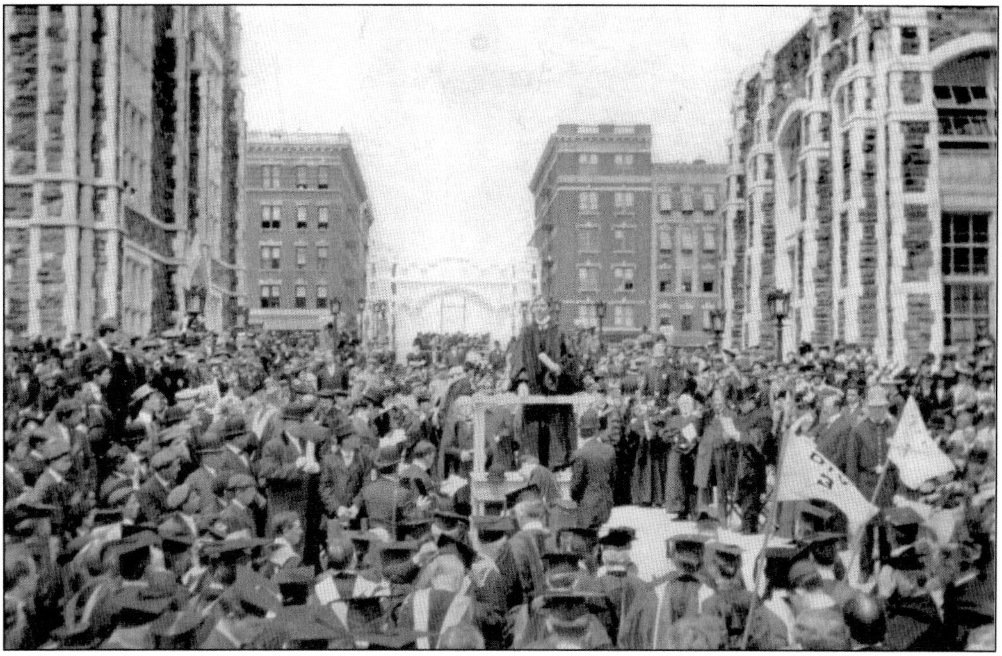

College president John H. Finley addresses the crowd on May 14, 1908, the occasion that marked both Charter Day and the Dedication Ceremony for the new buildings of the St. Nicholas Heights campus. Messages of greeting from Pres. Theodore Roosevelt and New York State governor Charles E. Hughes were read to the assembled group.

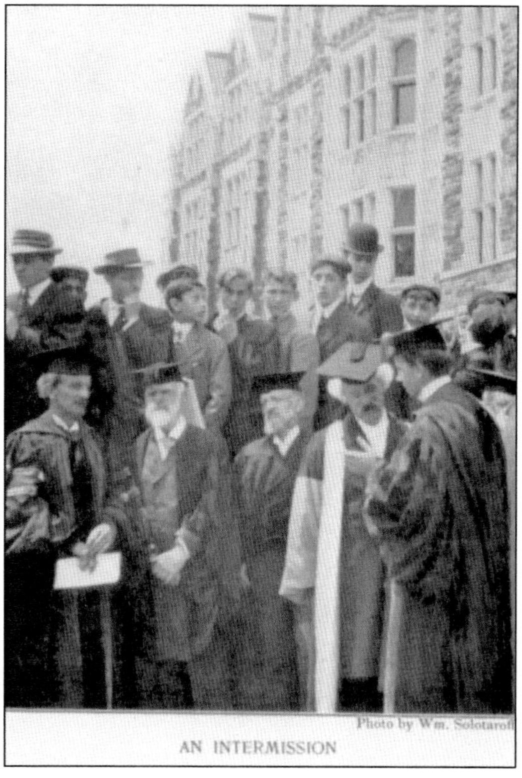

Samuel L. Clemens (Mark Twain) is shown in the academic procession, speaking to President Finley, at the dedication ceremony for the new buildings. That evening, he gave an address at the Associate Alumni Banquet at the Waldorf-Astoria.

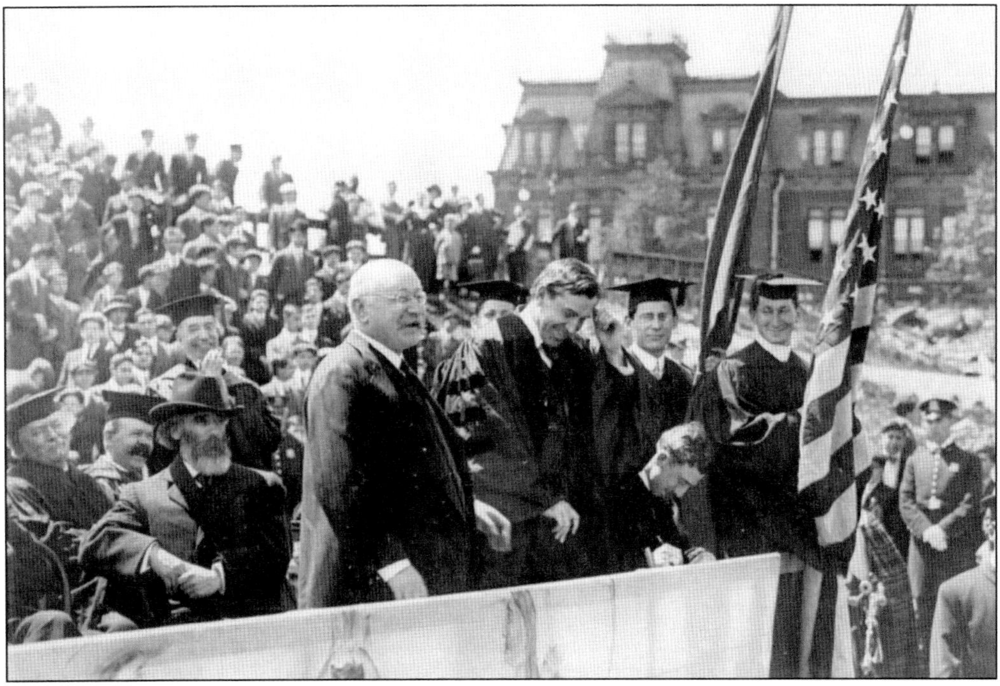

Charter Day in 1912 was held in the newly completed Lewisohn Stadium. Pres. John H. Finley stands with the benefactor of the stadium, Adolph Lewisohn, who donated the much-needed financial support to enable Finley to realize his plan for adding athletic facilities to the college.

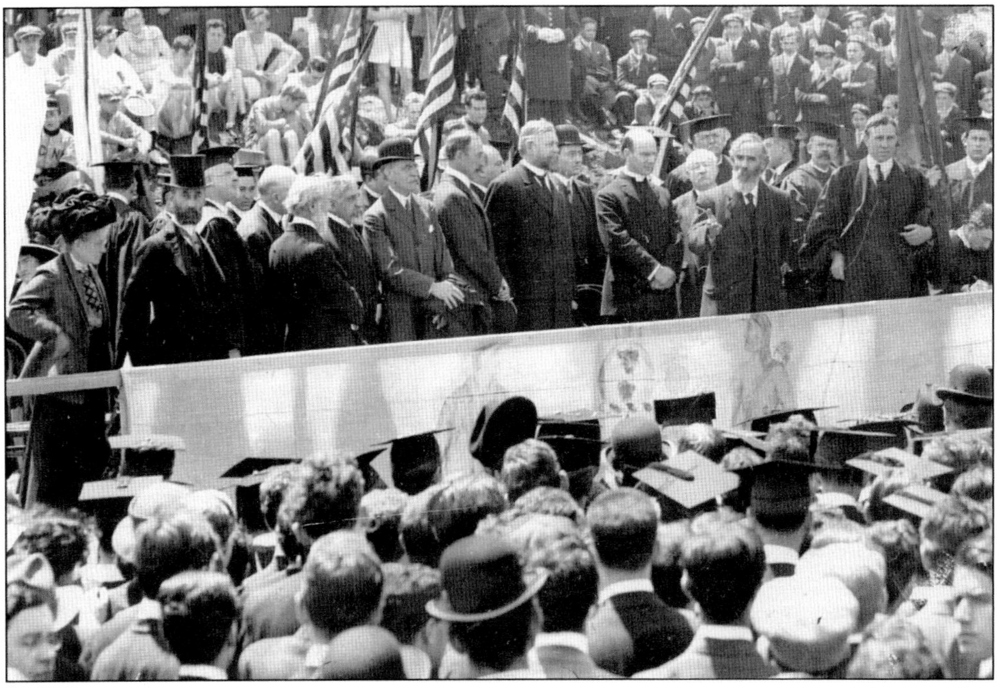

Those who attended Charter Day in 1912 included not only President Finley and Adolph Lewisohn, but the faculty, students, and athletic teams. Members of the track and field team, pictured in the upper left corner, would finally have a proper place to conduct their meets.

The ceremonies opening Charter Day were held in the Great Hall in 1925. Note the capacity crowd in the Great Hall, which could accommodate 2,200 people. This space was meant to be a gathering place for the college community and to echo the chapel that had served as the assembly hall for the community for the first 60 years of the institution's existence.

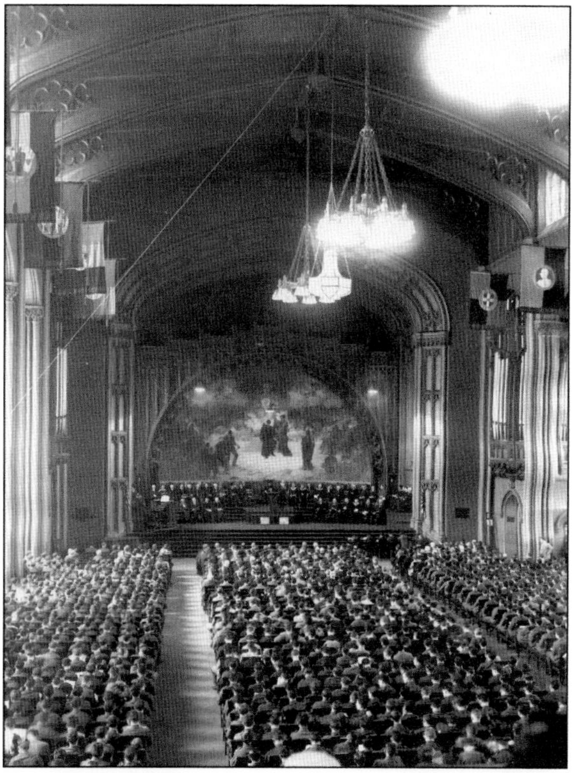

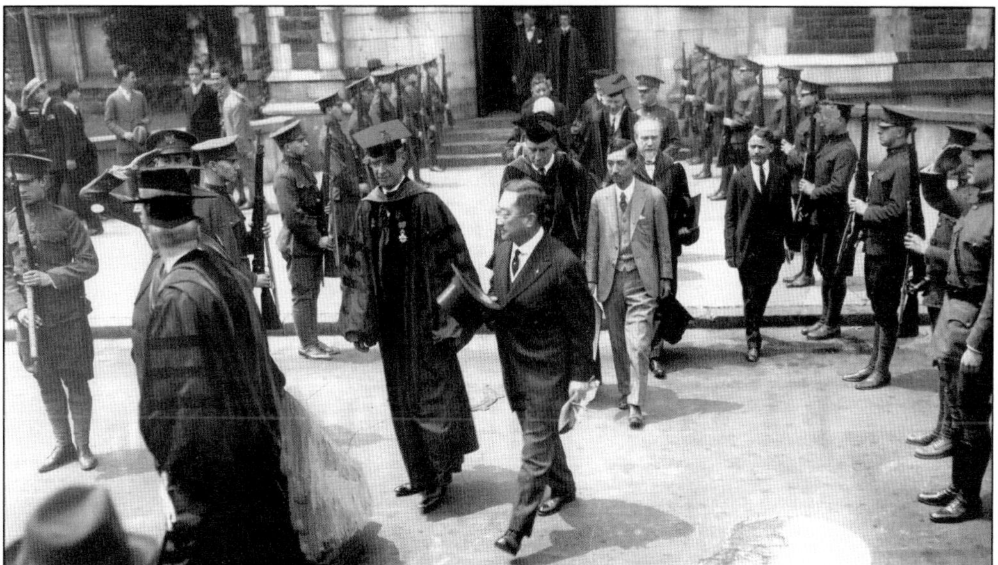

Ambassador Matsudairo with President Sidney Mezes, followed by former president John Finley with Consul-General Hirosi Saito, and Professor Mario Cosenza and Charlie H. Tuttle of the Board of Trustees march in the procession for Charter Day in 1926. This is one of many occasions over the years when the close ties between Japan and City College have been reaffirmed. The founder of City College, Townsend Harris, served as consul-general to Japan from 1856 to 1859 and then as minister resident from 1859 to 1862.

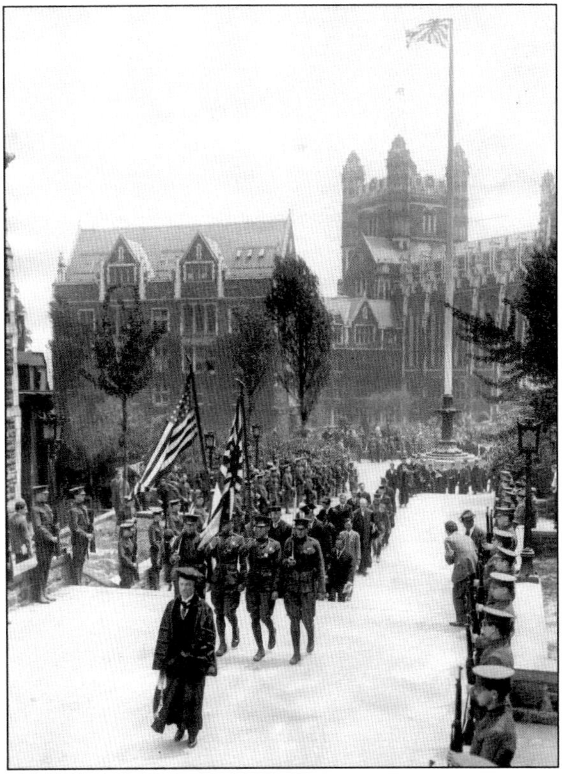

Members of the ROTC march from the quadrangle to Lewisohn Stadium to begin the festivities for Charter Day in May 1952.

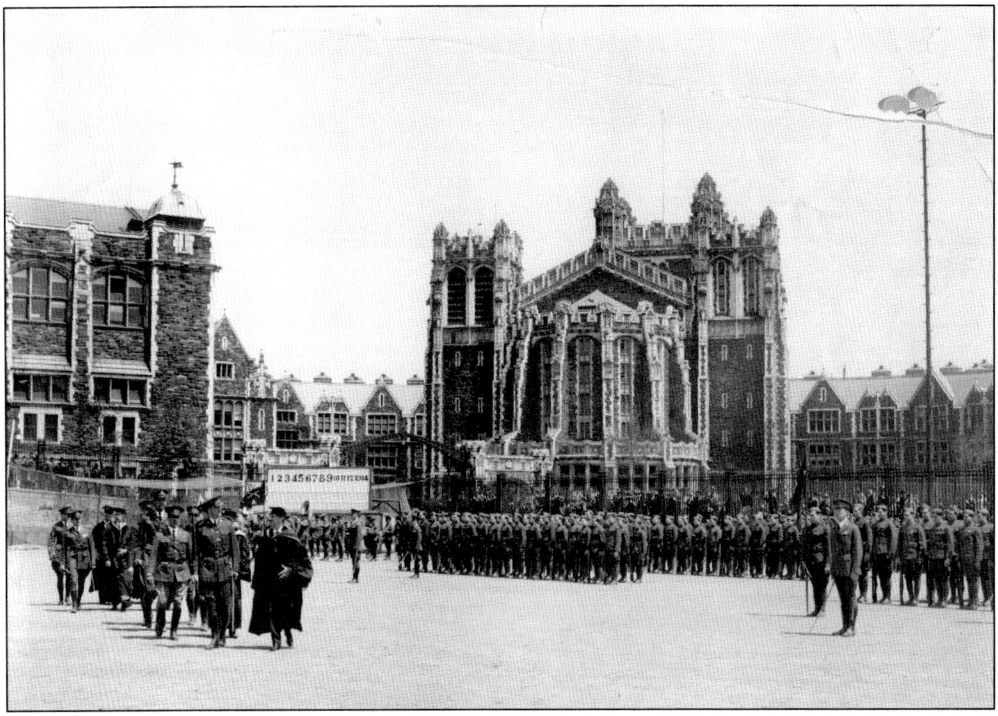

Pres. Frederick Robinson (class of 1904) reviews the ROTC drill held in Lewisohn Stadium in June 1928.

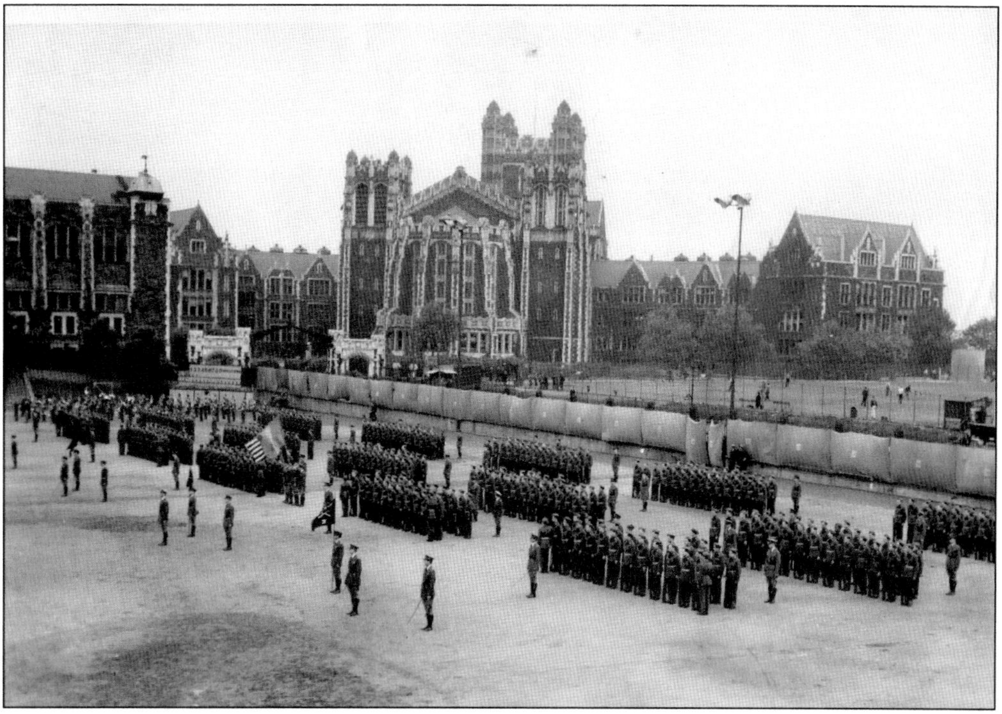

Members of the City College ROTC march in review in 1933.

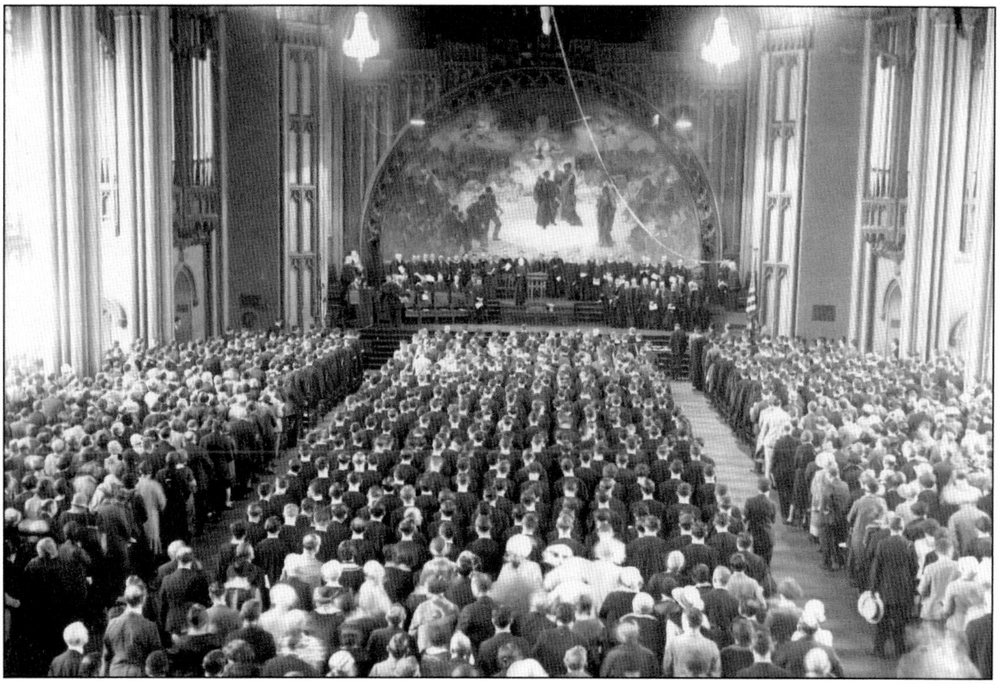

Felix S. Cohen, the son of Prof. Morris R. Cohen, graduated as valedictorian of the class of 1926. A ceremony saluting this class was held in the Great Hall. Felix Cohen served as editor-in-chief of the *Campus* and the 1926 *Microcosm*. Note the mural painting, *The Graduate*, by Edwin H. Blashfield at the end of the hall.

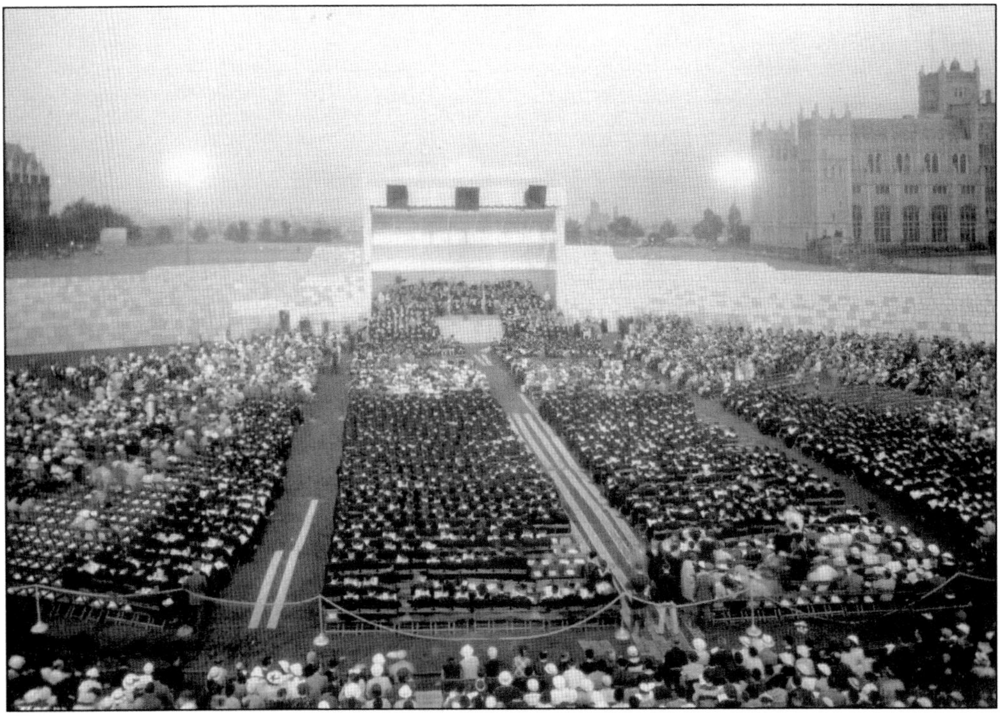

Commencement ceremonies for the class of 1931 are held in Lewisohn Stadium.

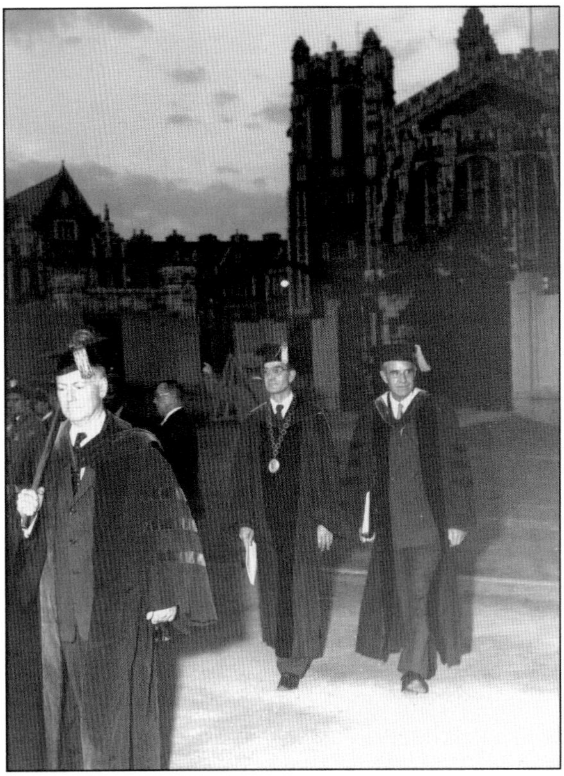

Pres. Buell Gallagher marches in the procession from Shepard Hall to Lewisohn Stadium during 1955 commencement exercises.

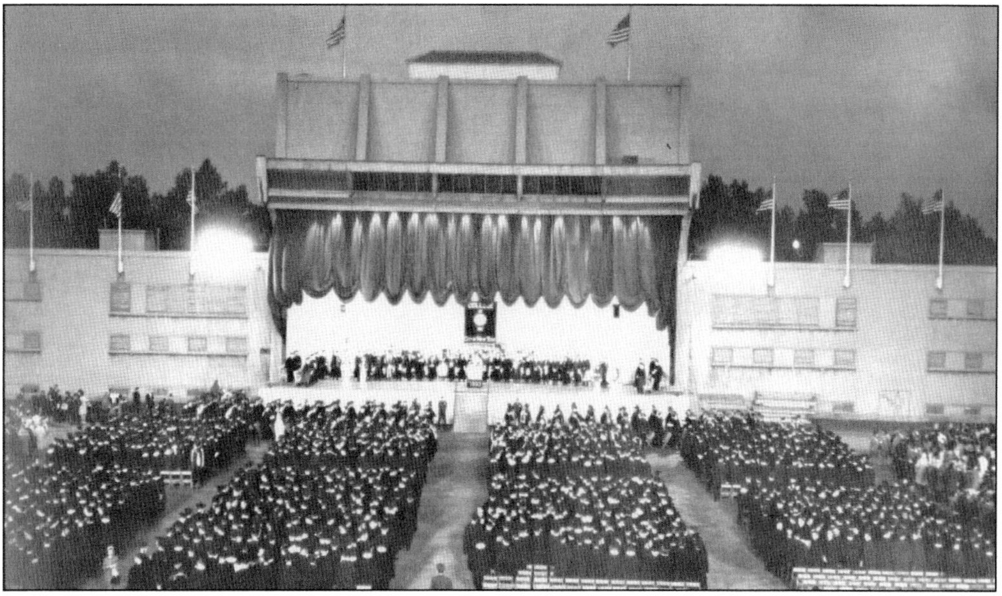

Dr. Martin Luther King Jr. was the 1963 commencement speaker at the Lewisohn Stadium ceremony. Andrew Grove, a graduate of the class of 1960, remembers Dr. King's address. In this speech, Dr. King stated there is a crisis challenging all men of goodwill to develop a world perspective. Dr. King continued by saying, "Education must enable a man to become more efficient and it must also humanize him . . . The moral dilemma posed by segregation must be addressed." In 1971, Coretta Scott King became the first female commencement speaker at City College.

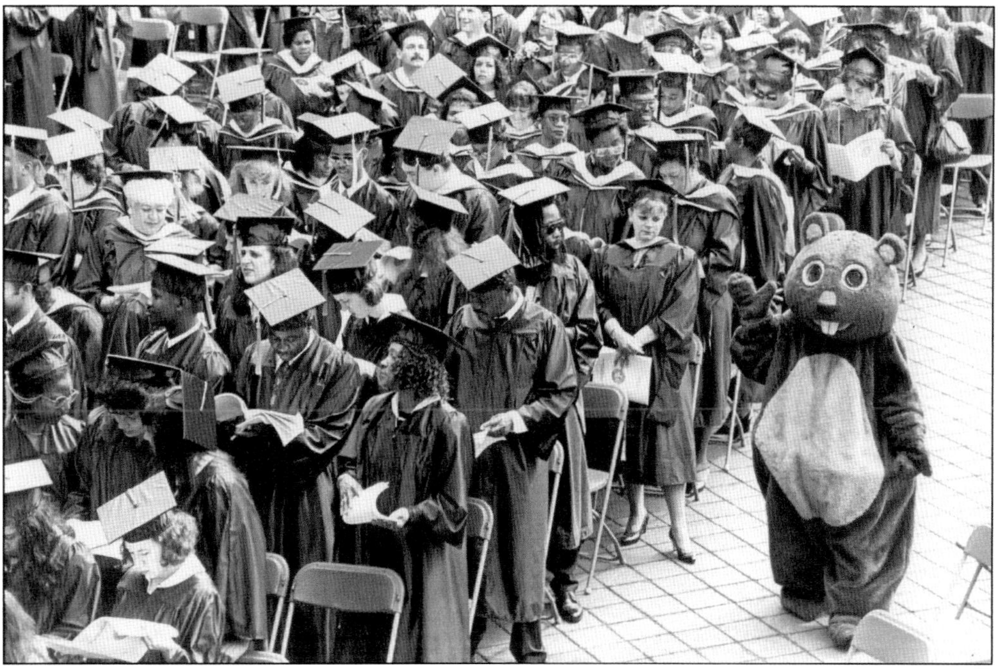

Members of the class of 1982 wait for the ceremony to begin, cheered on by the college mascot, Benny the Beaver. That year, commencement was held on the North Academic Center plaza. (Liza Schwair.)

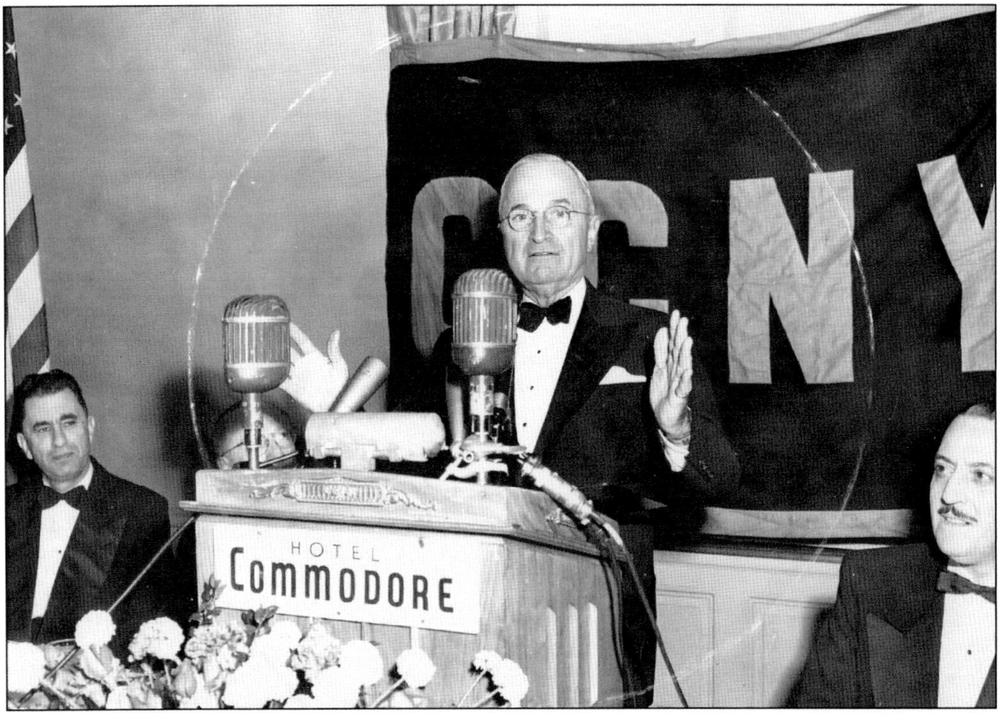

Pres. Harry Truman gave the Associate Alumni Association "hell" during the annual dinner at the Commodore Hotel in November 1955.

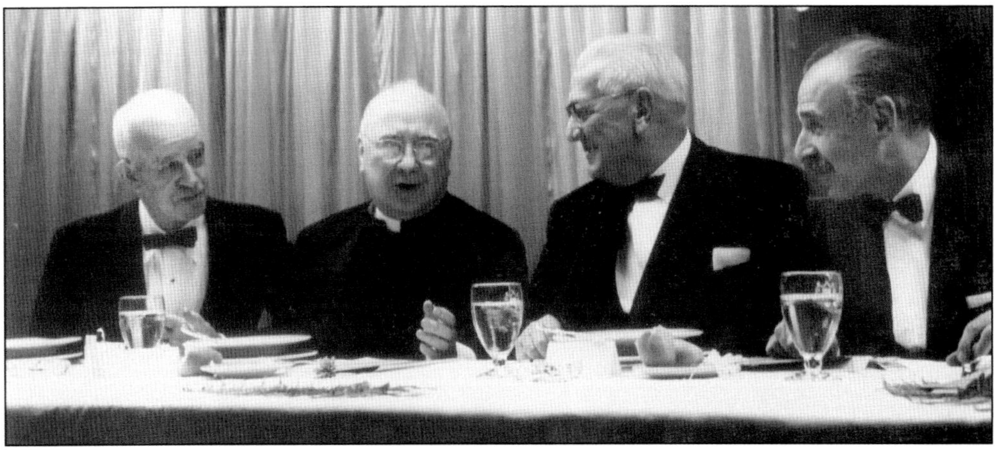

On November 2, 1960, some 1,300 City College alumni and New York dignitaries gathered at the Astor Hotel to celebrate Bernard M. Baruch's 90th birthday and attend the college's 80th Annual Alumni Dinner. Among the dignitaries were the following, pictured here from left to right: retired general Omar Bradley, speaking on Baruch's services to the cause of democracy as a "civilian-soldier" during World War II; His Eminence Francis Cardinal Spellman, who gave a moving benediction; Dr. Jacob Greenberg, former deputy commissioner of schools; and Dr. Gustave G. Rosenberg, chairman of the board of higher education, who spoke on Baruch's role as a trustee. Baruch and Greenberg were both recipients of the Townsend Harris Medal, the award for distinguished post-graduate achievement. The John H. Finley Medal, a recognition of service by non-alumni, was granted to Eleanor Roosevelt for her services on behalf of international understanding and for her work for the children of New York.

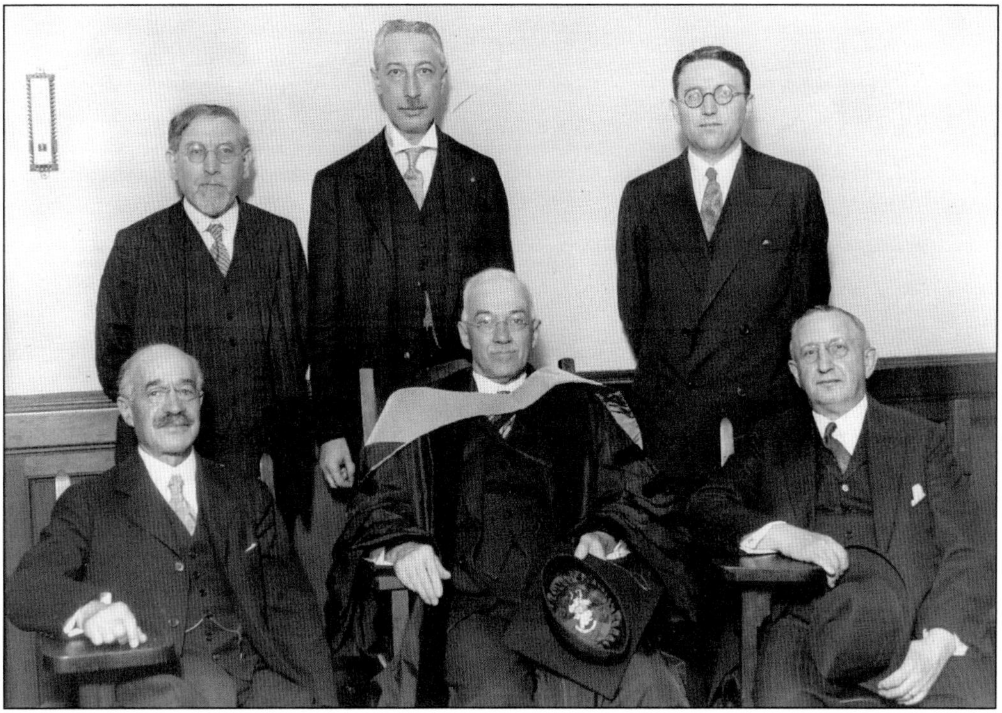

Six members of the class of 1899 were reunited in 1931 when they attended commencement. They reminisced about pranks they had perpetuated when they were students.

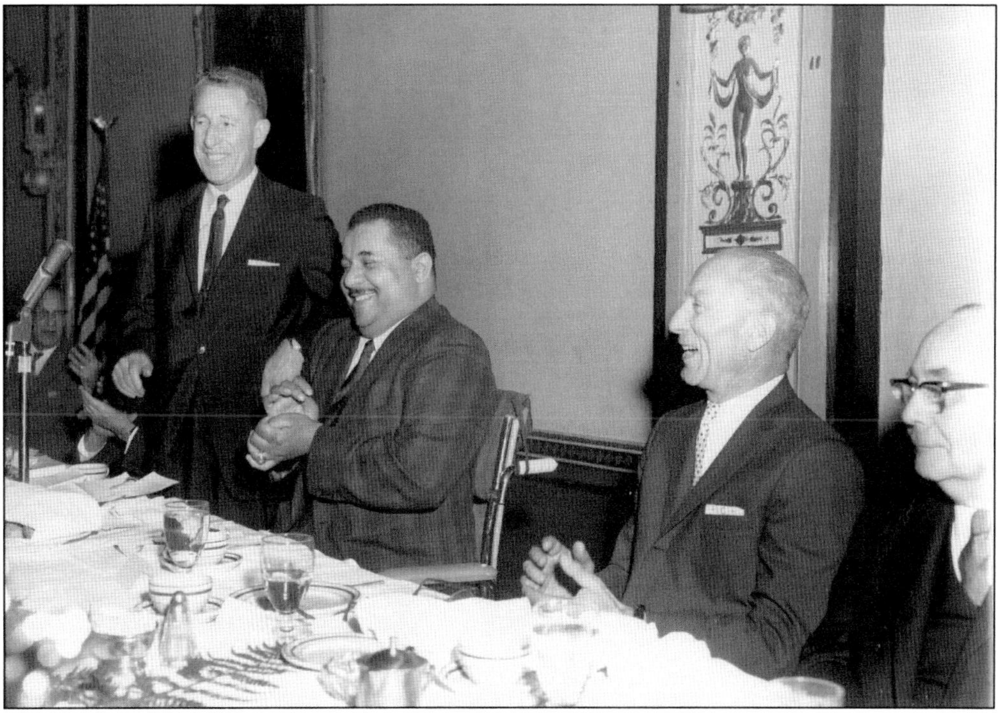

Milton Trupin, president of the Alumni Varisty Association, is seen introducing Roy Campanella, guest speaker, at the 1964 All Sports Dinner. (Conrad Waldinger.)

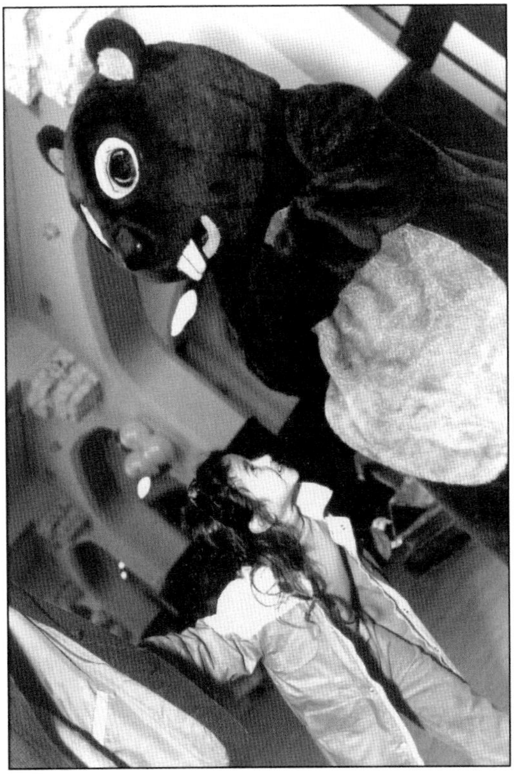

A young visitor attending the 1984 Homecoming event talks to the beaver mascot in the Lincoln corridor. Behind them, at the tops of the 12 pillars, are corbel personification figures. They could denote the muses or the seven liberal arts, the curriculum of Pythagoras.

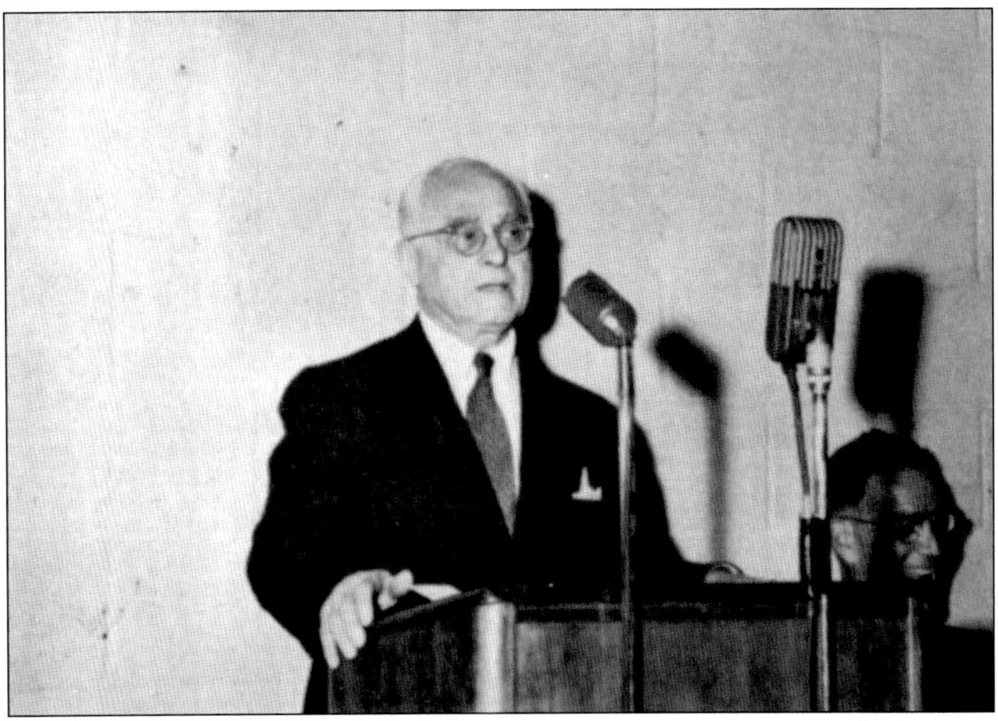

Felix Frankfurter (class of 1902) addresses the audience at the dedication ceremony for the Morris Raphael Cohen Library upon its opening in 1960.

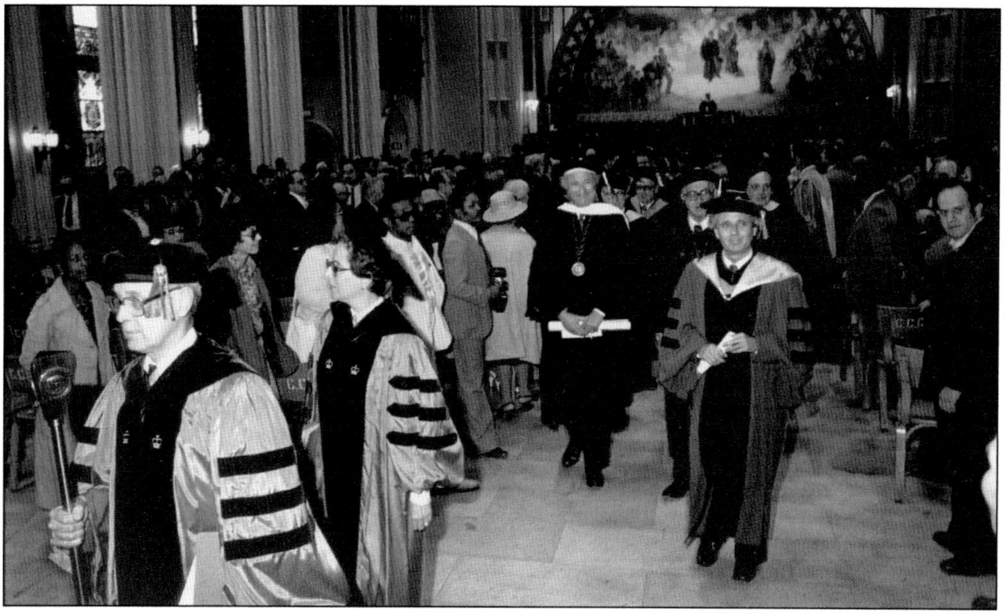

The science and physical education building, designed by Skidmore, Owings, and Merrill, received a double dedication when it opened in 1972. The tower structure with laboratories and classrooms for the scientific disciplines was named for a living person, Robert E. Marshak, the former college president. The street-level three-story section housing new indoor athletic facilities was dedicated to Jeremiah T. Mahoney. Here, the recession following the dedication on May 9, 1980, is led by Robert Mount, the chief marshal, carrying the college mace depicting the college seal. Mount is followed by acting president Alice Chandler; then Robert E. Marshak, Professor Emeritus; then Morris Silverberg (acting provost); and partly hidden by acting provost Silverberg is Robert Kibbee, the chancellor of CUNY.

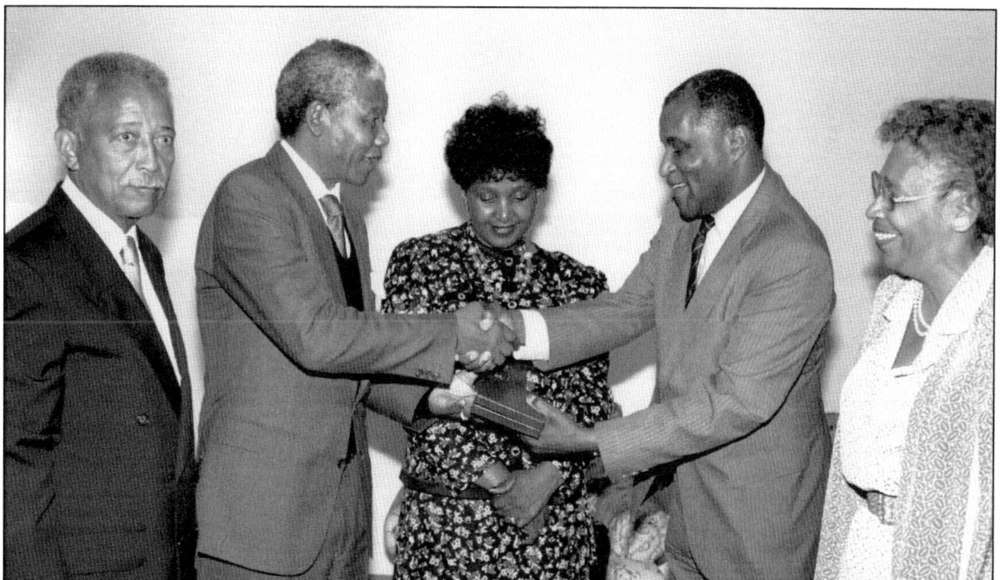

Nelson Mandela received the President's Medal from Pres. Bernard Harleston when he visited City College. New York City mayor David Dinkins looks on.

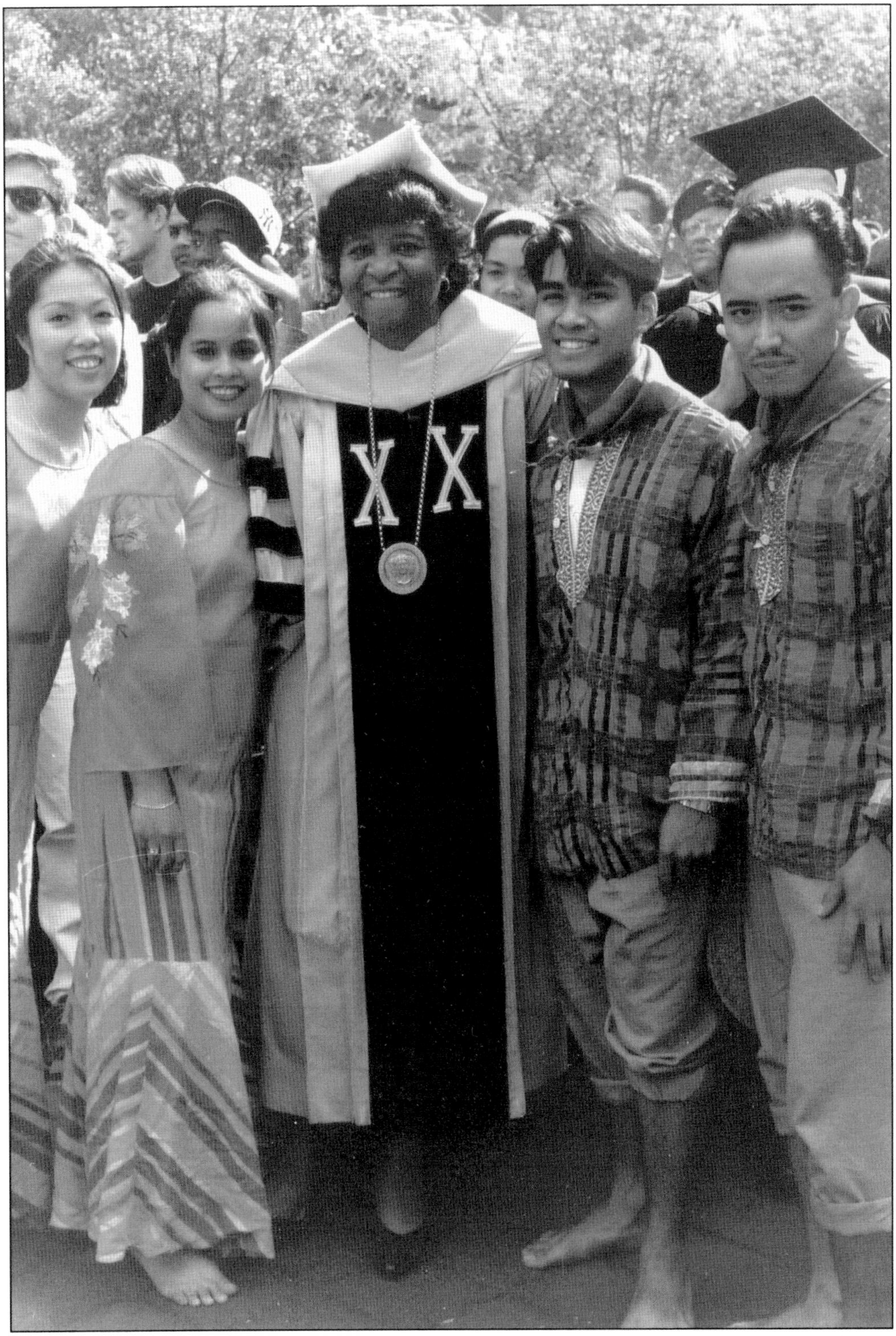

Pres. Yolanda T. Moses is flanked by students participating in the Student Cultural Festival held to celebrate pluralism and diversity at City College on her inauguration day in 1993.

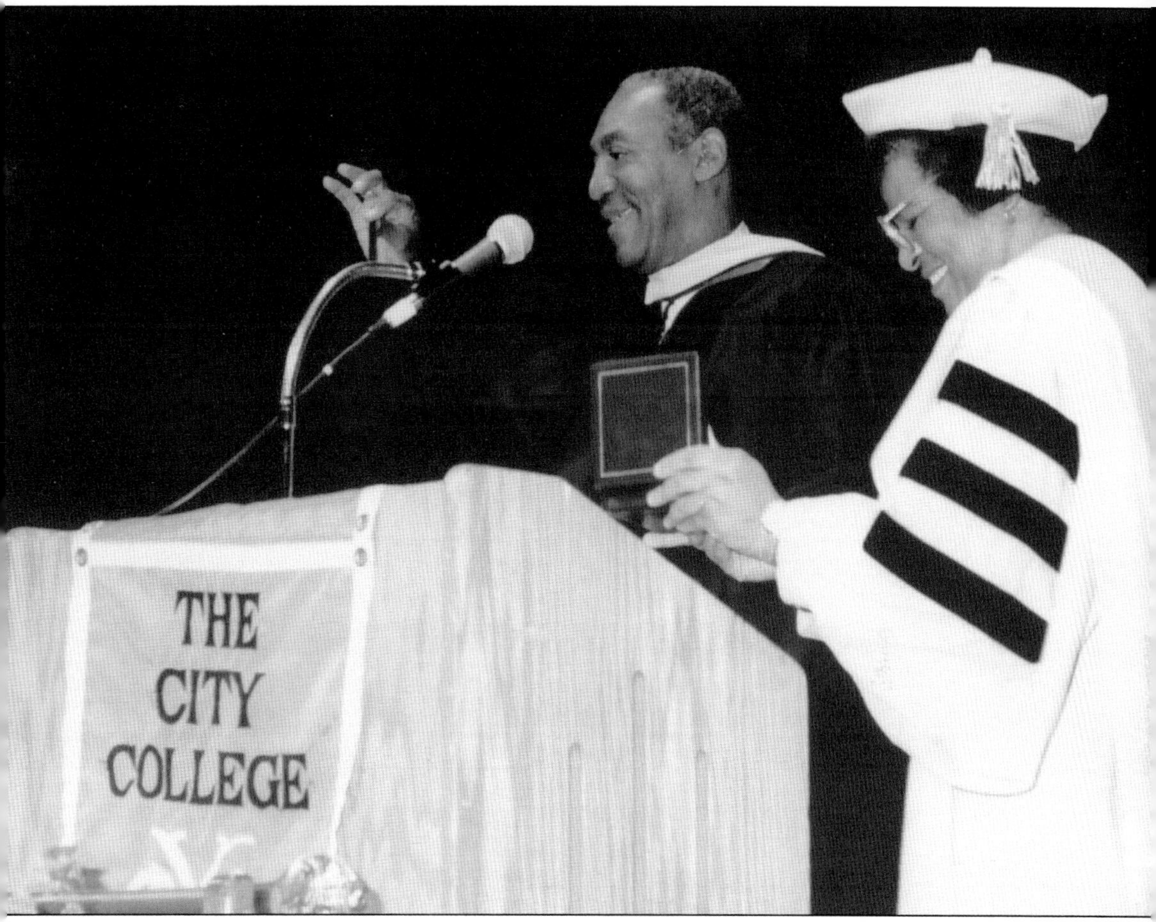

Bill Cosby received the President's Medal from Pres. Yolanda Moses on May 11, 1995. Bill Cosby was honored at the 13th annual Honors Convocation for his "lifelong commitment to education," according to President Moses. Bill Cosby, in turn, saluted seven of the students who had garnered honors that year.

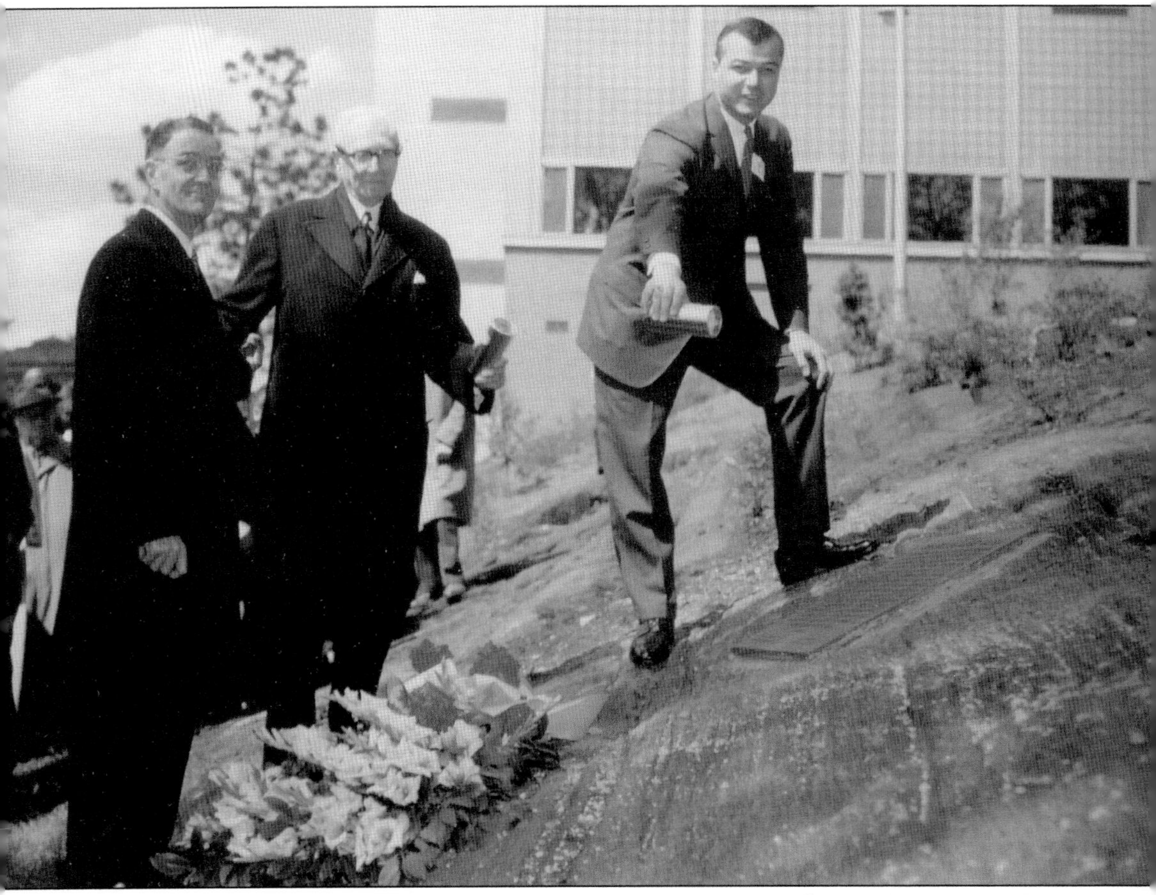

Pres. Buell Gallagher (left) participated in the ceremony held on May 16, 1959, for the remembrance of those felled in battle. He looked on with Bernard Baruch (center) while Army Air Corps veteran Albert Ragusa (right), class of 1950, scattered some sand from Omaha Beach onto the Remembrance Rock plaque, a gift of the class of 1958, that states that soil from the battlefields of Gettysburg, San Juan Hill, the Argonne Forest, Omaha Beach in Normandy, and Korea was poured onto this schist outcropping on south campus. Soil from the site of the original Free Academy building, New York tenements, and New York City Hall was also placed here. The original Cohen Library building can be seen in the background.

In honor of the 150th anniversary of the founding of City College, on May 7, 1997, a commemorative postcard was issued by the U.S. Postal Service.

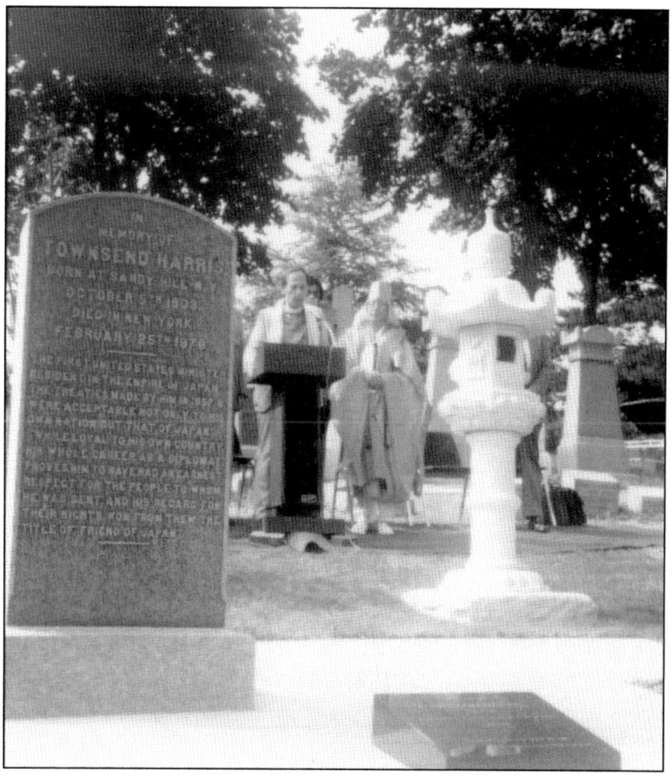

Services at the refurbished Townsend Harris grave site in Green-Wood Cemetery, Brooklyn, on July 24, 1986, were officiated by Rev. Yodo Murakami, resident priest at the Gyokusenji Temple in Shimoda, where Harris lived between 1856 and 1858. Murakami was assisted by Rev. Thomas Pike of St. George's Episcopal Church at Gramercy Park, which Harris attended between 1863 and 1878. (Philip Carvalho.)

BIBLIOGRAPHY

Berrol, Selma C. *Getting Down to Business: Baruch College in the City of New York, 1847-1987.* Westport, Connecticut: Greenwood Press, 1989.

Bowker, R.R. "The College of the City of New York, 1847-1895." *The University Magazine* (reprinted by permission).

Dunlap, Barbara J. "The City College Presidents: An Inaugural Celebration How it All Began." *Alumnus 90*, 1 (Winter 1995): 8-10.

Dunlap, Barbara J. "Here Come the Co-eds!" *Alumnus 87*, 3 (Summer 1992): 14-16.

Dyer, Conrad M. "The Protest and Politics of Open Admissions: The Impact of the Black and Puerto Rican Students' Community (of City College)." Ph.D. diss., The City University of New York, 1990.

Cosenza, Mario E. *The Establishment of the College of the City of New York as the Free Academy in 1847: Townsend Harris Founder.* New York: Associate Alumni, 1925.

Gordon, Sheila C. "The Transformation of the City University of New York, 1945-1970." Ph.D. diss., Columbia University, 1975.

Gorelick, Sherry. *City College and the Jewish Poor: Education in New York, 1880-1924.* New Brunswick, NJ: Rutgers UP, 1981.

Gross, Theodore L. *Academic Turmoil: The Reality and Promise of Open Education.* Garden City, NY: Anchor Press/Doubleday, 1980.

Heller, L.G. *The Death of the American University: With Special Reference to the City College of New York.* New Rochelle, NY: Arlington House, 1973.

Howe, Irving. *World of our Fathers: The Journey of the East European Jews to America and the Life they Found and Made.* New York: Simon and Schuster, 1976.

Jensen, Oliver. *A College Album or Rah, Rah, Yesterday.* New York: American Heritage Publishing Co., Inc., n.d.

Labin, David E. et al. *Right versus Privilege: The Open Admissions Experiment at the City University of New York.* New York: The Free Press, 1981.

Lebow, Eileen F. *The Bright Boys: A History of Townsend Harris High School.* Westport, Connecticut: Greenwood Press, 2000.

Middlebrook, Samuel M. (ed.) *Centennial Addresses: The City College of New York.* New York: The City College Press, 1950.

Mosenthal, Philip J., and Charles F. Horne. *The City College Memories of Sixty Years.* New York: Knickerbocker, 1907.

Neumann, Florence M. "Access to Free Public Higher Education in New York City: 1847-1961." Ph.D. diss., The City University of New York, 1984.
Pearson, Paul David. *The City College of New York: 150 Years of Academic Architecture*. New York: The City College, 1997.
Roff, Sandra Shoiock, et al. *From the Free Academy to CUNY: Illustrating Public Higher Education in New York City, 1847-1997*. New York: Fordham UP, 2000.
Rudy, S. Willis. *The College of the City of New York: A History, 1847-1947*. New York: City College, 1949.
Traub, James. *City on a Hill: Testing the American Dream at City College*. New York: Addison-Wesley Publishing Company, 1994.
Van Nort, Sydney. "From Matrimony to Mattresses, Shepard's Great Hall has Seen it All," *Alumnus, 96*, 3 (Summer 2001): 6-7.
Washingon, Eric. *Manhattanville: Old Heart of West Harlem*. Charleston, SC: Arcadia Publishing, 2002.
"Welcome Back, Mike." 89, 3 *Alumnus* (Summer 1994): 16-17.
Year of Dedication, 1955-1956. New York: The City College, n.d.